Neuroscience and Education

This volume makes a philosophical contribution to the application of neuroscience in education. It frames neuroscience research in novel ways around educational conceptualizing and practices, while also taking a critical look at conceptual problems in neuroeducation and at the economic reasons driving the Mind-Brain Education movement. It offers alternative approaches for situating neuroscience in educational research and practice, including non-reductionist models drawing from Dewey and phenomenological philosophers, such as Martin Heidegger and Merleau-Ponty.

The volume gathers together an international bevy of leading philosophers of education who are in a unique position to contribute conceptually rich and theoretically framed insight on these new developments. The essays form an emerging dialogue to be used within the philosophy of education as well as neuroeducation, educational psychology, teacher education, and curriculum studies.

Clarence W. Joldersma is Professor of Education at Calvin College, USA.

Routledge International Studies in the Philosophy of Education

For a full list of titles in this series, please visit www.routledge.com

Neuroscience and Education

A Philosophical Appraisal

Edited by
Clarence W. Joldersma

Foreword by Nel Noddings

Routledge
Taylor & Francis Group

LONDON AND NEW YORK

First published 2016 by Routledge

2 Park Square, Milton Park, Abingdon, Oxfordshire OX14 4RN
711 Third Avenue, New York, NY 10017

Routledge is an imprint of the Taylor & Francis Group, an informa business

First issued in paperback 2017

Library of Congress Cataloguing-in-Publication Data
Names: Joldersma, Clarence W., editor.
Title: Neuroscience and education : a philosophical appraisal / edited by
  Clarence W. Joldersma.
Description: New York : Routledge, [2016] | Series: Routledge
  international studies in the philosophy of education ; 39
Identifiers: LCCN 2015040969 | ISBN 9781138802636
Subjects: LCSH: Cognitive learning. | Cognitive neuroscience. |
  Education—Philosophy.
Classification: LCC LB1062 .N47 2016 | DDC 370.15/23—dc23
LC record available at http://lccn.loc.gov/2015040969

ISBN: 978-1-138-80263-6 (hbk)
ISBN: 978-0-8153-8198-3 (pbk)

Typeset in Sabon
by Apex CoVantage, LLC

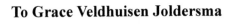

To Grace Veldhuisen Joldersma

Contents

PART II
Thinking Philosophically with Neuroscience and Education

Foreword

This is an important book for all educators. Neuroscience has made impressive progress over the past two decades, and it may in time make significant contributions to our understanding of such illnesses as Alzheimer's, autism, depression, and Parkinson's. But educators should be aware that many claims for its relevance to education are, at this time, exaggerations if not outright untruths.

Neuroscientists are doing fascinating work on the connections between perception and cognition, between environmental rhythms and brain rhythms, and between feeling and thinking. However, they face a tangle of problems not the least of which is figuring out whether the activity of specific neurons causes thinking or thinking causes the neuronal activity. If it is the latter, then what does cause thinking?

We are still far from an understanding of the human mind and its marvelous complexity. Is autism caused by a deficit in reactive capacity or by hyper-reactivity? Will an understanding of our minds emerge from a collection of knowledge about distinct parts of the brain, or will it turn out that, just as a smoothly functioning society depends on adequate communication among its groups and individuals, a smoothly operating mind depends on the well-ordered communication of its brain-parts provided by integrally working circuits?

Warning us about the overuse of mirror neutrons in past theorizing, Gregory Hickok, in *The Myth of Mirror Neurons*, writes: "Placed in the context of a more balanced and complex structure, mirror neutrons will no doubt have a role to play in our models of the neural basis of communication and cognition"; but neither they nor any other single structure is likely to tell the whole story. As the authors of this book suggest, you should read material on neuroscience and education with caution!

Nel Noddings
Stanford University

Preface

This book started with a chance conversation I had a few years ago with Francis Schrag at a presidential reception at a Philosophy of Education conference. As one does at such receptions, he asked me what I was working on, and I replied that in my reading at last I had been returning to my dissertation research in philosophy of mind, but I was interested in the mind's embodiment in living beings. He enthusiastically encouraged me to write something for PES on the subject, saying that philosophers of education were strangely silent on these matters. He related that he had just finished a book review in neuroscience and education, finding that this area really needed attention by people with philosophical expertise. I took his suggestion as a personal challenge. When I presented my first paper on neuroscience and education at the next PES conference, I was heartened by all the encouragement I received about the importance of this topic and thought I should continue.

A few months later, I received an e-mail out of the blue from a Routledge editor noting that I had just presented on neuroscience and education and asking whether I happened to have any book manuscripts hanging around on this topic. I replied that I didn't. However, I put to her an idea, suggesting that what was needed was an edited volume by leading philosophers of education using their existing expertise to think about the intersection of neuroscience and education. Within hours she replied, suggesting I gather together such a group. That summer, I developed the idea and contacted scholars around the world, some of whom I knew personally but others whom I knew only by their scholarship. I was struck by the positive and enthusiastic response I received from the scholars I e-mailed. It was clear to me that it was time for a book such as this. Although not everyone I asked was able to say yes, I was very pleased at how quickly I could gather an impressive set of chapter proposals for a book. The proposals clearly gave evidence of deep insights by philosophers about this intersection. I'm pleased to have been able to gather together leading scholars from around the world to begin this important conversation in philosophy of education.

Clarence W. Joldersma

1   What Can Philosophers of Education Contribute to the Conversations that Connect Education and Neuroscience?

Clarence W. Joldersma

The book *Neuroscience and Education: A Philosophical Appraisal* makes a philosophical contribution to an emerging if not burgeoning discussion about the relations between education and neuroscience. There are, as one might suspect, many books and articles that describe this interconnection, including thoughtful assessments about the propriety of applying neuroscience to education. Yet this book is unique: it offers a novel perspective by bringing to the conversation the voices of philosophers of education. They are in a unique position to contribute conceptually rich, theoretically framed, historically situated appraisals of this new development. There is little literature on this subject by philosophers of education.

As is by now well known that neuroscience as an emergent discipline is widely taught around the world, both at undergraduate and graduate levels.[1] There are also now a growing number of academic societies in (applied) neuroscience.[2] Further, neuroscience is increasingly being applied in many academic fields, including economics, philosophy, theology, and aesthetics. Of relevance to the current book, it has also made a visible entry into educational research and practice.[3] Neuroscience is increasingly informing teacher education, as evidenced by a number of undergraduate and graduate programs in educational neuroscience.[4] There is ample indication that neuroscience is becoming a major force in the field of educational research and practice—in fact, the field of education is rapidly being transformed by neuroscience.

The explosion of books that bridge education and neuroscience show this. For example, there are many thoughtful volumes that address this interconnection aimed at teachers and other educational practitioners. One interesting example is the book edited by Sergio Della Sala and Mike Anderson, *Neuroscience in Education: The Good, the Bad, and the Ugly* (2012). This work brings together (cognitive, neuroscience) psychologists and educational theorists to discuss possibilities, wrong turns, and simplistic suggestions of how neuroscience can help educators. In a similar vein, David E. Sousa has edited an informative volume, *Educational Neuroscience* (2011), a book that introduces basic brain science to K–12 teachers and suggests a series of instructional strategies making use of that knowledge.

It typifies the thoughtful application of neuroscience for teachers. A similar applicatory book is Louis Cozolino's *The Social Neuroscience of Education: Optimizing Attachment and Learning in the Classroom* (2013). This single-authored monograph is written for K–12 teachers, helping them navigate the information and possibilities of recent developments in social neuroscience. However, as might be expected, these 'applied' volumes do not address philosophical issues or even more generally possible critiques of the intersection between neuroscience and education.

There are also more scholarly books. Although it is impossible to do a comprehensive survey, a few examples of recent scholarly publications are worth noting. Kathryn Patten and Stephen Campbell's edited volume, *Educational Neuroscience: Initiatives and Emerging Issues* (2011), is a book version of a themed issue of the journal *Educational Philosophy and Theory*. The essayists are cognitive scientists, psychologists, and educational theorists specializing in neuroscience, and the essays are thoughtful and scholarly contributions to the discussion on a variety of theoretical and practical topics. Similarly, Paul Howard-Jones is also a prolific and important theorist in the intersection of education and neuroscience. For example, his book *Introducing Neuroeducational Research: Neuroscience, Education and the Brain from Contexts to Practice* (2010) introduces the interdisciplinary field, puts educators and scientists in dialogue, highlights current neuromyths, comments on methodology in this new field, clarifies neuro-educational ethics, and speculates about the future. Similarly, his edited volume, *Education and Neuroscience: Evidence, Theory and Practical Application* (2012), also exemplifies this approach. This book, which brings together neuroscientists and educators, considers current knowledge about brain functions that are important for areas of teaching, including reading, mathematics, music, and creativity. The volume tackles the way that neuroscience intersects with the various curricular subjects taught in K–12 school settings. In general, this genre of scholarship does important work in analyzing aspects of the intersection between education and neuroscience. But it isn't yet philosophical. These books don't typically utilize philosophical analysis, tackle philosophical themes, or seek out philosophical implications of neuroscientific developments. For example, although Howard-Jones does have philosophical insights, he is first of all an interdisciplinary scholar, and his work does not focus on philosophy as such. That is, his work is not a focused *philosophical* appraisal, and he does not develop insights for philosophy of education drawn from developments in neuroscience.

This short literature review of the intersection between neuroscience and education thus shows a philosophical lacuna. There is a dearth of literature that tackles philosophical issues around the interconnections between neuroscientific discovery and educational research and practice. Arguably, there is a need for philosophers of education to bring their expertise for an appraisal of the burgeoning educational neuroscience literature, including educational research, teacher education, and K–12 teaching. This book is thus uniquely situated, where leading philosophers of education do important philosophical analysis at this intersection. The book is premised on the idea that philosophy of education, a traditional field of research and teaching associated with most schools of education around the world, needs to address the philosophical implications of the topic of neuroscience and education. As educational research and the practices of teaching keep up with developments in neuroscience, education, and teacher training, it is important for philosophers of education to give philosophical appraisals of this emerging application of neuroscience to education. The book draws on the skills and expertise of philosophers of education to give a conceptual appraisal of neuroscience in education and the possibilities that it might offer to the philosophy of education. The present volume is one of the first forays into that conversation. There are currently *no* books, either edited volumes or monographs, in which philosophers of education focus on the interconnections between neuroscience and education.

Neuroscience and Education: A Philosophical Appraisal is a philosophical commentary on the interconnections between neuroscience and education. There are two main themes in the book. The first engages in a critique of aspects of neuroscience in educational research as well as problematic connections between neuroscience and educational practices. The second involves thinking creatively with neuroscience research to frame educational conceptualizing and educational practices in novel ways. Both of these themes run through all the essays. However, some focus more on critique and others more on possibilities. The book is therefore divided into two parts: "Critique" and "Possibilities." I will give a brief synopsis of each chapter in the two sections.

The essays in the first section of the book focus primarily on developing specific criticisms of neuroscience in its relation to education. These include a critical look at the economic reasons driving the Mind-Brain Education movement, albeit disguised as the science of cognitive psychology; a critique of educators offering simple solutions connecting neuroscience to education when the relation is actually complex; and an analysis of the interpretive pitfalls of reading neuroscience research for education, including its pervasive educational neuromyths. In addressing these concerns, the chapters are not merely critical but also offer creative alternative approaches for situating neuroscience in educational research and practice, including non-reductionist models drawing from Dewey and phenomenology. Further, two extended models developed in the section are based on the analyses of human experiences offered by phenomenological philosophers such as Martin Heidegger and Merleau-Ponty, as well as on the radical embodiment perspective of recent phenomenologists and cognitive theorists.

Emma Williams and Paul Standish's chapter opens the first section. They begin by pointing out that one of the major challenges facing those working in the field of educational neuroscience today is to bridge the 'gap' between knowledge about neuronal activity in the brain (or specific brain regions) and our everyday cognitive human activities, such as learning. Their point is that there seems to be a category mistake, where scholars talk about what the brain does, when it ought to be about what a person does. What remains to be developed in their view is an educational neuroscience today with a different model of the relation between mind and brain. They acknowledge that their concern is not new and that the relation has been a key concern within the field of neuroscience more broadly for some time. A number of neuroscientists have looked to philosophy to address this issue, including particularly the philosophical understanding of consciousness. In that context, Williams and Standish draw on Peter Hacker's arguments in his challenge to what he terms the 'consciousness community' and their adherence to "a mutant form of Cartesianism." Williams and Standish outline Hacker's critique of the current predominant conception of consciousness and suggest it is persuasive in its criticism of the consciousness community's commitment to a faulty (yet long-standing) metaphysic. The authors then build on Hacker's challenge to neuroscientific accounts of consciousness and the mind. In particular, they show that Hacker's challenge can be extended and developed in certain positive ways that he himself overlooks. Drawing upon the analyses of human experiences offered by Martin Heidegger and Ludwig Wittgenstein, they work to develop an account of the mind that goes beyond the predominant conception of consciousness in both its reductionist and non-reductivist forms. Through this, the authors open the way to a re-consideration of the relation between mind and brain. They argue that their account not only has significant implications for the project of educational neuroscience as a whole but also for pointing toward a better understanding of teaching and learning.

In the next chapter, **Paul Smeyers** focuses on the rhetoric of neuroscience in its attractiveness for educational research and practice. He acknowledges that neuroscience is 'hot,' that there are a growing number of academic positions, research projects, and fields with high expectations about neuroscience's application to education. To situate his argument, he briefly surveys a variety of reflections by leading scholars on the nature of this sub-discipline and approach, together with insights on how the findings are relevant for various educational contexts. Smeyers develops a meta-analysis of these findings and highlights criticisms by several philosophers of education of this move in education. He argues that the tempting rhetoric of what he calls 'the believers' reveals more about what neuroscience possibly *could* offer than what it actually *has* to offer. Drawing numerous examples from the themed issue of *Educational Philosophy and Theory* edited by Patten and Campbell (discussed in the beginning of this chapter), he relates that despite warnings from leading colleagues in the field of neuroscience and from some psychologists, educational researchers continue to believe in its potential for the educational context. Smeyers thus is interested in exposing this blind faith by identifying the flaws in the so-called arguments and by interpreting more generally the position the believers embrace. As an alternative, he argues that a more balanced approach, one that invokes the particularities of the situation as well as a broader concept of practical rationality, is required for the study of education. This means, he believes, that educational researchers should reclaim their territory and thereby do justice to their responsibility in this area. This could be done in part by highlighting the importance of understanding social practices in terms of reasons and intentions. Smeyers suggests that although researchers and practitioners rely upon various sorts of knowledge, one of which he draws from Wittgenstein in particular is important, something he calls "knowing how to go on." He acknowledges that this invokes something that is different from what one normally understands by 'knowledge' but that, nevertheless, it is strategically crucial in reclaiming the territory for education. His overall concern is that because education is complex, the scholarly discipline addressing this field should resist the many simple solutions connecting neuroscience and education, however tempting they may be.

Bruce Maxwell and Eric Racine's chapter is next. Their interest is the interpretive pitfalls involved in reading neuroscience research, in particular for its application to social practices, such as teaching or parenting. Maxwell and Racine offer two examples of transferring neuroscience knowledge to social practices. Their goal is to uncover ways of tempering the general over-enthusiasm for, and unexamined acceptance of, neuroscience's applications to everyday educational practices. Their first case, which at first glance isn't as explicitly neuroscientific as one might expect, concerns what they call behavioral ethics, namely, moral reasoning. Here they draw on cognitive science research in the area of moral behavior, arguing that this research challenges the commonsense idea that ethical behavior is, and should be, based in conscious moral reasoning. Rather, this approach suggests that unethical behavior is largely from influences outside of the moral agent's conscious control, situated rather in cognitive biases and situatedness that operate more at a subconscious level, concluding that teaching moral reasoning is not effective nor desirable as part of education. This example, broadly speaking, draws on research in neuropsychology. Maxwell and Racine develop a critique of this approach, arguing that its emphasis on instruction in ethical 'blind spots' of moral behavior comes up short, and that more deliberate moral reasoning still has a crucial place in education. Their second case study draws more explicitly on neuroscience research. In it they examine the potential for neuroscientific evidence to change the way parents might raise their children. They do so by looking at a set of 'evidence-based' practices called 'responsive parenting.' The critique emerging from this example includes the idea that we need to distinguish levels of knowledge, understand the nature of neuroscientific evidence, recognize that some applications of neuroscience to parenting can have negative consequences, and that we need to question the uncritical public trust in neuroscience and its quick translation into social practices. With this example, they want to establish respect for levels of empirical evidence, the appropriateness of applying such evidence in educational settings, possible negative effects of improper applications, and the role of public trust in such applications. Their overall aim is not to dismiss neuroscience research in education. Rather, when the limits of neuroscience research are appreciated, and especially when brain-level research is conducted in close consultation with research in other social sciences, they suggest the potential is great for neuroscience to contribute in meaningful ways to a better understanding of teaching and learning processes and to improving practice and policy in education. But their caution is that, as educational neuroscience's record shows, when these conditions are not met, the marriage of education and neuroscience can lead to short-sighted approaches and direct harm to children, youth, and their families.

Deron Boyles's chapter continues the critique section of the book, with a chapter that focuses particularly on the interplay between neuroscience's reductionism and its commercialization. He begins with an exploration of the recent fascination with neuroscience. His argument is that neuroscience, including particularly its 'application' to education, is separated from history and philosophy but is cast in technological, biological, and cognitive terms. His goal is to resituate neuroscience within Deweyan pragmatism. The first part of the chapter sketches out this approach, including overviews of pragmatism, neopragmatism, and the recent neuropragmatism. In the second part of the chapter, he sketches out neuroscience, neuropsychology, and the Mind-Brain Education movement (MBE). His (somewhat controversial) claim is that MBE has a commercial subtext, including particularly the idea that following evidence-based practices will enhance education's administrative control—a domestication or taming function. His point is that neuroscience evidence used in schooling is a political act. He states that they do so by reducing what teaching and learning mean to physical and behavioral phenomena in laboratory settings—his reductionism thesis. Boyle's response to such reductive moves is to argue for a revised understanding of classical pragmatism and neopragmatism, developing something he calls neuropragmatism. He concludes that this is the most defensible way to situate neuroscience in the realm of authentic and generative education.

The section's concluding chapter, written by **Clarence Joldersma**, continues Boyles's theme by connecting the application of recent developments in neuroscience to education and the ideology of neoliberalism. His argument is that especially popular understandings of neuroscience can easily be co-opted by the political ideology of neoliberalism. The chapter begins with a short sketch of neoliberalism and its connection to education. Joldersma characterizes neoliberalism as, at first glance, a vision of reducing the size of government through market-based approaches. However, he argues, as a vision, it is also an ethics to guide human behavior, one of functioning as a rationally self-interested subject obligated to accept the risks of participating in market exchanges. Following Michael Peters, he calls this "responsibilizing the self," something he connects to Foucault's idea of governmentality. As an ideology, he outlines, this appears in education in the ideology of lifelong learning. Joldersma then turns to a sketch of neuroscience, with a particular focus on the emergence of 'brain plasticity.' He points out that this recent discovery is being applied to education in many ways, including through commercial projects. However, he is wary of the simple applications of plasticity in education. He shows there are methodological reasons for being wary of claims about plasticity. But his main critique is based on critical neuroscience, an emerging field that focuses on the socio-political interests that frame neuroscience research and its ready application in society. Joldersma turns to Victoria Pitts-Taylor's idea of the neuronal self to argue that the idea of brain plasticity, in its application to education, gives neoliberalism another—powerful—area to 'responsibilize the subject,' especially in connection to lifelong learning. Accepting oneself as a 'neuronal self' makes it all-too-easy to accept the obligation that it is one's economic and political duty to manage one's brain for the sake of the changing economy. This has implications for the growing economic inequality within societies.

The essays in the first section have at least one strong recurrent theme. The authors all give cautions about the problem of reductionism associated with many claims about the appropriateness of applying neuroscience to educational research and practice. Williams and Standish put this as the brain versus person issue, Smeyers as the overreach of claims about the science itself, Maxwell and Racine as a problem with levels of knowledge, Boyles as the connection between a reductionist view and the commercial subtext, and Joldersma as the popular understandings that can be co-opted by neoliberalism. Although each of these articulations is not reducible to the others, nevertheless, the worry about reductionism—oversimplifications, levels of explanations, etc.—has strong family resemblances. And the alternatives offered by the authors typically point to something more complex, often at the societal level: person rather than brain, science as social practice, social level of knowledge, neuropragmatism, and socio-political contexts.

The essays of the second section are included to highlight philosophically informed possibilities developed in the intersections between neuroscience and education. The chapters of this section, as those of the previous one, develop both critiques and alternatives, but they are placed in this section because of the focus on positive possibilities. In this section, essayists develop new philosophical insights about educational matters in their conversations with neuroscience and education. Extended examples include: drawing on neuroscience to think about the formation of moral education, using recent developments in neuroscience to understand how rhythm can serve to enhance learning in the area of music education, problematizing Dewey's notion of flexibility and habituation and exploring the implications of neuroscience to support the idea of radical eruptions as learning, relying on neuroscience to help push a construal of social cognition toward an embodied hermeneutics of interpreting others, thinking about hermeneutics and pedagogy in the context of philosophical discussions in neuroscience, and developing a more dynamic idea of mind and cognition to address problems with representationalism.

The first chapter of the book's second section, written by **Derek Sankey and Minkang Kim**, is in the educational area of moral education. The authors argue that neuroscience can both inform *and* misinform the educational task of cultivating moral values, contending that educators should view neuroscience with critical eyes. The authors begin with a caution against proliferating neuromyths in education and the use of neuroscience to support pet theories in ways that can appear highly contrived. They also criticize neuroscience in its adherence to hard determinism and ontological reductionism. However, the main focus of the chapter is their use of neuroscience for uncovering the biological origins of moral values and exploring the nature of moral intuition. Educationally, the authors' emphasis is on cultivating moral *values,* rather than instilling moral norms, teaching children to be good, or with relativistic values clarification. They define moral values in terms of "guiding principles, beliefs, and sensitivities," and it is these they say need to be cultivated in education, both consciously and subconsciously, involving both reason and intuition. Further, they have conceived the educational task as enhancing moral 'connoisseurship.' Their conclusion is that moral judgment is always a form of connoisseurship, whether it involves reasoned deliberation and/ or intuition, and whether it occurs consciously or subconsciously. Biology ensures that living creatures are born with the necessary equipment to care for and cooperate with others. Humans develop a set of guiding principles and beliefs that form a remembered backdrop for our thoughts and actions. However, what humans think and do in any given situation results from a sense of what is best and what is not so good, what is right and not right. These are acts of tacit discernment that can be refined and cultivated through constant practice and rehearsal. In that sense, the authors argue, moral development is emergent and self-organizing; that it is highly dynamic, variable, context-sensitive, and somewhat unpredictable. This does not make the educational task of cultivating moral values easy. Instead, the authors provide a model of moral development that is complex and always in flux, developmental but often not predictable, and that's the educational challenge.

The next chapter, by **Pradeep Dhillon**, focuses on aesthetics and judgment. She explores the neuroscientific basis of aesthetic forms such as shapes, lines, an edges in order to argue for a transcultural basis for making aesthetic judgments. She begins with an exploration of Zangwill's idea of non-aesthetic properties supervening on what she calls narrow, formal aesthetic properties in an artwork. She holds that moderate formalism is the best approach to see stable patterns across cultural and historical differences. Using examples from India, including Sher-Gil and Raza, she argues for a way to make aesthetic judgments in a non-hegemonic manner. She turns to an aesthetics version of supervenience theory to depict a way of relating narrow, formal aesthetic properties with non-aesthetic ones such as line and color. This approach, she says, allows us to compare works of different periods or cultures in the way that they afford people similar aesthetic experiences. She turns to neuroscience, and in particular discoveries of certain clusters of cells in the brain that seem to respond selectively to lines and other visual cues oriented in specific spatial ways. Her point is that neuroscience has discovered basic building blocks of visual representation and processing. Although she cautions that drawing attention to specific correlations between neuroscientific findings and specific features of particular artworks is not yet to explain why someone would have an aesthetic experience, nevertheless she suggests that these neuroscientific building blocks lead to ways of exploring the idea of aesthetic appreciation beyond specific historical periods or cultures. She suggests that her approach has fruitful implications for a variety of areas, including curatorial practices of artworks from various periods and cultures. This might lead to new ways of seeing and judging across cultural differences. Her conclusion is that we can rightly turn to science to shed light on some of the more vexing and abiding issues in aesthetic theory, the resolution of which can enrich not only art education but education more generally.

Tyson Lewis's chapter continues the section with an educational and philosophical exploration of the notion of plasticity. He starts by exploring Althusser's exploration of the relationship between philosophy and science, drawing attention to his idea of philosophy's role of drawing demarcation lines. This intervention, as Lewis calls it, is the philosophical gesture that Catharine Malabou also employs in her work on the question of neural plasticity. Lewis's goal is to demonstrate that we still need a philosophical theory of the brain in order to prevent certain ideologies from taking over. Lewis turns to the recent work of philosophy of Catherine Malabou, who, he argues, seriously challenges many of the assumptions of the flexibility thesis. She does so not by rejecting neuroscience, but rather by historicizing its major claims, connecting the scientific investigation into flexibility with the overarching rise of flexible, transnational capitalism. Lewis points out that for Malabou the mind is capable of radical eruptions that are not cumulative or continuous. Drawing on examples taken from brain trauma, literature, and philosophy, Malabou posits that flexibility actually underestimates the brain's radical potentiality for reinvention, rupture, and the production of unprecedented new forms of life and subjectivity. Indeed, there is a utopian possibility for breaking with the past found in the very architecture of the brain. Lewis draws out several implications of this insight, which are far reaching for education. For one, Malabou poses a challenge to Dewey's theory of mind that was both plastic and adaptable; Dewey's idea of habituation is a kind of open-ended process of becoming which was continuous and cumulative. Lewis's critique is that instead of promoting the society of tomorrow, as Dewey would have liked, a progressive education predicated on a notion of the flexible, plastic brain is actually a symptom of modern industrialization, scientism, and global capitalism. Teachers interested in promoting educational experiences over and above mis-educative experiences typically employ a philosophy of mind that conceptualizes the flexible nature of the brain and its functioning. Lewis argues that contemporary neuroscience on the whole supports Dewey's philosophy of mind, emphasizing the brain's plastic nature and its malleability. For another, if we move beyond the flexibility model inherited from Dewey and now given scientific 'legitimacy' by neuroscientific research, new possibilities emerge for education. If the brain can undergo transformations as Malabou suggests, this suggests that education might act as a catalyst for events. And, Lewis asks, if it can, should it? He ends by addressing what it might mean if radical education is, on the level of the brain, a traumatic experience and if so, what are the ethics of an education that provokes such trauma.

The next chapter in this section, by **Clarence Joldersma**, develops an alternative philosophical model of mind, one that he suggests is more adequate for understanding possible contributions of neuroscience to education. He begins with a critique of the philosophical model of mind that typically frames our understanding of cognitive science, neuroscience, and the application of neuroscience to education. Joldersma argues that in the emerging field of neuroeducation, there is an implicit set of philosophical assumptions about the relation between mind and brain, one that in traditional cognitive science is termed a 'representational theory of mind.' He enters the discussion through John Bruer's recent neuroscientific construal of learning in terms of neural correlates to mental representations. Joldersma spends the first part of the chapter developing an argument that a representationalist approach is inadequate to the task and then introduces another philosophical perspective, that of radical embodiment. Radical embodiment involves the idea that we cannot understand the brain and mind in isolation from the body and its environment. The chapter develops this perspective by interpreting brain states as fundamentally involving dynamic sensorimotor coupling of the lived body and its surroundings, rather than being construed as rule-based computations over abstract symbols (mental representations). Drawing especially on philosopher Evan Thompson's groundbreaking book, *Mind in Life*, the chapter describes an enactive approach to cognition based in a radical embodiment approach. Rather than the computational manipulation of mental representations, enactive cognition involves something brought forth in the deliberate, intentional interaction between a bodily subject and its world. Moreover, the chapter draws on the phenomenological tradition—including particularly Merleau-Ponty—to construe such sensorimotor dynamics in terms of a lived body, i.e., as a bodily subject that responds to situations in the world. The chapter briefly turns to dynamic systems theory as well as to J. J. Gibson's idea of affordances to model how the bodily subject generates and maintains coherent patterns of activities in its interaction with the world. Learning is subtended by the neural dynamics of sensorimotor coupling. Thus, on the enactive approach, learning is fundamentally something humans do by an extended process of skillful probing, one in which the world makes itself available to the reach of the learner.

The last chapter of the section, by **Shaun Gallagher**, participates in an ongoing philosophical discussion about the mind in the area of embodied cognition. One aspect of this philosophical debate is about social cognition, where one side has developed a 'simulation' understanding of social cognition, and the other a more direct and interactive approach. Gallagher is part of the second approach, developing his position from a phenomenological perspective. He frames the debate in terms of different understandings of hermeneutics—between 'neural hermeneutics' and 'enactive hermeneutics.' He begins by asking: in the context of the scientific study of intersubjective interaction and social cognition, how should we conceive of the interpretation of others? He depicts the first approach, neural hermeneutics, as understanding the brain's interpretive function in terms of predictive coding, both as the mechanism for and the model of intersubjective understanding. Chris Frith is a proponent of this view, who says, "Neural Hermeneutics is concerned with the mechanisms, instantiated in the brain, through which people are able to understand one another." Gallagher points out that Frith equates the predictive coding loop with the hermeneutic circle and cites Schleiermacher in defense of his conception of how we understand others. Gallagher then contrasts his own approach to that of Frith, proposing an 'embodied hermeneutics.' This model emphasizes the dynamics of face-to-face interaction rather than internal brain processes. He draws on studies that highlight social and cultural factors in social interpretation, suggesting that there are cultural variations in brain mechanisms that sustain perception and emotions. He argues that these studies undermine Frith's simulation approach to social cognition and point to the idea that the brain needs to be understood as part of a larger set of dynamic relations, one that includes the body and environment. This enactive hermeneutics aligns with a Gadamerian view of understanding others. Gallagher then moves to education, examining the concept of 'natural pedagogy,' a term that he borrows from developmental studies (Csibra and Gergely) as a way to understand how we gain generalizable knowledge. He interprets this idea enactively. He concludes that education involves a hermeneutic circle consisting of body-brain-environment, rather than merely an isolated brain.

Together, the essays of the second section showcase creative possibilities that occur when philosophers of education turn their attention to neuroscience and its connection to education. The chapters are not meant to develop a uniform or common perspective or even ones that are necessarily consistent with each other. Rather, they highlight important and creative philosophical possibilities that emerge when philosophers engage educational neuroscience. Although a first foray into this conversation, the insights developed by the essayists are interesting and worthwhile.

The book concludes with a synthesizing, retrospective essay by **Nicholas Burbules**. His chapter engages the previous chapters of the book by categorizing into five themes the previous chapters' various criticisms of neuroscience research in education. He clusters the criticisms into five areas: methodological, conceptual, theoretical, political, and educational. What emerges through the five clusters is a coherent set of philosophical criticisms that jointly show a new voice in the discussion of the intersection of neuroscience and education. Burbules's interpretation of the state of philosophy of education in its engagement of neuroscience and education shows why philosophers of education are important to this conversation. And, albeit indirectly, Burbules's analysis also suggests future directions for philosophy of education, given the work of this current volume, for equally, any particular critique is also an opportunity to develop alternative modes of thinking. And so his chapter is at the same time a sketch of new possibilities for engaging with neuroscience in its application to educational research and practice.

NOTES

1. Examples include Harvard, Stanford, MIT, Yale in the US; Cambridge, University College London, Oxford in the UK; Dusseldorf, Zurich, Bonn, Gottingen, Amsterdam, Milan, Kaorlinska in continental Europe.
2. For example, the Society of Applied Neuroscience and the Applied Neuroscience Society of Australasia.
3. This is evidenced by, if nothing else, the increasing number of educational research centers: Mind, Brains and Education at Harvard; the Neuro Education Initiative at Johns Hopkins; Stanford Education Neuroscience Program at Stanford; the Centre for Neuroscience in Education at the University of Cambridge; Centre for Educational Neuroscience at the Institute of Education, University College, London; the Neurocognitive Development Unit at the University of Western Australia; Numerical Cognition Laboratory at the University of Western Ontario (Canada); Center for Neuroscience and Learning at the University of Ulm (Germany).
4. These include Vanderbilt University; Teachers College, Columbia; Harvard; Stanford; Cambridge; Oxford; VU University Amsterdam.

REFERENCES

Cozolino, Louis. 2013. *The Social Neuroscience of Education: Optimizing Attachment and Learning in the Classroom*. New York: W.W. Norton & Company.

Della Sala, Sergio, and Mike Anderson. 2012. *Neuroscience in Education: The Good, the Bad, and the Ugly*. Oxford: Oxford University Press.

Howard-Jones, Paul A. 2010. *Introducing Neuroeducational Research: Neuroscience, Education and the Brain from Contexts to Practice*. London and New York: Routledge.

Howard-Jones, Paul A. 2012. *Education and Neuroscience: Evidence, Theory and Practical Application*. reprint. London: Routledge.

Patten, Kathryn E., and Stephen R. Campbell, eds. 2011. *Educational Neuroscience: Initiatives and Emerging Issues*. Hoboken, NJ: Wiley.

Sousa, David A., ed. 2011. *Educational Neuroscience*. Thousand Oaks, CA: Corwin.

Part I

A Critique of Neuroscience in Educational Research and Practice

2 Out of Our Minds
Hacker and Heidegger contra Neuroscience

Emma Williams and Paul Standish

On the current neuroscientist's view, it's the brain that thinks and reasons and calculates and believes and fears and hopes. In fact, it's human beings who do all these things, not their brains . . . .

(Hacker 2012)

BRAINS, MINDS, AND MYTHS

Is the brain of educational interest? Read in a positivistic sense, this question is easy to answer. For, in education today, there is palpable interest in the human brain. In lots of ways, such interest is understandable. Many working in the field of education have long been convinced that our understanding of how human beings develop and learn can be advanced by insights gleaned from empirical investigations into cognitive functioning. Hence the long-standing link between education and psychology. Yet, in recent years, the emergence of more biologically advanced understandings of neural structures in the brain—the field of what is now called 'cognitive neuroscience'—has propelled this interest in new and controversial directions.

The impact of this has been especially felt in educational practice, where a number of packages for enhancing students' learning and performance, which claim to be grounded in scientific knowledge of the brain, have emerged. Enter the 'brain-based learning' program Brain Gym, which prescribes twenty-six physical movements, purported to trigger "whole brain learning" in school children (Brain Gym 2011). Among Brain Gym's more remarkable claims is that children have special areas on their bodies known as 'brain buttons' which, when stimulated, can trigger a heightened focus for their visual systems of reading and writing. While the Brain Gym website itself admits "it is not clear yet 'why' these movements work so well" (2011), such packages continue to flourish, heralded as important and innovative educational 'tools.'

Academic researchers working in newly formed Centers for Educational Neuroscience have been more cautious. In fact, many specialists in educational neuroscience are now keen to expose the 'neuromyths' they perceive to be at work in education and particularly within the 'brain-based learning' industry.[1] And it is worth noting that programs such as Brain Gym constitute only one portion of this. As Usha Goswami (2006) suggests, the neuro-mythology might well extend to ideas as familiar as critical periods of learning development, notions of visual, auditory, and kinaesthetic 'learning styles,' and the well-worn view that the left and right hemispheres of our brains are responsible for different types of thinking. It seems, then, that those working in education and neuroscience are currently involved in a complex cleanup operation.

At the same time, researchers are somewhat optimistic about what the new knowledge of the brain rendered by neuroscience can offer to education. Hence a recent report entitled *Neuroscience and Education: Issues and Opportunities* (Teaching and Learning Research Programme 2011) concludes by affirming that "neuroscience has a fundamental and increasing relevance to education" and that "to ignore the relevance of present neuroscientific understanding to education flies in the face of a common-sense connection" (24). The pressing task thus seems to be one not of justifying *whether* neuroscience is of educational interest, but rather of forging the best *way* this utility can be realized. In this spirit, a strongly advocated approach is the fusion of neuroscience, the biological and physiological account of the brain, with psychological concepts of the mind and mental processing. As the report recognizes, a big challenge for educational neuroscientists is to bridge the divide between the biological/physiological picture of the brain presented by science and the actual or 'direct' processes of thinking in human beings. And it is here that the neuroscientist must turn to the psychologist and vice versa, "for when cognitive models and our knowledge of biological processes inform each other, we can feel more confident about both" (17).

Let us return to our opening gambit. We asked if the brain is of educational interest, and immediately we saw that surely it is. Is this all there is to say? Certainly not. For, as is so often the case in such matters, the fact that something actually *is* of educational interest begets a further question, namely, whether the brain actually *should be*, or *is worthy of holding*, such interest. Here our question becomes an explicitly philosophical one. Of course, as we noted earlier, those working in the field of educational neuroscience believe there to be a 'commonsense' connection between brain science and education—thus suggesting it is taken-as-read that the brain should be of interest to educators. We do not want to deny such a view wholesale here. Nevertheless, we do want to suggest that this interest should be acutely aware of its limits: for there are areas in which the extension of biological knowledge of the brain does not make *philosophical* sense—and in fact constructs a picture that holds pernicious influence over education and its associated practices.

Before spelling out our position in detail, let us bring into view the picture that holds the educational neuroscientist captive. We have just noted that one of the largest problems facing educational neuroscience today is how to bridge the 'explanatory gap' and translate the physiological account of the brain, which is increasingly being unfolded via scientific investigation of neural networks, into education. In other words, one of the major issues facing educational neuroscience is one of the key problems facing the discipline of cognitive neuroscience more broadly: that of showing how the new scientific knowledge of the brain can be used to say something meaningful about the cognitive capacities of human beings. What tends to happen is that this task gets adjudicated by way of psychology. Hence cognitive neuroscientists—and, as we saw earlier, educational neuroscientists follow this lead—attempt to assimilate a biological understanding of the brain with psychological concepts and categories of concepts.

How exactly does this work out? Max Bennett and Peter Hacker (2003) have suggested that while early neuroscientists ascribed psychological attributes to the *mind*, contemporary neuroscientists reject dualisms and thus work to ascribe psychological attributes to the *brain* (14). Perhaps one of the most celebrated illustrations of this is the work of Benjamin Libet, whose experiment into voluntary decision making was taken to demonstrate that the *brain decides* (or rather *a specific neural network within the brain decides*) to begin to act at least 2000 milliseconds before one becomes 'consciously aware' of having made such a decision. Such a characterization of the brain is shared by a number of leading neuroscientists: indeed both Blakemore and Young suggest that "the brain *knows* things, *reasons* inductively, *constructs* hypotheses on the basis of arguments, and its constituent neurons are *intelligent*, can *estimate probabilities* and *present arguments*" (Bennett and Hacker 2003, 17). What the 'interface' between neuroscience and psychology appears to come down to, then, is a particular mode of ascription of "psychological attributes to the brain and its parts," which is then used "*in order to explain* the possession of psychological attributes and the exercise . . . of cognitive powers by human beings" (2003, 7, emphasis in original).

We have already seen how such a picture has come to take hold in certain areas of education. Indeed, the 'brain-based learning' phraseology that has been on the rise in recent years in educational practice works, in a similar vein, to attribute cognitive powers of learning to the *brain* rather than the human individual. Yet it is worth noting here that a shared tendency is evident in the work of those academic researchers who, as we noted earlier, want to distance themselves from such pseudo-scientific programs and their 'neuromyths.' For example, the earlier-cited report references a recent study into the fostering of creativity that has revealed that the degree of creativity a student's story was judged to possess was directly "linked to increased 'creative' brain activity"—that is, to a heightened activity in those areas of the brain "associated with creative effort" (Teaching and Learning Research Programme 2011, 23). Here, then, we find a clear illustration of the picture Hacker bring into view, wherein "operations of the brain . . . are being advanced as explanations for human behaviour" (2012). Indeed, the report itself suggests that cognitive neuroscience operates with a model of 'brain → mind → behavior' in seeking to explain human activity—although it recognizes that such a model may well need to be 'extended' and amalgamate insights from the social sciences (Teaching and Learning Research Programme 2011, 23).

At this point, question marks over the neuroscientific approach may well start to arise. Let us imagine that we want to explain why certain students have been able to produce stories that are more 'creative' than others (setting aside for now questions regarding the criteria of creativity). The neuroscientist comes along and tells us she has the answer: an fMRI scan has revealed that it is because those students have increased activity in the part of the brain associated with creative effort. Is this a good explanation? Hacker would argue not. In fact, Hacker suggests, what the neuroscientist gives us here is *no explanation at all.* For what the neuroscientist seems to be suggesting is that certain students have been more creative because their brains (or a certain part of their brains) have been more creative. Aside from seemingly making the classical logical blunder of shifting back, rather than solving the problem, we might also ask, does talk of the creativity of the brain itself make sense? Of course, we might talk in ordinary parlance about someone having a 'creative brain,' but we do not usually interpret this to mean that the 'little gray cells' we all have inside our skulls are creative. For *human beings* are creative: not brains, not neurons, not cells.

This last point might seem trivial, but the principle aim of this chapter is to bring out its significance. In other words, and we shall aim to show, while Hacker's critique is focused on linguistic analysis, we should not misinterpret his point as *merely linguistic.* For making the point that it is human beings who think and reason, rather than their brains, does more than just clarify the language and terminology of the neuroscientist. The philosophical move being made here is not a janitorial one. Rather, the linguistic point has *metaphysical significance*: it opens up something important about the nature of human beings and the world they live in. This is something Hacker himself attests to within his account.[2] Notably, however, as we shall also come to see, Hacker's account in important ways also stops short of drawing out the full implications of this. To take the analysis further, then, in the later stages of this chapter, we shall take a path through aspects of the philosophies of Wittgenstein and Heidegger. In doing so, we will work to show more fully how challenging the *language* of neuroscience constitutes a significant challenge to neuroscience as a whole. For the false pictures that it sets up and sustains of how human beings go on, in educational settings and elsewhere, are not to be explained in terms of its succumbing to neuro-mythologies: these are tantamount to neuro-*mystifications.*

METONYMS, METAPHORS, AND MYSTIFICATIONS

Let us now recommence our consideration of Hacker's analysis. As we have already seen, Hacker's key objection to neuroscience is built upon a point of linguistic clarification. Neuroscientists, he states, have illegitimately extended psychological concepts—thinking, reasoning, perceiving, willing, and so forth—to the *brain*. Yet the brain, Hacker (2012) claims, is not "a logically appropriate subject for psychological predicates"; and we can, as he points out, see this quite clearly from the fact that it makes no sense to talk of "the brain's thinking or knowing, seeing or hearing, believing or guessing" (19). Notably, Hacker adds to his critique by providing two explanations for this illegitimate move. The first is that it is rooted in an "unthinking adherence to a mutant form of Cartesianism" on the part of contemporary neuroscientists (2012, 20–21). What Hacker means here is that the way neuroscientists use and ascribe psychological predicates follows the usage first laid down by Descartes in the seventeenth century. Of course, Descartes ascribed psychological predicates to an *immaterial mind*— a notion that is intractable to the contemporary neuroscientist. However, in ascribing these predicates instead to the *biological brain*, neuroscientists merely repeat the Cartesian move on another (physical/material) level. We shall pick up the threads of this point a little later in this chapter. For now, let us focus our attention more on the second explanation Hacker provides for the illegitimate move committed by contemporary neuroscientists. This, in a way that is not unrelated to the first, consists of the claim that neuroscientists have fallen prey to what Hacker terms the 'mereological fallacy.' This means that they have come to ascribe to constituent parts of human beings attributes that logically apply to the *whole* (22). Thus psychological predicates, Hacker suggests, properly apply to the "whole living animal" and not particular parts of that animal (22). To say otherwise is tantamount to suggesting that the *eye* is what sees, rather than recognizing that it is *we* who see "with our eyes" (and a whole host of other things as well).

It is important to attend carefully to what Hacker is saying here, not least because certain possible objections to what he is saying quickly come into view. Indeed, it might be pointed out that there are circumstances in everyday life when it is entirely appropriate to speak of parts of our *bodies* doing (or not doing) things, rather than our 'whole person.' Consider for example the person who, after screwing up her eyes in the optician's chair declares, "it's no good, my eyes are too weak to see the bottom line." Of course, this person might equally have told the doctor "I can't see the bottom line," but the former way of talking is not reprehensible—and in fact it might be entirely appropriate, given the circumstances, to draw attention to and describe the physical impairment in such terms. And in a similar way, we might point out that people have in fact come to speak in meaningful ways about the brain 'doing' certain things we might equally attribute to the whole person. Suppose I am teaching a philosophy class in the first lesson of the day. One of my students asks me a tricky question—say, "Could you re-explain Russell's paradox about set theory?" I might well respond by saying, "I'll tell you in a moment, when my brain grinds into gear." Of course, I might equally say, "I can't think right now because it is 8:25 a.m. and way too early for me," but the point is that the former way of talking is *not inappropriate* given the circumstances (and the question!). And perhaps, later on in the same day, a friend is telling me a particularly startling piece of information to which I reply, "My brain needs to process what you have just said!" Once again, this is not a misconceived way of speaking, and it would surely be mistaken to say that the person is simply in error. Indeed, in cases like these, there is a metonymic usage of language at work—which is part and parcel of our everyday way of thinking and speaking with others.

Furthermore, it can be said that such a point may also be made with respect to the neuroscientific usages of language. Indeed, as Hacker himself points out, in key places, neuroscientists *themselves* suggest that their usage of language is figurative or, more specifically, metaphorical. A good illustration of this is given by neuroscientific talk about 'maps' of the brain—now a fairly commonplace notion within this field. These 'maps' are rule-governed nerve firings—'topographic patterns of activity'—and have been described (by J. Z. Young among others) as the brain's language or grammar. In other words, brain maps are thought of as systems of representation through which the brain interprets the world. Hence, as Colin Blakemore suggests, brain maps are mediums of interpretation, in the same way that the maps of an atlas are mediums used by human beings to understand and interpret the world. Notably, however, Blakemore himself argues that this way of talking about the brain is not meant to be *literal*: it does not suggest there is "a ghostly cartographer browsing through the cerebral atlas." Rather, he claims, the notion of brain maps is invoked as "metaphorical imagery," the result of "empirical description, poetic license and inadequate vocabulary" (as quoted in Hacker and Bennett 2003, 31).

From this, Hacker's objection seems to be on shaky ground. For one, Hacker cannot be against or deny the usage of metonym in everyday speech. Ordinary language philosophy, after all, profoundly influences his thinking, and the acknowledgment of ordinary usage must at some point pull in favor of such contemporary forms of expression. Now, we could contend that Hacker would agree with this and would not seek to outlaw metonymic usage in everyday parlance as merely fallacious ways of talking. However, and this is a key point, we would also contend that *the matter is quite different when we come to consider the use of figurative or metaphorical language in the field of neuroscience*. In other words, we would contend, there is a difference to be drawn between ordinary-language ways of talking and the ways language is used in neuroscientific circles. And this is because, in a way that is quite distinct from metonymic usage in ordinary language, what happens in neuroscientific parlance is that the metaphor is made to stand for the whole in some *reified sense*—as though the brain *actually is* the (only) thing that is 'doing' the thinking, processing, believing, and so on. Of course, as we have just seen, neuroscientists such as Blakemore want to deny this and claim that they know 'full well' that the way they are using language is metaphorical. And yet—and this is the key point—it is difficult to see how neuroscientists really can defend such a claim. Hacker himself makes this point, stating as he does that while we might well grant that Blakemore et al. do not *really* believe that there is a 'ghostly cartographer' who reads maps within the brain and that the phrase 'brain maps' is used by virtue of poetic license or inadequate vocabulary, when we look a little more closely at what is being said by the neuroscientist, it becomes clear that the metaphorical language runs *much deeper* than is recognized. For, even when they try to jettison the talk of the brain as a ghostly cartographer, they still suggest that the brain, or some part of brain tissue at least, "makes use" of the maps in its navigation of the world; they still suggest that the brain, or some part of it, "operates with" maps in order to "interpret and represent" the world. In this way, then, it seems that however much Blakemore et al. want to claim they are *just* using language metaphorically or figuratively, their claims about the brain are *so steeped* in this metaphor that it is difficult to see how they are *not* engaged in reification and thinking of the brain as *really* what is 'doing' all of these (psychological, mental, human) activities. A *non-ghostly* cartographer is still, after all, a cartographer.

Perhaps we can make this point a little more strongly here and suggest that, in the language of neuroscience, the metaphorical uses of language *have ceased to be recognized* as metaphorical at all. Such a charge might fruitfully be compared to Nietzsche's critique of the epistemological drive to truth, in which we come to call 'truths' those illusions that we have forgotten are illusions: "metaphors which are worn out and without sensuous power; coins which have lost their pictures and now matter only as metal, no longer as coins."[3] And it is perhaps fair to say that, in a similar way to those envisaged by Nietzsche, the *conditions* for the neuroscientific reification—the forgetfulness of metonym and metaphor that we have just identified—lie in our own scientific culture and its associated epistemology, where scientistic and reductivist explanations for human behavior have become so entrenched, often with misleading consequences.

Before moving on to say more on this last point, let us note that it is possible to put the challenge we are leveling here against the neuroscientist in another way. For the process of reification that we have just suggested the neuroscientist is involved in becomes equally (if not more) apparent when we take the following into consideration. In ordinary usage, it is usually possible to substitute a literal expression for the metaphor in question. For example, it would be possible to re-interpret the phrase "life is a roller coaster" in a more literal sense as "life is full of ups and downs, highs and lows." Is it possible to do the same with the metaphorical statements used in the field of neuroscience? Perhaps not, or at least not as easily. For in the language of the neuroscientists, it is not clear what the *literal expression* we would want to substitute in would be. Consider a sample phrase from the neuroscientist's repertoire such as "the brain operates with maps in order to interpret the world." Now, what is the corresponding literal expression for this claim? If the neuroscientist says it is to be found in some description of electric-chemical changes in the brain, this would surely undercut the very move (to the mental) that they are trying to make. And, from this, another—somewhat more pernicious—challenge to the neuroscientist might be envisaged. For, we may well come to question whether the language of the neuroscientist is, in the end, *metaphorical at all*, rather than *mystification*.[4]

Can we take these challenges any further? Indeed we can. As we stated at the beginning of our chapter, our aim here is to show how the linguistic challenges we can make against neuroscience have a *metaphysical significance*: for they open up something important regarding the way we understand human beings and how they go on—in educational settings and elsewhere. Now, as we also outlined earlier, while Hacker's account can take us *some of the way* toward seeing this, it does not take us as far as we would like to go in this chapter. And, at this stage, it is perhaps worth noting that the reason for this is that Hacker does not, in our eyes, fully draw out what is *wrong* with the forgetfulness of metaphor—or indeed the mystifications— that we have just charged the neuroscientist with being engaged in. What we are appealing to here, more specifically, are problems that arise from both (i) the picture of the human being that is *sustained* by neuroscientific metaphors and mystifications and (ii) the picture of the human being that simultaneously is *effaced*. As we have intimated, to develop this point, we will bring our analysis to cross paths with the philosophies of Wittgenstein and Heidegger. Let us now see how this transition can be made.

PRACTICES, CONVENTIONS, AND RULE FOLLOWING

To begin with, let us follow a further thread from Hacker's own analysis. In particular, let us consider the way Hacker elaborates his aforementioned critique of the neuroscientist's use of the cartographical metaphor. Now, Hacker expands upon the reasons why he feels it is mistaken to use the phraseology of 'maps' to apply to procedures in the brain when he says:

> [A] map is a pictorial representation, made in accordance with conven-
> tions of mapping and rules of projection. Someone who can read an
> atlas must know and understand these conventions, and read off, from
> the maps, the features of what is represented. But the 'maps' in the brain
> are not maps, in this sense, at all. The brain is not akin to the reader of a
> map, since it cannot be said to know any conventions of representation
> . . . or to read anything off the topological arrangement of firing cells in
> accordance with a set of conventions. For the cells are not arranged in
> accordance with conventions at all.
>
> (2012, 33)

Hacker's point here is that something fundamental and intrinsic to a map being what it is—functioning *as* a map—means that this notion is not well applied to the domain that concerns the neuroscientist. For the neuroscientist is concerned with activities of the brain (such as clusters of brain cells), and these are mechanical or, we might say, disengaged and abstracted processes. Yet the process of reading a map is categorically different to this. And the key difference, as Hacker emphasizes in the earlier quotation, comes from the fact that map reading is an activity that is made possible by virtue of certain *conventions*. Cartography, as we might say, is a human *practice* (to the extent that 'practices' can be defined as activities that are conditioned by conventions: which may extend from the simple practice of sitting in a chair to the more complex practice of driving a car or playing tennis). Yet the mechanical workings of clusters of brain cells do not operate in accordance with conventions at all. Hence any talk of the brain having 'maps' is a misapplication of the concept: brains don't read maps, human beings do.

Notably, Hacker does not take this account much further at this stage—a move that is perhaps defensible, given the overarching aim of his work in this area is to expose the "conceptual errors" within the field of neuroscience or, more specifically, within the description of the results that follow from the neuroscientist's experiments and investigations. For Hacker, without such conceptual clarity, the neuroscientist "will not have understood what he set out to understand" and will hence be unable to publicly communicate, in any meaningful way, the genuine positive results that this field can have (2012, 33). But it is perhaps worth *our* while dwelling on the account we have just opened here, by way of Hacker, a little more. For much remains to be said and in ways that brings us more explicitly to see that what happens when neuroscientists 'misunderstand' the results of their investigations is that they come to set up a false picture of the human being—and one that can efface the ways human beings actually go on.

To see this, let us now cross over more explicitly to Wittgenstein and, in particular, his account of rule following—a move that does not constitute too much of a leap at this stage, given Wittgenstein's account is surely not far from Hacker's own mind when he invokes the notion of *convention* to differentiate between the human activity of map reading and the firing of brain neurons in the earlier quotation.[5] What, precisely, does Wittgenstein have to say on this? Charles Taylor (1997) offers us a helpful summary. We want to know how it is possible that human beings are able to follow rules. To find the answer, Wittgenstein asks us to consider what it would mean to say that a human being knows how to follow arrows (one example of rule following). Now, on the strength of a traditional (or what Taylor calls 'intellectualist') reading, it might be claimed that the person who knows how to follow the arrows has in their mind (consciously or unconsciously) a certain premise that instructs them on the right way to follow arrows. Indeed, the presence of such a premise seems to be exemplified by the fact that, if a stranger appears on the scene who follows arrows in the wrong way (they intuitively follow the direction of the feathers, for example, rather than the point), our right-minded person can explain their mistake to them. In this way, one (intellectualist) answer to the question of what it means to say a human being knows how to follow rules is to say that they have within themselves an *explanation* of the right way to follow said rule, which can be articulated to others on the occasion that they go wrong.

However, for Wittgenstein, this intellectualist explanation leads to insurmountable difficulties. To see why, consider first that in any situation of rule following, any given run of cases, there is a host of different ways of 'following-on' that are available. For example, the sequence 2, 4, 6, 8 may be followed by 10, 12, 14, 16 or by 12, 14, 16, 18, etc., or by 102, 104, 106, 108, etc. We cannot foreclose in advance the question of what following-on might mean to someone who is taught with the initial sequence, provided that some sense can be made of the ensuing sequence. Sequences and rule following are, we might say, open to development. Notably, however, one of the upshots of this is that, for any given explanation of rule following, there will remain an infinite number of points in the sequence at which someone could misunderstand (Taylor 1997, 166). Put otherwise, *explanations* (of how to follow a rule) are themselves open-ended and partial, because "every explanation leaves some other potential issues unresolved" (166). If we now return to our intellectualist account of rule following, we start to see the problem. For this account suggests that, to be able to follow a rule, what we need is some articulable understanding of what it means to follow on correctly in any given situation. And yet, on the basis of what we have just seen, it becomes clear that possessing such an understanding would also require us to understand all the *wrong* ways of carrying on, at the same time. In other words, we would need to have formulated and discounted in our heads in advance all possible permutations and combinations of a particular run of cases. And yet, given rules are themselves open to modification and development, this would mean that to follow even the *simplest* of rules, we would need to possess an infinite number of thoughts in our heads in advance. Obviously, this is impossible. This is not to make a skeptical point about rule following. We are not here moving toward the conclusion that we do not or cannot know how to follow rules—or that there are no rules and everything can be interpreted in any way we like. Plainly, human beings successfully follow rules: we get it right, most of the time. The upshot is, however, that we need a different and more adequate account of rule following than that offered by the intellectualist.

We can move toward such an account by appealing to a point that brings us back into direct contact with the analysis offered by Hacker earlier: the intellectualist account appears to lose sight of the part played by *convention* in the following of rules. To develop this, let us return to our example of map reading. More particularly, let us consider, in ordinary terms, how a human being might come to learn how to read a map. Now, surely one of the obvious ways this happens is through their being guided by someone more skilled than themselves. (We set aside, for brevity's sake, the multiple ways in which a child's attention might first be guided by the movement of a finger and subsequently be drawn to looking at representations or patterns on paper, perhaps in the context of trying to find the way to a destination and so forth. All this would be stages in learning what a map *is* and, hence, preparatory to our example here.) The guide helps the novice to see when they are getting it wrong and making mistakes with their reading, and they will help the novice to *correct* their reading when such mistakes arise. And such correction—and this is the crucial point—is made possible by the fact that there is a *community* that sustains there being the correct way of reading the map, through the *conventions* that they agree upon and put into practice. Another way of putting this is to say that it is through what people do together that rules and possibilities of correctness come into view and come to be.[6]

To some extent, what we have said here fleshes out in more detail what we have already seen earlier by way of Hacker. Yet we can also add further detail to this account here. For it is important to note that conventions and practices are also flexible and fluid. Hence the correct way of reading a map might well be different if one's concerns or purposes are different; the appropriate way to read a map can alter and change according to one's priorities. Thus, we might say, there is never any *totalized* reading of the map—there are multiple ways in which a map might be used, all of which are sustained by human practices. In addition, and pushing this further still, we can say that rules and conventions themselves can change and be modified. Indeed, it can be said that such flexibility is a key part of what it means to follow a rule and to have understood the meaning of the practice to which the rule applies in a number of situations. For we would not think that someone has learned the meaning of 'being a musician' if they simply played music by relying just on what is written in the score. Such an act might well produce accuracy, but it would fail to demonstrate the need for appreciation of the nuances of a piece and the possibilities of interpretation. Hence, as Charles Taylor puts it, a rule does not stand 'behind' the practice, as an underlying formula. Rather "[p]ractice is, as it were, a continual interpretation and reinterpretation of what the rule really means" (1997, 178).

Of course, and as might already be clear, what we are saying here is not meant only to apply to the practices of map reading (or following arrows or playing music). Our aim in developing this analysis is to show in more detail what is at stake in human activities *in general*. Now, it might be objected that we are leaping here too quickly. More specifically, it might be objected that taking what happens in map reading as an illustration of human activity *in general* is controversial. This is, not in the least, because a map is a tool of abstraction. In other words, a map presents the world in *representational* form, which is quite distinct from the embodied, embedded way we relate to the world in our everyday lives (where our sense of the very same place, for example, might be different depending on which direction we are going in, what our purposes are in going this way, what has previously happened to us along this way, and so on).[7] Perhaps, then, it might reasonably be objected that reading a map does not work as an adequate illustration of human life in general. We would have been better off using a more 'everyday' example. Yet we would suggest quite the opposite. In fact, we would argue that our use of map reading as an illustration of what goes on in human life more generally works to demonstrate that *even when* human beings are engaged in abstractions (making representations, dealing with objective 'states of affairs'), their activity is still fundamentally imbricated in conventions and practices. For representations can only function as representations on the basis of certain accepted rules and understandings about what sorts of things legitimately count as such. Hence it can be said that even the more apparently 'objective' human practices such as map reading or mathematics are made possible and sustained through community, convention, and purposes in the ways that we demonstrated earlier.

Let us, then, start to draw out some of the implications from our discussion thus far. For one, we have seen that human activities are, *par excellence*, governed by conventions, rules, and purposes. As we might put it, human practices are *conditioned* and *made possible* by conventions and rule following. Second, we have also now seen what is at stake in this idea more fully—we have started to see the nature of convention and rule following, which included an appeal to their flexibility and fluidity in the face of our concerns and purposes. And this brings us, as a third point, to see more fully just how problematic it is to talk, as neuroscientists are apt to do, about the *brain* carrying out activities that are normally ascribed to the human being: activities that require conventions, communities, and concerns to make them possible. Of course, this is not to say that we cannot talk about events in the brain as operating in accordance with certain rules or patterns. Indeed (in a way that somewhat reopens the point about the usage metaphor we examined earlier), it has become somewhat commonplace now to use the phraseology of 'rules' and 'patterns' within science, and the science of the brain is no exception to this. Yet what our foregoing analysis highlights to us is that what is meant by a rule or pattern in this sphere should be understood quite distinctly from what it means to follow a rule or a pattern as a human being. For the notion of rule we invoke in relation to brain activity is understood after the notion of a rule in natural sciences where, as Charles Taylor points out, what we are conceiving of is some sort of timeless, universal, "which dictates movements of all bodies everywhere" (1997, 176). Yet rule following in the realm of human affairs, as we have shown, is only properly understood with reference to communities and conventions: of which the brain has neither. Hence we must thus resist the intellectual temptation to equate what happens in the human world with what happens in the causal world of physical science. To make such an equation, we might say, is scientistic and hence profoundly misleading: it creates a false picture of what makes it possible for human beings to go on in the way they do.

HUMANS, PURPOSES, AND WORLD

Can we take our critique any further? We think we can. However, before we do this, let us make a slight detour and entertain the possibility that our own account may have laid us open to certain problems.

As we saw at the start, a prevailing aim among advocates of neuroscience is to bridge the divide between the biological/physiological picture of the brain presented by science and the actual or 'direct' processes of thinking in human beings. The purpose is to *explain* the possession of psychological attributes and the exercise of cognitive powers by human beings. Our response to this has been to draw attention to the rule-following nature of human practices in which purposiveness, concern, and use come together in an internal relation. Brains or clusters of brain cells, we have said, do not themselves have purposes. But have we missed something important here? It has become quite common in biology to talk in semiological terms—about 'messages' being transmitted from one part of the body to another. Is this metaphorical? At first blush, our answer might well be yes, but perhaps things are more complicated than they seem. Biology operates teleologically: the purpose of the lungs is to absorb oxygen from the air. Of course, without some further elaboration, this sounds markedly incomplete: why is it that oxygen needs to be absorbed? In response, we then come up with something about the circulation system, and we end up by couching this, quite reasonably, in some notion of normal animal or human functioning. So if we admit, as it seems we must if we are doing biology, purposes at this level (that is to say, if we accept that explanations at the micro-level depend holistically upon macro-level accounts that identify a *causa formalis* or *telos* of some kind), can we keep purposiveness out so insistently when we are doing neuroscience (that is, when we are describing neurological reactions)? And given that the neuroscience in question purports to deal with mental processes as well, a negative response to our question would seem to play into its hands.

Now certainly, at this point, we can be tempted by the thought that the neuroscientists' purported explanations might work in the case of simpler animals' interactions with their habitat, although the description would need to take account of the affordances of the environment and, hence, be holistic in that respect, and it would be purposive in terms of the forms of life described. So if this might conceivably be a valid approach for simpler animals, could it not be scaled up to account for human psychological reactions? What is there to separate humans from animals? Bringing our argument to bear on these problems will involve three inter-related moves.

First, then, a distinction needs to be drawn between the extension of the idea of purpose through biology, with its semiological ramifications, and the use of the term in relation to human beings themselves. The crucial difference here lies in the fact that it is impossible to make any sense of the life of human beings without reference to *their own sense* of what they are doing:

that human beings have purposes includes the fact that they entertain them, and this is part of what characterizes their mindedness. Animals of various levels of complexity can be said to have purposes too, but only in descriptive terms—that is, from the point of view of a human observer—and with a degree of anthropomorphism.

Second, the line that we have begun to draw here takes us back to the account of rule following that is central to our discussion. If, to avoid unnecessary elaboration, we confine our attention to the rule-following behavior of higher animals, we can see that their relation to rules and the use of signs is markedly different from that of human beings. For the animal, the sign functions with a regularity that is cause-like in its effects; for the human being, the sign remains open to interpretation. Hence, if we recall that 2, 4, 6, 8 can be followed not only by 10, 12, 14, 16 but also, say, by 11, 14, 17, 20, and so on, we get some glimpse of the open possibilities of human practices. Quintessentially, language functions in this way, and this is the very engine of culture. To say this, it is worth noting at this point, takes us beyond what comes to the fore in Hacker's treatment of language.[8]

A leap is made in self-consciousness where rules are opened to new possibilities and where interpretation and convention function there at the heart of the sign. The child does not just follow the rule but *knows* she is following the rule. How else could children's play-acting be explained?[9] And weighing the consequences of this can take us further than has been apparent in the insights from Wittgenstein upon which we have been drawing. The point is not that Wittgenstein's account is limited (although, as we shall see shortly, there is a sense in which it is), but that too much, or the wrong, emphasis on practices as language games can give the impression of a holistic, smooth functioning and self-containment that obscures the broader perspectives within which this familiar feature of Wittgenstein's thought comes to the fore. It is helpful to consider how a different approach to our topic, via the thought of Heidegger, might have led us to a similar juncture.

In fact, taking this line of thought will quickly lead us into the third of our moves, which will bring together purposiveness and rule following in relation to a better understanding of world. Heidegger's opposition to the Cartesian picture is every bit as strong as Wittgenstein's, and the phenomenology of the examples that he advances early in *Being and Time* challenge the intellectualist position in particularly telling ways (Heidegger 2005/1927). The purposiveness of the 'in-order-to' and the 'for-the-sake-of-which' in his account is crucial to his wider position. One hammers a nail in order to fix a doorframe as part of a house or a church . . . . By the end of that book, however, it becomes clear that this ellipsis must be filled in by the being-toward-death that is fundamental to, and distinctive of, the ontology of what he calls *Dasein*. Indeed animals in a sense do not die—that is, their deaths are not preceded by anticipation, by that terror in the middle of the night at the thought of becoming nothing. And lacking this self-consciousness, the consciousness that calls into question what their purposes might be, they lack a sense of *world*. The notion of 'world' or the 'worldly' character of *Dasein* is worth emphasizing here, and it forms a key part of Heidegger's account of human existence in *Being and Time* and elsewhere. Crucially, this notion should not be understood merely as an optional extra: it is not as though human beings *incidentally* or *accidentally* have a world. Rather, the world is constitutive of human existence itself; as Simon Glendinning (2007, 78) highlights, it is "a 'wherein,' a 'whereabouts' or a 'there' where Dasein always already finds itself." The world concerns *Dasein's* "familiarity with existence," and human existence is fundamentally a "being-in-the-world"—which means, an existence that takes place within language, culture, and so forth (80). The stone, in contrast, is without world; the animal is world-poor. Animals have only a habitat, not a world. Hence there is something encompassing, self-conscious, invoked by the notion of 'world' in Heidegger—which also brings into view an *unsteadying* dimension within human existence, a crucial aspect that can be obscured where emphasis on the holism of Wittgenstein's language games allows them to become picturesque.

There is good reason to think that something similar can be found in Wittgenstein's thought—say, in his response to skepticism, where, recurrently, peace is achieved only to be disturbed again, or in his remarks regarding religion and the understanding of other cultures in, for example, his *Remarks on Frazer's* Golden Bough (Wittgenstein 1993). Nevertheless, the thought remains recessive. Heidegger, by contrast, expresses this with a boldness that can itself appear excessive. And it is here that there is perhaps a limitation in Wittgenstein's account of language, as Rush Rhees has tried to show: Wittgenstein nowhere recognizes that a crucial feature of language is that we say things *about the world*.[10] Against the Cartesian picture, the impression one is given is of language in use—that is, in carrying out transactions, praying, telling jokes, etc. But in the richness of the plethora of examples, the sheer fact that we can say things about the world, and that the world is something about which things can be said, is obscured. That the world is something about which things can be said is, on this account, definitional of world. It is in the absence of this, most crucially, that the mental life of animals is different from that of human beings. And it is in the absence of the kind self-consciousness implied in this that the neuroscientists' attempt to ascribe psychological attributes to the brain and its parts, or to understand human mindedness by scaling up from simpler animal lives, is most disastrously exposed.

The 'explanatory gap' we identified at the start needs, then, to be placed differently, with greater emphasis given to the difference between the mental lives of human beings and those of animals. For while it would be wrong to deny connections, of course, it is from the top downward that our ordinary psychological concepts are secured, and it is this larger picture that gives sense to expressions such as 'see,' 'perceive,' 'anticipate,' 'hope,' and 'fear'— even to the idea of *thinking* itself. And, it is in this way that we come to show

how, we would argue, Hacker's analysis can be extended and strengthened. For by appealing to the notion of *world*, we have sought to bring the larger picture into view and to give a sense of the reach of the linguistic point with which we began. Let us now move to see where this discussion has taken us.

EDUCATION, NEUROSCIENCE, AND BEYOND

What conclusions can we now draw about the question we posed at the start of this chapter, viz. the justification of educational interest in the *brain*, which has, in recent years, been given a new life by the emergence of cognitive neuroscience?

We have argued throughout against the utility of invoking biological descriptions of the *brain* as useful tools for explaining what human beings do with their *minds*—which is to say, what human beings *do* (for surely all human action—save bodily movements such as blinking and breathing—is minded, in some sense). We began to build a case for this through an emphasis on ordinary language, and in particular the analysis of the language of neuroscience offered by Peter Hacker. This helped us to show that when those in the field of neuroscience—and those in educational neuroscience who follow suit—talk about the *brain* doing things and performing actions (e.g., a 'creative *brain*'), they engage in misleading reifications that, *at best*, perpetuate myths that have pervaded our understanding of the human mind since at least the time of Descartes and, *at worst*, beget new and more pervasive mystifications that halt progress and prevent more adequate understandings from coming to the fore. Not only, then, can it be said that such linguistic errors succeed in founding neuroscience on highly questionable philosophical assumptions, they also work to obscure the valuable evidence that neuroscientific investigations can bring. Furthermore, and more directly linked to education, it can be said that such modes of talking succeed in perpetuating the *instrumental* and *functional* conception of learning and thinking that has, in recent years, come to prominence; thus bringing neuroscience under the sway of a certain reductive conception of education, rather than allowing this new field to unfold its own possibilities and openings. Indeed the present context of practice, where policy makers are keen to wrest judgment from teachers, in combination with the prevailing empiricist climate of research, where the medical model is recurrently held up as the best orientation for inquiry, make education peculiarly susceptible to the allure of neuroscience, whose glamor is only enhanced by the huge research funding it currently attracts. These are circumstances in which opportunistic claims are made for neuroscience in education.

Through our exploration of rule following, purposes, and practices, we strengthened our critique by providing a positive account of human activity that again demonstrated its difference from the workings of the brain (however much these may be described, in biological terms, as operating according to certain rules, patterns, or teleological principles). We came to appreciate the reach of this point when we turned to consider the notion of *world*. This brought into view the larger, 'top-down' picture that needs to be invoked in any account of human activity, again emphasizing the incommensurability between this and the kind of explanation we are given on the basis of the somewhat linear neuroscientific account of brain → mind → behavior. Of course, as much as we can say that neuroscience, through this, becomes complicit in the instrumental and functional conception of education that holds sway today, we can also say that the messier, top-down model we have brought into view here becomes obscured. This certainly seems to be the case in areas such as the development of 'critical thinking' or 'thinking skills' which, as the present authors have shown elsewhere, are entrenched in a reductive and instrumentalist conception of human thought and human beings themselves.[11] Of course, this is not to suggest that neuroscience as a discipline is incommensurable with this larger picture—and perhaps if the project of neuroscience became more aware of its own philosophical foundations, it could find a way toward the sort of picture we have sought to elaborate here, which does more justice to the rich nature of human existence. This is an issue for a different essay. What we have sought in the present chapter, rather, is to show the vigilance that must be maintained in the face of current educational interest in the brain. And we have done so by seeking to demonstrate the full reach of the idea—misleadingly trivial in its appearance—that *brains* don't think, *human beings* do.

NOTES

1. See for example the commentary by Teaching and Learning Research Programme, *Neuroscience and Education: Issues and Opportunities*, whose contributors include: Sarah-Jayne Blakemore, Guy Claxton, Anne Cook, Richard Cox, Uta Frith, John Geake, Usha Goswami, Christine Howe, Paul Howard-Jones, Ute Leonards, Carol McGuinness, Pat Mahony, Claire O'Malley, Sue Pickering, Iram Siraj-Blatchford, and Aaron Williamson.
2. Of course, the point we are making here is one that invokes more generally to the procedures of Ordinary Language Philosophy, wherein clarifying the appropriate usage of a term is itself not seen as a trivial task, but rather one that has metaphysical significance regarding the way we think about and understand concepts (the present authors have expanded upon this approach elsewhere—see, for example, Standish and Cavell 2012; Williams 2014). The inheritance of this procedure in this chapter is not out of place, given Ordinary Language Philosophy profoundly influences Hacker's own philosophy.
3. Hacker, given his philosophical allegiances, may well dispute the comparison with Nietzsche.
4. It is perhaps worth emphasizing here that neuroscience—conceived as it is as an approach informed by materialism and physicalism—in many ways styles itself as offering a polar opposite account of the mind to that presented by Descartes (and those who inherited his account), which has been charged with turning the mind into a non-material, 'ghost in the machine.' However, as Hacker has argued elsewhere, neuroscientific accounts of the mind—alongside

modern philosophy of mind which attempts to 'hang on the white coat-tails' of contemporary neuroscience—does not, in fact, succeed in overcoming the Cartesian-based picture so easily. For the picture of the mind that is established by what Hacker terms the 'consciousness community' continues to rest on what he identifies as a 'thoroughgoing confusion'—which has resulted both from the knots that have been tied in language and the inherited Cartesian mystifications (most notably, that 'consciousness' represents an inner, subjective world) that neuroscience continues to labor under. For more details see Hacker 2012.

5. Although, it is perhaps worth noting that Hacker's reading of Wittgenstein may well be more conservative than the account we develop in the following sections.

6. Of course, this is also the rationale behind Wittgenstein's "Private Language Argument," which shows the impossibility of having a private language, given that words get their meaning from the way they are used by communities.

7. As Charles Taylor puts it, the map of a terrain relates all points to each other "without discrimination," for it lays everything out "simultaneously" (1997, 176).

8. What we are suggesting here is brought out in Heidegger's later account of the 'poetic' nature of language, which should not, of course, be misinterpreted as a romanticized valorization of poetry, but rather is suggestive of the way that language has the potential for creating new possibilities and thoughts and that this fundamental quality of language is perhaps most clearly evident in poetic writings (see Heidegger 1971 [1959]). Furthermore, it invokes the notion of the 'iterability' of the sign—its ability to be repeated and re-used in new and different ways, which Jacques Derrida emphasizes in his account of the functioning of language. For more on this, see Williams (2014).

9. Children see their parents washing vegetables and cooking them. They are given a toy vegetable set and duly wash the plastic vegetables. They will not eat the plastic vegetables: the nature of the activity is that they are self-consciously following the rule adopted by their parents (i.e., wash vegetables before cooking). For elaboration of this point, see Standish 2015b.

10. Rhees writes: "When he can speak, we may be delighted because 'He can say things himself now—not just repeat.' But what is important is that he can *say* things: not just that he can construct new sentences—as it were in an exercise. You can set him exercises if you want to test his vocabulary. But this is not how you find out whether he can speak . . . The point, roughly, is that if he can speak he has got something to tell you or to ask you. In arithmetic it is different. 'Telling you things' is not part of his achievement when he learns to multiply, whereas it is his principal achievement in learning to speak" (Rhees 2006, 159). For further discussion, see Standish 2015a.

11. See for example Williams (2015) and Standish (1992).

REFERENCES

Bennett, M., and Hacker, P.M.S. 2003. *Neuroscience and Philosophy: Brain, Mind and Language.* New York: Columbia University Press.

Brain Gym. 2011. "What Is BRAIN GYM?" *Brain Gym International.* Retrieved April 03, 2015 from http://www.braingym.org/about

Goswami, U. 2006. "Neuroscience and Education: From Research to Practice?" *Nature Reviews Neuroscience* 7 (5): 406–413.

Glendinning, S. 2007. *In the Name of Phenomenology.* Oxford: Routledge.

Hacker, P.M.S. 2012. "The Sad and Sorry History of Consciousness: Being Among Other Things a Challenge to the 'Consciousness Studies Community.'" *Royal Institute of Philosophy Supplements* 70: 149–168.

Heidegger, M. 1971 [1959]. *Poetry, Language, Thought*. New York: Harper & Row.

Heidegger, M. 2005 [1927]. *Being and Time*. Kundli, India: Blackwell Publishing.

Rhees, Rush. 2006. *Wittgenstein and the Possibility of Discourse*, edited by D.Z. Phillips. Hoboken, NJ: Wiley.

Standish, P. 1992. *Beyond the Self: Wittgenstein, Heidegger, and the Limits of Language*. Aldershot: Ashgate.

Standish, P. 2015a. "Crying and Learning to Speak." In *Mind, Language, and Action*, edited by Danièle Moyal-Sharrock, Analisa Coliva, and Volker Munz, 481–494. Berlin: De Gruyter.

Standish, P. 2015b. "The Disenchantment of Education and the Re-Enchantment of the World." *Journal of Philosophy of Education* 50 (1).

Standish, P., and Cavell, S. 2012. "Stanley Cavell in Conversation with Paul Standish." *Journal of Philosophy of Education* 46 (2): 155–176.

Taylor, C. 1997. "To Follow a Rule." In *Philosophical Arguments*, edited by C. Taylor, 1–19. Cambridge, MA: Harvard University Press.

Teaching and Learning Research Programme. 2011. *Neuroscience and Education: Issues and Opportunities*. London: Economic and Social Research Council. Retrieved from http://www.tlrp.org/pub/documents/Neuroscience%20Commentary%20FINAL.pdf

Williams, E. 2014. "Out of the Ordinary: Incorporating Limits with Austin and Derrida." *Educational Philosophy and Theory* 46 (12): 1337–1352.

Williams, E. 2015. "In Excess of Epistemology: Siegel, Taylor, Heidegger and the Conditions of Thought." *Journal of Philosophy of Education* 49 (1): 142–160.

Wittgenstein, L. 1993. *Remarks on Frazer's* Golden Bough. In *Philosophical Occasions, 1912–1951*, edited by J. Klagge and A. Nordmann, translated by J. Beversluis, 119–155. Indianapolis, IN: Hackett Publishing.

3 The Attraction and Rhetoric of Neuroscience for Education and Educational Research[1]

Paul Smeyers

PSYCHOLOGY, EDUCATIONAL RESEARCH, AND NEUROSCIENCE

Psychology studies a great variety of processes (for example, conflict, aggression, frustration, memory, learning, etc.) and is used in different fields or areas (for example, labor relations, mental health, advertising, human resources management, the courts, people's private lives). Among these, one also finds education and child rearing. In this context, it tries, for example, to understand how learning takes place and what its mechanisms are, including attempts to identify how this process can be more effective or more pleasant or run more smoothly. Insofar as psychological processes play a role in education, its relevance and attraction in general is straightforward. It is an understatement to claim that psychology nowadays favors a particular methodology and the use of particular methods. Although it loves to refer to itself as embracing 'post-positivism,' it can be asked whether it really has parted from a logical empiricism characterized by the invariance of perception, meaning, and methodology. Randomized field trials and (quasi-) experiments are paradigmatically recognized as the preferred way to proceed. It is true that parts of the discipline are no longer wary of the use of qualitative methods and are sometimes even interested in 'the particular,' but it can be questioned whether this is anything more than the use of qualitative data within a design that is foremost aimed at explanation (whether causal, quasi-causal, or probabilistic) and which is looking for the general, i.e., to be able to generalize its insights. The discipline thrives in the present climate of research output that almost exclusively values publications in 'Web of Knowledge' journals. The higher the impact factor of a journal, the more prestige is ascribed to the successful author; such rankings are also applied to evaluate groups of researchers and indeed whole departments. Research and research opportunities (i.e., funding) also operate along these lines. It can hardly be denied that in these terms, the discipline is flourishing. Moreover, it has penetrated many domains of society and its vocabulary and discourse has become part of our everyday conversations. The number of psychology researchers is growing and so is the number of job opportunities requiring qualifications in psychological research and the areas in which those who have studied psychology are employed. Such a success story is likely to attract researchers working in other areas who gladly take the lead from those who work in a booming field. Educational researchers are no exception to this, but in their case, more needs to be said. Psychology not only carries with it the promise that it will deliver insights into human behavior, it is also widely believed that it can help to address the problems human beings are confronted with. Of course, 'address,' although not necessarily excluding problem redefinition, in general really means 'solving,' in the sense of resulting in either the disappearance of these problems (through an adequate way of dealing with them in an anticipatory manner) or making the way to handle the problems more manageable.

It should be observed, however, that the study of education collective involves theoretical approaches that overlap with other disciplines, including sociology, ethics, and history. Now, since all of these approaches often come together at the level of the practitioner and the policy maker in the educational field, it is clear that all of them should have a place in educational research that is intended to inform practitioners and policy makers. Yet it is also important to recognize that they also have a place in the study of education and child rearing as an academic discipline in its own right. Further, although there have been many debates about the boundaries between academic disciplines, these often have not proved to be very helpful. There are, for example, sociological approaches taken by educational researchers and sociologists who focus on educational phenomena. In these cases, it may not be easy or even possible to identify clearly whether a particular example is a case of educational research rather than sociological research. This is not particularly significant if it simply means that in the context of education and child rearing many elements have to be taken into account, some of which can also be (part of) the focus or interest of another discipline. But this is not the end of the story. By studying educational phenomena from different angles, methods are also borrowed from other fields of study. And thus a new debate is given ammunition: which are the proper methods by which to study education? Although it may not be easy to determine all the relevant aspects of an educational problem (in fact, opinions differ considerably concerning this), surely all of them have to be given a place in educational research. From this it follows that educational research has to accommodate various methods or methodologies.

Recently, this debate got a new impetus from the area of neuroscience. One could argue that there is a new hype in educational research, called educational neuroscience or even neuroeducation (and neuroethics)—there are numerous publications, special journals, and an abundance of research projects together with the advertisement of many positions at renowned research centers worldwide. To see the gist of what is argued for, an interesting starting point is offered by a number of position papers published in a special issue[2] of one of the philosophy of education journals (*Educational Philosophy and Theory*). Incidentally, the contributors are not philosophers of education but researchers working in the area of neuroscience. The guest editors identify as a common aim of educational neuroscience "to produce results that ultimately improve teaching and learning, in theory and in practice" (Patten and Campbell 2011, 6). I hasten to add that the articles are full of warnings, for example, not to misapply science to education, that filling the gulf between current science and direct classroom application is premature, and insisting against exaggerating what this area could mean for education, thus to work in close collaboration with . . . . Yet almost all also express the hope (and the confidence) that a lot may be expected from what some are calling an emerging sub-discipline. Here are some typical quotes from these papers.

> The "holy grail", for a transdisciplinary educational neuroscience as I see it, would be to empower learners through the volitional application of minds to consciously perceive and alter their own brain processes into states more conducive to various aspects of learning.
>
> (Campbell, in Patten and Campbell 2011, 8–9)

> The question is not whether there are connections between minds and brains. There clearly are. The evidence is insurmountable and growing. The question then is to what extent, subject to intrinsic theoretical and practical limits of measurement and analysis, can we identify changes in mental states as changes in brain and brain behaviour, and vice versa.
>
> (Campbell, in Patten and Campbell 2011, 11)

Working in the area of mathematics education, Stephen Campbell, who has a particular interest in the nature of mathematics anxiety and mathematical concept formation (for example, in ways in which the former impedes the latter), outlines that he has in his educational neuroscience laboratory (the ENGRAMMETRON[3], Faculty of Education at Simon Fraser University) equipment to record[4]

> electroencephalograms (EEG), electrocardiograms (EKG), electrooculograms (EOG), and electromylograms (EMG), which pertain to brain activity, heart rate, eye movement and muscle movement . . . . All these psychophysiological metrics are augmented with eye-tracking technology, screen capture, keyboard and mouse capture, and multiple video recordings of participants from various perspectives. These data sets can then be integrated and synchronized for coding, analysis,

and interpretation, thereby affording comprehensive observations and insights into the learning process.

(Campbell, in Patten and Campbell 2011, 13)

According to Campbell:

The main challenge has been to muster evidence and rationale to justify this initiative to funding agencies traditionally supporting educational research.

(Campbell, in Patten and Campbell 2011, 14)

In the same issue, Howard-Jones refers to an Organisation for Economic Co-operation and Development (OECD) Brain and Learning project and to the UK's NeuroEducational research network at the University of Bristol (NEnet, www.neuroeducational.net). He argues in favor of a multiperspective approach (from neuroscience and education) and refers, for instance, to work within NEnet, i.e., an fMRI study of creativity fostering strategies:

This imaging study, which included a focus on the biological correlates of creativity, was useful in revealing how those parts of the brain associated with creative effort in a story telling task were further activated when unrelated stimulus words had to be included. Results provided some helpful indication, at the biological level of action, of the likely effectiveness of such strategies in the longer term.

(Howard-Jones, in Patten and Campbell 2011, 26)

Similarly Ferrari argues:

unlike cognitive neuroscience—which aims to explain how the mind is embodied—educational neuroscience necessarily incorporates values that reflect the kind of citizen and the kind of society we aspire to create . . . What are the biological foundations of authentic and deep understanding? Of an appreciation of art and beauty? Or of compassion for those in need at home and around the world? All these concerns reflect different values that matter to particular communities and neuroscience could inform us about all of them.

(Ferrari, in Patten and Campbell 2011, 31 and 35)

As I said, the papers also include clear warnings; for example, Ansari, Coch, and De Smedt write:

close inspection of these claims for a direct connection between particular 'brain-based' tools and teaching approaches reveals very loose and

often factually incorrect links . . . the direct application of neuroscience findings to the classroom has not been particularly fruitful.
(Ansari, Coch, and De Smedt, in Patten and Campbell 2011, 41)

Nevertheless, they too remain 'believers' when they identify, for example, as a topic for research:

How might non-invasive neuroimaging methods be used to measure the relative success of educational approaches?
(Ansari, Coch, and De Smedt, in Patten and Campbell 2011, 42)

A CHARACTERIZATION OF THE EMERGING FIELD OF NEUROSCIENCE

The emerging sub-discipline of neuroscience is conceptualized in various ways and with various degrees of caution. Some offer it as support for what is 'known,' i.e., a neuronal 'explanation.' For instance, Geake argues that

Teachers have long suspected that IQ tests, although predictive of academic success, do not reveal all there is about a child's cognitive potential. Our findings, in supporting conjectures that the brain might develop separate working memory systems for general intelligence and fluid cognition offer an explanation of such skepticism.
(Geake, in Patten and Campbell 2011, 46)

Others are particularly interested in identifying brain activity in order to draw curricular implications. For example, Lee and Ng report on investigations in their laboratory concerning heuristics commonly used, for example, to teach algebraic word problems (respectively, the model method and symbolic algebra).

Despite the lack of behavioural differences, we found difference in the degree to which the two methods activated areas associated with attentional and working memory processes. In particular, transforming word problems into algebraic representation required greater access to attentional processes than did transformation into models. Furthermore, symbolic algebra activated the caudate, which has been associated with activation of proceduralised information . . . . Findings . . . suggest that . . . Both methods activate similar brain areas, but symbolic algebra imposes more demands on attentional resources. . . . If symbolic algebra is indeed more demanding on attentional resources, one curricular implication is that it is best to teach the model method at the primary level and leave symbolic algebra until students are more cognitively matured.
(Lee and Ng, in Patten and Campbell 2011, 83–84)

Some educational neuroscientists seem to label 'standard' educational research as 'neuroscience.' There are, for example, the cohort studies on language acquisition, brain development, and language education (Hagiwara, Tokyo Metropolitan University). Although their objectives are to propose a guideline for second language learning and education (especially for English, including the optimal ages and conditions surrounding it), they phrase this as 'a cognitive neuroscience-based guideline.' Other educational researchers speak of 'bringing frameworks together' (respectively from educational research and from neuroscience), which they believe will offer opportunities to deepen our understanding. For example, Tommerdahl writes:

> It is highly doubtful that any single given study in neurology will have a direct application to the classroom but, on a more hopeful note, it is almost certain that aggregations of findings from several studies, mediated through higher levels culminating in the behavioural and educational levels will indeed provide new teaching methodologies.
>
> (Tommerdahl 2010, 98)

Similarly, Hardiman et al. claim that

> Although applying research from the neuro- and cognitive sciences to classroom practice certainly remains a challenge, interdisciplinary collaboration has yielded considerable educationally-relevant information about learning mechanisms that could not have been acquired solely through behavioural methods.
>
> (Hardiman et al. 2012, 137)

Finally, one could say, for some, 'the sky is the limit' in their evaluation of what they perceive is an emerging sub-discipline.

> Since the emergence of dispositions and basic emotions are to a large degree autonomic and unconscious, they cannot be recognized nor stopped until they become conscious feelings. However, they can be attenuated and avoided in the future through emotion regulation by recognizing their emergence triggers and enacting preventive measured related to specific object and situations . . . . This model [Somatic Appraisal Model of Affect] identifies quintessential functions, components, and facets of affect necessary to provide a new research domain, namely educational neuroscience, with a basis on which to build a dynamic model of affect serving to challenge current pedagogy and inform and build a new praxis, called neuropedagogy.
>
> (Patten, in Patten and Campbell 2011, 94)

In sum, what many feel is an emerging sub-discipline of neuroscience is characterized in various ways and with various degrees of optimism about what it can offer as educational research.

NEUROSCIENCE, EDUCATIONAL RESEARCH, AND THE EDUCATIONAL FIELD

There are a number of philosophically informed observations and comments that should be made at this point about the methods and approaches of neuroscience and educational research.

First, the studies are correlational. It is often assumed that, for instance, fMRI techniques offer 'visual proof' of brain activity. However, as Narvaez and Vaydich argue, few studies test theories and most are primarily correlational. Far too often readers assume that fMRI techniques enable researchers to capture 'visual proof' of brain activity without taking into account the complexities of acquiring the data and processing the images. To ease the task of interpreting and reporting results, neuroimaging studies often highlight responses in specific brain regions; however, these regions are rarely the only ones that produced activity. Moreover, every human brain is distinctive, so the fMRI studies look at areas of agreement across brains, which often vary greatly. In fact, laboratories often use their own techniques to test and analyze the messy and inconsistent data across participants and trials. Due to limited knowledge, few studies test theories and most are primarily correlational. Moreover, correlative approaches, such as human brain imaging and psychophysiology, are not sufficiently robust to adjudicate what is 'basic about basic emotions' because 'autonomic physiology is regulated by generalized sympathetic and parasympathetic controls' which are not measurable through fMRI. Activation can vary for a range of reasons. (Narvaez and Vaydich 2008, 291)

Second, several philosophers have pointed to problems with the nature of the concepts that are used: for example, they speak of a reductionism or of a confusion of 'activity' and 'content.' Reference is made to Wittgenstein's position concerning the 'inner,' and to Ryle's notion of 'category mistake,' moreover to the issue of 'underdetermination.' Purdy and Morrison refer to Bennett and Hacker (2003) who, following the work of the later Wittgenstein, have asked whether we know "what it is for a brain to see or hear, for a brain to have experiences, to know or to believe something." That the brain thinks, believes, etc. is for them the result of a conceptual confusion. Thus they point to the separation of the inner and the outer "a 'mutant form of Cartesianism' where psychological attributes once ascribed to the mind, Descartes' immaterial *res cogitans*, are now ascribed unreflectively to the material brain instead" (Purdy and Morrison 2009, 105–106). For them, the brain is not a logically appropriate subject for psychological attributes (the expression "the brain sees" lacks sense), and thus they conclude "While neuroscience can reveal what is happening in the brain . . . the imagery is never more than a neural concomitant of that thinking . . ." (Purdy and Morrison 2009, 106).

Third, unless the neurological mechanism that lies behind the phenomena (and which is made explicit) could be directly influenced, it is not clear what the educational implications are that surpass those already available on the basis of relevant research in, for example, educational psychology. That neuroscience offers a description (or even explanation) in terms of neurological concepts and theories does not in itself warrant an *educational* surplus value. This remains still to be argued and established. It is of course possible that the techniques, methods, concepts, and theories of psychology will be replaced by those of neuroscience, in which case, there could be some gain in our understanding of learning. This presupposes, however, accepting that the object of study of psychology coincides with that studied by neuroscience. And as dealt with in the previous point, this is doubtful. Nevertheless, neuroscientific explanations have a particular seductive character. In a 2008 article, Weisberg, Keil, Goodstein, Rawson, and Gray discuss an experiment they have set up concerning the seductive allure of neuroscience explanations. Explanations with logically irrelevant neuroscience information had a particularly striking effect on non-expert's judgments of bad explanations.

Fourth, concerning what is frequently argued for, i.e. 'bringing frameworks together,' if this is supposed to be more than the expression of what is always true, it needs to be shown in what way this is helpful. What is argued for is only true if (for example) one of these provides information at an earlier time than the other one. There are examples of this, but they are scarce. Goswami argues along these lines and provides such an example. Neural variables can be used to identify those who might be at educational risk: "a child may be at risk because aspects of sensory processing are impaired, and biomarkers could show the presence of the processing impairment before any behavioural symptoms have appeared" (Goswami 2008, 394–395). It is not enough that complementary information is gathered and the outcomes interpreted against two different backgrounds—one predominantly using a quantitative approach and an experimental setting,[5] the other qualitative data from a classroom-based 'design research.' Except for very specific cases, the gains of such an approach, i.e., 'bringing frameworks together' therefore remains doubtful.

Last, there is always the further step to 'education,' as implicit in, for instance, the idea that improved knowledge about how the brain learns should assist educators in creating optimal learning conditions—not to mention issues concerning desirable outcomes in general educational content and processes. Some scholars realize that the possible contribution is limited, others seem to be inclined to forget, and proclaim the need for such an approach:

Cognitive neuroscience is important for education because it enables a principled understanding of the mechanisms of learning and of the basic components of human performance. It also enables componential understanding of the complex cognitive skills taught by education. Many of the principles of leaning uncovered by cognitive neuroscience might appear to support what teachers knew already. For example, aspects of pedagogy such as the value of multi-sensory teaching approaches or of crating safe and secure environments for learning are highly familiar. Nevertheless, cognitive neuroscience offers an empirical foundation for supporting certain insights already present in pedagogy and disputing others. The evidence from neuroscience is not just interesting scientifically. It enables an evidence base for education in which mechanisms of learning can be precisely understood.

(Goswami 2008, 396)

In general, my observations are meant to be somewhat deflationary, expressing explicit caution if not skepticism about the optimism many researchers have about current methods and approaches of neuroscience and educational research.

ONCE AGAIN, PSYCHOLOGY, EDUCATION, AND EDUCATIONAL RESEARCH

Before offering some further analysis and conclusions concerning neuroscience, I want to say something more general about the relationship of psychology and the educational field. The popularity and presence of psychology in society at large and its success in academia combined with its general relevance for education and child rearing has considerably influenced educational research, educational practice, and policy. This concerns issues of what should be studied in educational research and the way these issues should be studied (i.e., questions of methodology and methods). Traditionally, education had deep roots in philosophy, religion, and more generally in questions of value and in what it means to lead a life that is worth living. Various societal processes (secularization, communication patterns, growing mobility) have weakened the importance given to these questions and from this, labeled by some 'the erosion of values,' a new age has arrived, characterized by performativity, output, and efficiency. According to many scholars, the debate is now more about means than it is about ends, where every element has value almost exclusively for its contribution to something else and other things for something further, and so on. For some people, the ends themselves are no longer part of a rational debate. They are for them, to put this bluntly, just a matter of opinion (or taste). And thus education is seen as having value only insofar as it assists in acquiring a good (or a better) job, as it prepares young people for society. It is not just lifelong learning that proceeds along those lines, but more conventional education is also narrowed down almost exclusively to instrumental learning.

Compared to fifty years ago, a lot of the elements of educational practice have been questioned, adjusted, or improved, but the present too comes at a price. It may be the case that it has to be left to future generations to determine more fully what is involved, but currently (perhaps as in other fields of endeavor) it is clear that in a general climate of uncertainty, the emphasis naturally shifts to short-term results in educational research. Thus there is a tendency to mark out limited areas of investigation that are relatively uncontaminated by independent variables and by broader questions. If this is done in the name of 'objectivity,' it is understandable that researchers want to be 'objective.' But there is always a price to be paid when investigations are pursued within very limited parameters. The result is that a lot of research, for instance, in psychology and in many aspects of education and child rearing, addresses a context, a process, a variable separated as much as possible from broader questions and deals with only a small, even a miniscule part of what is at stake. Yet clearly, addressing an educational problem, be it language learning or bullying, requires a wide spectrum of knowledge; some of it relies on theoretical insights (based on laws or law-like regularities or other theoretical approaches), while some of it comes from the particularities of the situation. Moreover, as all of that has to come together, in order to make wise decisions, a lot of contextualization of laws and regularities is required. In deciding what to do (what changes to institute, what policies to put in place, what alterations to classroom practice to make), matters cannot be left exclusively to the operation of a deductive, nomological model of educational research.

One can see the attraction of the kind of research that is studied in laboratory conditions and the relation between independent and dependent variables in the hope of achieving general insights and conclusions with the assistance of statistical reasoning. Yet the truth is that in social sciences much more than in natural sciences, its laws (or quasi-laws) or regularities can only be applied *ceteris paribus* (everything being equal). They are in desperate need of contextualization. Attending to matters of meaning and intention, from what something *means* for us as the material out of which our decisions are composed (and which should therefore be taken up by the relevant academic disciplines), will push us even further away from laws and regularities. In a model where meaning is central, attention must also be paid to the need for a balance between all kinds of things that are important in our lives (and in education) and thus to questions of value. Yet it is the model of causality and the predictability and elements of manipulation that go with it that many find irresistible. No wonder educational research has been eager to adopt such a methodology and the methods that go with it. And it comes equally as no surprise that to a large extent, similar ends are pursued in the area of education more generally. Since part of the attraction of psychology may be explained, in my opinion, in terms of the methods it uses and the methodology it embraces, I will say something more about different kinds of research.

In quantitative research, one typically looks for a distribution of variables (how many are there with this or that characteristic) and for explanations, which can be of a deductive-nomological kind, incorporating universal laws, or be of an inductive nature, which employ statistics. Because it is subsumed under its own set of laws, quantitative research can offer explanations of two kinds: one is in terms of an argument; namely, a logical structure with premises and conclusions governed by some rule of acceptance—although, incidentally, many doubt whether it is possible to find universal laws within the context of the social sciences; the other is a presentation of the conditions relevant to the occurrence of the event and a statement of the degree of probability of the event given these conditions.

Qualitative research can be differentiated into two kinds. On the one hand, one may be interested in common features in different cases. Here the purpose is not only to describe categories but also to deal with the relationships between different categories. In many cases, this kind of research is generally analogous to a quantitative design (including hypotheses), with the difference being that qualitative data are gathered—for example, data about what people feel, what their experience is with particular things, or what they say that their reasons (or desires and intentions) are. On the other hand, distinct from the first, is another kind of qualitative research. Here, for example, the researcher arranges events and actions by showing how they contribute to the evolution of a plot. The plot is the thematic line of the narrative, the narrative structure that shows how different events contribute to a phenomenon seen as a kind of story. Writing this research involves an analytical development, a dialectic between the data and the plot. The resulting narrative must not only fit the data but also bring out an order and significance not apparent in the data as such. This is not so much an account of the actual happening of events from an objective (i.e., something we agree about intersubjectively) point of view. Instead it is the result of a series of particular constructions or (perhaps more accurately) reconstructions by the researcher. Not only is the researcher *present* in the conclusions that are offered, but she is also involved all through the process (although differently as compared with the practitioner's involvement). This kind of 'interpretive research' is distinct from educational research grounded in the empirical traditions of the social sciences, such as theoretical, conceptual, or methodological essay. Rather, this 'interpretive research' comes close to those areas of scholarship and studies grounded in the humanities, including areas such as history and philosophy of education, where in general interpretation is involved. In such a holistic approach, the relation of the elements that are involved is given not only a more prominent but also a different place. Variables are not so much studied on their own, but the researcher is focused on the complex relationships between them. Here the presence or absence of any particular element may change the whole picture and, consequently, the conclusions that can be drawn from and for a particular setting.

Quantitative empirical research belongs to the paradigm of causality, which cannot give a place to the reasons human beings invoke for doing what they do (or only at great pains and by changing the meaning of causality incorporating 'reasons'). It may battle to contain interaction effects, yet it is in danger of falling short, because it starts from the idea that variables can be studied in isolation and put together again later with other variables. Perhaps too it presupposes too much homogeneity. Here the result, the full picture, is seen as a matter of the accumulation of variables. But in qualitative research, starting from a meaningful action or conversation we get a completely different starting point. In such a holistic approach where the full picture is the starting point, the meaning of the parts are defined in terms of their contribution to the full picture. Psychology has to a large extent departed from trying to give an account of *what makes sense* in human life; it no longer seems interested in studying human self-consciousness and intentionality, imagination and moral responsibility, human experiencing of the natural and social world and human understanding of the rules which they live by, as well as the cultural and historical framing of all these. It has directed its attention to theories that identify variables and combines them with an ever-growing approach inspired by neuroscience, thus giving priority to the natural over the social world. This may be a legitimate interest, but its utilitarian value, one that is celebrated so highly in its means-end reasoning, seems to be rather limited in the field of education. In that context, it may be in danger of imploding or melting down. This would happen once it is realized that quantitative educational research becomes no more than a bubble because it is not based on what is really at stake in education, and this because it cannot take its lead from the more holistic, quantitative methodology. The methodology of independent and dependent variables comes with certain presuppositions we referred to in general at the beginning of this paper. The reduction necessary in every scientific endeavor is, however, particularly in danger of an oversimplification in the 'causal' model and of reducing originally rich concepts to very thin concepts indeed. John Elliott (2006) claims that when positivism's picture of science dominates (where researchers adopt the standpoint of an impartial spectator), "this also implies that such a stance is in the interest of social practitioners, for it is a condition of practical rationality, conceived in instrumentalist terms" (Elliot 2006, 180). And he continues: "Positivism, therefore, links theory and practice in terms of a logic that marries an objectivist view of knowledge, an *episteme*, with an instrumentalist view of practical reason" (180). He summarizes Nussbaum's characterization of the four constitutive claims of such a 'science of measurement': *metricity*, in a particular choice situation there is a particular value, varying only in quantity, that is common to all the alternatives; *singularity*, the idea that one and the same metric or standard applies in all situations of choice; *consequentialism*, the notion that the chosen actions only have instrumental value as a means of producing good consequences; and *maximalization,* the idea that there is a particular single value that in every case it is the point of rational choice to maximize (see Elliot 2006, 180). Elliott refers to Sen's conclusion

> that we need a broader conception of practical rationality that reaches beyond the maximisation principle to include a "critical scrutiny of the

objectives and values that underlie any maximizing behaviour" and an acknowledgement of values that constitute "*self-imposed* constraints on that behaviour."

(Elliott 2006, 182)

Thus he argues that "both forms of practical reasoning—*techne* and *phronesis*—need to be set alongside each other within a broad conception of educational research as a discursive and democratic process" (182). Obviously, this more balanced approach not only departs from the 'causal chain' aspired to in psychology in general and more typically dominant nowadays in educational research, it also invokes much more knowledge and understanding that draws on the particularities of the situation one is studying. It accepts that empirical, quantitative social science does not give us fixed and universal knowledge of the social world, but rather that it contributes to the task of improving our practical knowledge of ongoing social life. It does not help to address the existential condition in which one finds oneself, a condition characterized and increasingly undermined by uncertainty and doubt, to look for laws, regularities, statistical reasoning, because these would offer only the illusion of certainty and offer us nothing in our search for existential meaning. Thus there are grounds for resisting the tendency to look for expert advice, which would bracket the personal commitment of those involved and abandon their responsibility in favor of what is neutral and 'objectively true.' There is nothing wrong with trying to achieve as much knowledge as possible provided such knowledge takes into account all the relevant aspects, observes a balance when applied, and invokes various interests and therefore a plurality of methods. This replaces 'being effective' by seeing all the relevant aspects and invites all (practitioners, policy makers, and researchers) to be part of a dialogue and take up their responsibility. It may still be of interest to know how much regularity can be observed concerning human behavior or in what sense it is indeed underpinned by laws. But it will no longer be the case that on the basis of this, certainly not exclusively on this basis, it can straightforwardly follow what needs to be done. That the development of a particular child can be explained in terms of what is normally to be expected may give us some confidence that nothing is going wrong in the particular child's case. Yet the opposite should not necessarily invite all kinds of measures, but start with a more inclusive appreciation of her behavior that may or may not lead to specific interventions. Psychology and educational research that puts itself in the currently dominant tradition presupposes too much that normal development administers a normative background and generates aims that have to be observed and aspired to at any cost.

It goes without saying that there are many psychologists and educational researchers who apply their insights wisely and who do not exclusively rely in their advice on the limited insights particular research has to offer. But it seems that when they refer to their specific expertise (as psychologists or as educational experts) or when they talk about what their subject should address, they invoke a particular concept of science (laws and regularities) and use what is 'scientifically established,' thus putting themselves in danger of ignoring other relevant aspects as well as the particularities of the problem they want to address. Their approach carries a promise they cannot live up to. Of course, the illusion of certainty that they uphold is very attractive, indeed almost irresistible to all those who struggle to decide what to do. Yet their help, well intended as it is, cannot do away with the responsibility and the requirement to offer a justification for the way we interact on behalf of those who are put in our trust. It cannot do away with the normative stance they themselves are necessarily embracing as researchers.

NEUROSCIENCE: THE FUNDAMENTAL PROBLEM

The methods and conclusions of the emerging sub-discipline of education neuroscience has been lurking in the background of the previous discussion. What goes missing in any third-person, physical description of the brain is, Bakhurst (2008) argues, the subjective dimension: "all that is observable are the neural correlates of mental activity, not mental activity itself" (422). To this he adds that from a personalist position, beginning from the premise that the human mind is a psychological unity, a person's mental states are not just a rag-bag collection of representations.

> One way to put this argument about psychological unity is to say that brainism [the view (a) that an individual's mental life is constituted by states, events and processes in her brain, and (b) that psychological attributes may legitimately be ascribed to the brain, 415] struggles to make sense of the first-person perspective. A person does not typically stand to her own mental states as to objects of observation.
>
> (Bakhurst 2008, 422)

Our observing is always charged with agency. He adds to this personalism an insight he gets from McDowell, namely, a distinctive view of human development:

> As the child matures, however, she undergoes a qualitative transformation. She enters a distinctively human, essentially social form of life and acquires distinctively human psychological capacities that enable her to transcend existence in the narrow confines of a biological environment and to hold the world in view. With this, natural-scientific modes of explanation are no longer adequate to explain the character of the child's mindedness.
>
> (Bakhurst 2008, 423)

And he continues:

> The human mind constantly transcends its own limits; it does not simply apply old techniques to new problems. On the contrary, we set ourselves problems precisely to develop the methods to address them, a process that in turn uncovers new questions, creating new problem-spaces demanding further innovation and so on. To understand this dialectical process, we cannot represent the mind as determined by antecedent conditions.
>
> (Bakhurst 2008, 423–424)

Instead, following McDowell's argument, Bakhurst holds that human beings think and act in the light of reasons:

> The relations in which rational explanation deals are normative in character. When I decide that Jack must believe that q because he believes (a) that p and (b) that p entails q, I am not making a causal claim. I am assuming that Jack believes what he ought to believe if he is rational.
>
> (Bakhurst 2008, 424)

These sort of relations are not of the sort that are characterized by natural-scientific theories. Rather, they are different from what goes on in the brain, which is exhaustively open to scientific explanation. Mental states and processes occupy a different logical space—the space of reasons. Human beings inhabit a social world because their world is full of objects created by human beings for human purposes. For Bakhurst, psychological talk represents a fundamentally different discourse from talk of the brain. Obviously, brain science can illuminate learning in the explanation of dysfunction, deficit, and disorder (a matter often referred to in the literature, see, for example, Davis 2004, 22) but, he argues, "Once we adopt the causal perspective on the child's problems, we cease to see her as a rational agent, at least in this respect, and absolve her from responsibility, and hence blame, for her failings" (Bakhurst 2008, 426). Thus he concludes that as there is as much reason to avoid crass biological determinism as there is to eschew *a priori* nurturism, there "are no *a priori* grounds to declare brain science irrelevant to educational issues, or relevant only in 'deficit' cases" (Bakhurst 2008, 428). He goes on to say,

> What is critical, however, is that interest in the brain should not distract attention from the fact that education is a communicative endeavour, not an engineering problem. Education is not about getting information into students' heads or of implanting skills in them . . . Once again, information and skills are not all that is at issue. Machines may possess those, or close surrogates, but machines have no practices and crafts.
>
> (Bakhurst 2008, 428)

If Bakhurst's position carries weight, it is doubtful that a lot may be expected from what is frequently argued for in the neuroscience sub-discipline, i.e., 'combining frameworks.' The so-called frameworks that have to be brought together are fundamentally different. Moreover, there is something strange going on in the debate about neuroscience and education: the methods that are used are correlational, i.e., the tools measure only indirectly brain activity. Hence there is conceptual confusion in more than one sense, and yet the proponents do not stop to argue that a lot can be expected from such an approach.

So why is it then that neuroscience is so attractive? Interestingly, one may be tempted to find an answer in the discussion this field offers itself when discussing certain so-called neuromyths of which examples are that one only uses a fraction of one's brain, namely 10%, or that people or either right- or left-brained (see Geake 2008). There is even a specific label coined for this: neurophilia (the appetite for neuroscience). Pasquinelli (2012) discusses several issues of neuromyths (the misconceptions about the mind and brain functioning), such as the origin, persistence, and potential side effects in education. There is, according to her, in the media "the tendency to offer irrelevant information, sensationalism, and the omission of relevant information" (Pasquinelli 2012, 90). She also refers to the biasing effect of images: "because neuroimages appear as compelling as eyewitness, they are persuasive" (Pasquinelli 2012, 91). Thus she argues, "The ignorance of basic facts about the making-of of brain images can mislead the layperson into believing that an image of the brain is sufficient to prove the existence of a mental state—an attitude described as 'neurorealism'" (Pasquinelli 2012, 91). And she refers to the blossoming of projects, reports, and studies on the social, political, and educational implications of neuroscience, looking in the latter field for guidelines and/or easy fixes for education. She talks about the example of Brain Gym (based on the idea that when different parts of the brain do not work in coordination, learning can be impaired) and argues that, although there is no evidence that its exercises are effective, they are globally well received in the domain of education (Pasquinelli 2012, 92). It is therefore really disappointing to find toward the end of the paper an answer to the question what actions one can take, *only* that "knowledge must be pursued, conveniently disseminated, and taught" (Pasquinelli 2012, 93), ending with the mantra "From this collaboration [an effective interbreed between science and applicative domains (such as education)], compelling theories and practices can see the light that are at the same time true of science and meaningful for educators" (Pasquinelli 2012, 94).

Granted, neuroscientific studies can eradicate mistaken views about how the brain works. But that does not go very far to justify a legitimate educational interest, not to mention what needs to be done in educational contexts. It does not justify the direction a lot of educational research has taken, not to mention the amount of money that is made available. It may be a field that merits interest on its own strengths, surely on that argument there are many areas that are interesting. But it should not be 'sold' as highly relevant for education. Indeed, something very remarkable is going on there, with an argument something like this: never mind the possible problems, we are aware of that, so let's continue 'business as usual,' and therefore the mantra sounds "at lot may be expected from this field!" It is easy so see how educators may be tempted to find an easy fix for educational problems, as they are overwhelmed by neurorealism and the aura of doing real science offering the prestige that goes with it and the so-called expertise demanded by educators and no less by parents. My arguments have been directed against such a neuromyth, which I offer as a reminder that education, including educational research and the discipline of education, should reclaim its territory.

NOTES

1. The paper is an elaboration of some of the ideas that are developed in Smeyers, P. and Depaepe, M. (2012), "The Lure of Psychology for Education and Educational Research," *Journal of Philosophy of Education* 46: 315–331 and Smeyers, P. (2013), "Making Sense of the Legacy of Epistemology in Education and Educational Research," *Journal of Philosophy of Education* 47: 311–321.
2. The special issue (Patten and Campbell 2011) contains the following contributions: "Introduction: Educational Neuroscience" (pages 1–6), by Kathryn E. Patten and Stephen R. Campbell; "Educational Neuroscience: Motivations, Methodology, and Implications" (pages 7–16) by Stephen R. Campbell; "Can Cognitive Neuroscience Ground a Science of Learning?" (pages 17–23) by Anthony E. Kelly; "A Multiperspective Approach to Neuroeducational Research" (pages 24–30) by Paul A. Howard-Jones; "What Can Neuroscience Bring to Education?" (pages 31–36) by Michel Ferrari; "Connecting Education and Cognitive Neuroscience: Where Will the Journey Take Us?" (pages 37–42) by Daniel Ansari, Donna Coch and Bert De Smedt; "Position Statement on Motivations, Methodologies, and Practical Implications of Educational Neuroscience Research: fMRI Studies of the Neural Correlates of Creative Intelligence" (pages 43–47) by John Geake; "Brain-Science Based Cohort Studies" (pages 48–55) by Hideaki Koizumi; "Directions for Mind, Brain, and Education: Methods, Models, and Morality" (pages 56–66) by Zachary Stein and Kurt W. Fischer; "The Birth of a Field and the Rebirth of the Laboratory School" (pages 67–74) by Marc Schwartz and Jeanne Gerlach; "Mathematics Education and Neurosciences: Towards interdisciplinary insights into the development of young children's mathematical abilities" (pages 75–80) by Fenna Van Nes; "Neuroscience and the Teaching of Mathematics" (pages 81–86) by Kerry Lee and Swee Fong Ng; "The Somatic Appraisal Model of Affect: Paradigm for Educational Neuroscience and Neuropedagogy" (pages 87–97) by Kathryn E. Patten; "Implications of Affective and Social Neuroscience for Educational Theory" (pages 98–103) by Mary Helen Immordino-Yang.
3. See http://www.engrammetron.net/about.html. "ENGRAMMETRON facilities enable simultaneous observation and acquisition of audio data from talking-aloud reflective protocols; video data of facial and bodily expression; and real-time screen capture. Instrumentation most notably supports: multi-channel electroencephalography (EEG); electrocardiography (EKG); electromyography (EMG); and eye-tracking (ET) capability. Orbiting this constellation of observational methods around computer enhanced learning

platforms allows for unprecedented flexibility of educational research experimental design and delivery, and for subsequent data integration and analyses."
4. It may be interesting at this point to point out some of the characteristics of the tools used by neuroscientists.

> *PET scan* (positron-emission tomography): a radioactive isotope is injected that allows the amount of glucose being metabolized in the brain to become visible (indicative of the amount of blood in each part of the brain which in turn represents brain activity); it provides an image of the working brain. Disadvantages: the need for radioactive material, the high cost of use.
>
> *fMRI* (functional magnetic resonance imaging): measures blood flow in the brain; provides an image of the working brain.
>
> *EEG* (electroencephalogram) shows cortical activity of the cortex in the form of electrical signals directly harvested from groups of thousands of neurons through electrodes placed on the scalp; there are no images of the brain but instead detailed information about the time course of neural activity and indications of where brain activity is being carried out.
>
> *MEG* (magnetoencephalogram) measures the magnetic field outside the brain caused by electrical activity; there are no images of the brain but instead detailed information about the time course of neural activity and indications of where brain activity is being carried out.

5. "Before the trials begin, the researcher fits a cap on the child's head with electrodes that register brain activity. This non-invasive EEG technique informs the researcher about the onset and duration of brain signals for particular stimuli and motor and perceptual responses. ANOVAs help determine differences in the brain activation and in the reaction times and additional analyses give more insight into the nature of interference and facilitation effects in the different experimental conditions." (Van Nes, in Patten and Campbell 2011, 78)

REFERENCES

Bakhurst, D. 2008. "Minds, Brains and Education." *Journal of Philosophy of Education* 42 (3–4): 415–432.

Bennett, M.R., and P.M.S. Hacker. 2003. *Philosophical Foundations of Neuroscience*. Malden, MA: Blackwell Publishing.

Davis, A. 2004. "The Credentials of Brain-Based Leaning." *Journal of Philosophy of Education* 38 (1): 21–35.

Elliott, J. 2006. "Educational Research as a Forum of Democratic Rationality." *Journal of Philosophy of Education* 40 (2): 169–185.

Geake, J. 2008. "Neuromythologies in Education." *Educational Research* 50 (2): 123–133.

Goswami, U. 2008. "Principles of Learning, Implications for Teaching: A Cognitive Neuroscience Perspective." *Journal of Philosophy Education* 42 (3–4): 381–399.

Hardiman, M., L. Rinne, E. Gregory, and J. Yarmolinskaya. 2012. "Neuroethics, Neuroeducation, and Classroom Teaching: Where the Brain Sciences Meet Pedagogy." *Neuroethics* 5: 135–143.

Narvaez, D., and J.L. Vaydich. 2008. "Moral Development and Behaviour Under the Spotlight of the Neurobiological Sciences." *Journal of Moral Education* 37 (3): 289–312.

Pasquinelli, E. 2012. "Neuromyths: Why Do They Exist and Persist?" *Mind, Brain, and Education* 6 (2): 89–96.

Patten, K.E., and S.R. Campbell, Guest eds. 2011. "Educational Neuroscience." *Educational Philosophy and Theory* 43 (1): 1–6.

Purdy, N., and H. Morrison. 2009. "Cognitive Neuroscience and Education: Unravelling the Confusion." *Oxford Review of Education* 35 (1): 99–109.

Tommerdahl, J. 2010. "A Model for Bridging the Gap Between Neuroscience and Education." *Oxford Review of Education* 36 (1): 97–109.

Weisberg, D.S., F.C. Keil, J. Goodstein, E. Rawson, and J.R. Gray. 2008. "The Seductive Allure of Neuroscience Explanations." *Journal of Cognitive Neuroscience* 20 (3): 470–477.

4   Two Cases in Neuroeducational Knowledge Transfer
Behavioral Ethics and Responsive Parenting

Bruce Maxwell and Eric Racine

There has been spectacular growth of interest in the neuroscience of learning, memory, attention, and other abilities crucial to the developing child and the world of education. This area bears different names depending on the authors and their perspectives (e.g., neuroscience of education, neuroeducation) but reflects a concerted effort to bridge the gap between the findings of basic research in neuroscience and cognitive psychology and practices and habits of educators, be they teachers in schools or parents raising young children at home. Although in the domain of health, knowledge transfer and translational research are intensely scrutinized from an ethics standpoint, clearly there are also high stakes involved in the ethical translation of neuroscience to the world of education (Levin 2004). These stakes include the responsible use of material resources, how well children and young people are being prepared for social life and work, and developmental outcomes directly influenced by the day-to-day choices of educators and caregivers. Given the ethical perils of underestimating or overestimating neuroscience's contribution to various fields of research (Illes and Racine 2005), it is crucial to examine closely epistemological standards used as the basis for claims made about the educational implications of neuroscience and what it means to use neuroscience evidence in an ethically sensitive and responsible way.

This chapter offers a critical analysis of two cases of neuroeducation knowledge transfer in which the findings of research on the brain and cognitive functioning are appealed as justification for specific educational practices. The first case—which underlines the potential for neuroscience to transform how we view moral reasoning, deliberation and choice, and, consequently, ethics education—concerns behavioral ethics. More specifically, we consider a particular position that has emerged in behavioral ethics on the teaching and learning objectives of professional and practical ethics. According to this view, 'moral reasoning' should be deprioritized as an objective of ethics education in light of large amounts of converging research in the cognitive science of morality, which challenge the previously dominant view that ethical behavior is more likely to occur when conscious moral reasoning leads the way. The second case—which underlines the potential for neuroscience to transform the way people raise their children and understand the reasons why certain childcare practices might be preferable to others—involves examining the use of findings in neuroscience to justify a specific set of early childcare practices known as 'responsive parenting.' This second case reviews and discusses four practical issues based on examples from developmental neuroscience research: (1) respecting levels of evidence and the nature of neuroscience evidence, (2) applicability of basic neuroscience research to the context of education, (3) possible negative implications of neuroscience on education and parenting, and (4) public trust in developmental neuroscience and responsible translation of research.

BEHAVIORAL ETHICS: ALIGNING ETHICS EDUCATION WITH COGNITIVE SCIENCE

A superficial review of ethics course books and course plans from fields as diverse as medicine, teaching, accounting, and journalism will confirm that the teaching of 'moral reasoning' and associated skills is a well-established objective of practical ethics education. Ethics educators and moral psychologists have long held reservations about moral reasoning as an educational aim and few today would subscribe to the view that even the most advanced ethical deliberation skills constitute, in and of themselves, a prophylactic against unethical behavior or guarantor of ethical choice. However, these classical educational concerns about moral reasoning—that it falsely represents ethical deliberation as a mechanical process (Bull 1993; Howe 1986), that it underplays other aspects of ethical experience like emotions, motivation, or character (Blasi 1980; Rest 1986), that it encourages cynicism or moral relativism among students (Bowie 2003), etc., are of a different order from those emerging from behavioral ethics and the cognitive science of morality. Converging evidence produced by dozens of broad research programs in various fields in the social sciences and humanities—behavioral economics in business (De Cremer and Tenbrunsel 2012), social intuitionism, moral foundations theory in psychology (Haidt and Kesebir 2010), and experimental philosophy (Knobe and Nichols 2008)—make it clear that behavior, both ethical and unethical, is rarely the product of careful, conscious reflection on moral reasons. Instead, it is primarily driven by a diverse set of intuitive processes over which individuals have little conscious control.

Behavioral ethics, a current movement in teaching and research in business ethics, advances a strong position on the content focus of ethics education. We need a model of ethics education, behavioral ethicists claim, that focuses not on directly modeling good ethical reasoning but which emphasizes how bad people are at thinking clearly and impartially about ethical problems. A more promising approach to ethics, in their view, is to concentrate on teaching about the social and psychological processes that lead to unethical behavior, rather than those that lead to ethical behavior (for various articulations of this position, see Ariely 2008, 2012; Bazerman and Tenbrunsel 2011; Keefer 2013).

To assess this proposal, our first step is to reconstruct and make explicit arguments that are often tacit or presented in a fragmented way in the behavioral ethics literature. At least two compelling arguments are invoked in support of the view that the teaching of skills in moral reasoning should not be considered a key priority in ethics education: (1) unethical behavior is mainly caused by cognitive biases and situational influences that operate largely outside agents' conscious control and (2) reasoning in social situations is overwhelmingly used to rationalize people's preconceived ideas and intuitions and as device for social positioning. Both arguments are backed by a substantial body of research literature in social and cognitive psychology spanning several decades. This is what makes the claim of behavioral ethicists that ethics educators need no longer be overly concerned with promoting ethical reasoning skills such a fascinating case in neuroeducation knowledge transfer. Epistemologically speaking, the basic body of research on which the claim rests is extremely strong. Yet, as we will argue, problems emerge at the stage where educators draw implications for practice from the basic research.

Let us now consider in turn two major, robust findings in the cognitive sciences of morality that recur in the behavioral ethics literature as grounds for rejecting ethical reasoning, a central aim of ethics education.

Situational Factors Are Reliable Predictors of Ethical Behavior

The first is that ethical behavior is heavily determined by factors that are outside individuals' conscious control. It is safe to say that the basic finding has been reproduced hundreds of times in the social psychology literature, but the classic reference in connection with research on the situational determinants of social behavior is Philip Zimbardo's 1971 Stanford Prison Experiment. A lesser-known study on helping behavior conducted during the same period by John Darley and Daniel Baton (1973) is equally illustrative. Sometimes referred to as the Good Samaritan study, the researchers set up a controlled situation to identify contextual and personality variables that predicted helping behavior. A sample of theology students at Princeton University were divided into four experimental groups: in a hurry to give a presentation on a religious topic related to helping (i.e., the Good Samaritan parable), in a hurry to give a presentation on a religious topic with no direct link to helping, not in a hurry to give a presentation on the Good Samaritan parable, and not in a hurry to give a talk on a religious topic unrelated to helping. On the way to the presentations, the subjects encountered a confederate dressed as a vagabond, slumped in a doorway, and showing signs of ill health by gently coughing. The study's striking finding was that neither the topic of the talk nor the level of personal religiosity predicted whether participants stopped to help. The predictive variable was whether subjects were in a hurry.

Moral Reasoning is Predominantly Ad Hoc

A second finding from psychology research that is commonly invoked in the behavioral ethics literature to raise doubts about whether a central aim of ethics education should be to promote skills in ethical reasoning is that reasoning is overwhelmingly used to rationalize people's preconceived ideas about ethical issues and in the service of social ends (e.g., demonstrating to one's peers that one endorses some socially accepted point of view on an ethical issue), rather than to find the ethically 'right' answer to ethical problems.

The key reference in regard to the idea that ethical reasoning typically follows rather than leads to ethical judgment is Jonathan Haidt's (2001) well-known social intuitionist model of moral judgment. Haidt's model draws explicitly on a deep well of previous research in social and cognitive psychology on the multiple functions of reasoning besides the epistemic one of finding the truth. It draws, for instance, on Nisbett and T. D. Wilson's (1977) review of the independence of the social judgment process from the social justification process. One of the major conclusions of this review was that people generally have poor insights into the reasons why they arrive at social judgments. In support of this conclusion, they cite, among numerous other papers, Ben and McConnell's (1970) study, which exposed participants to arguments against their personal view on a controversial contemporary social issue—in this case, busing (the policy of increasing racial or social diversity in schools using a targeted school children–transport system). At the end of the experiment, the researchers asked the participants who changed their view on the issue to recall their original position. As it happened, the participants who changed their minds recalled that their initial views on the issue were far more moderate than they actually were. This kind of result not only suggests that explicit moral reasoning is not a single psychological process. It suggests that the parallel psychological processes playing a major role in shaping moral judgments are opaque to reasoners themselves.

Does the Centrality of 'Moral Reasoning' Need Rethinking?

In light of findings like the ones sketched here, behavioral ethicists attempt to build the case that the traditional reasoning-focused conception of ethics education conveys a distorted picture of the psychological processes that lead to ethical action (Ariely 2008; Bazerman and Tenbrunsel 2001). They claim that the emphasis on reasoning skills as a teaching and learning goal in ethics relies on the naïve, pre-psychological notion that moral reasoning processes typically precede the formulation of a moral judgment, which in turn becomes the basis of action or choice. But research has shown that this is not the way moral deliberation works. In other words, a pedagogical approach centered on coaching learners through a rational ethical deliberation procedure may even be considered mis-educational insofar as it conveys an inaccurate picture of how ethical judgment works in the real word (Ariely

2008; Bazerman and Tenbrunsel 2001). It distracts learners' attention from the real causes of ethical behavior. Proponents of this argument claim that, in order to intervene effectively in ethical judgment processes and hence improve our chances of achieving better behavioral outcomes—our own and those of others—the most important thing we need to understand are the "forces that really drive us" (Ariely 2012, 8). Ethics education should focus on the social and environmental factors that lead to unethical behavior and the processes involved in ethical irrationality rather than showing learners how to emulate some idealized model of ethical reasoning. Research in the cognitive sciences of morality suggests that learners will, in any case, abandon the epistemic use of moral reasoning as soon as they are faced with a real-life ethical situation.

As convincing as this position may seem on the face of it, there are two reasons why we should not endorse the behavioral ethics perspective on the importance of teaching about moral reasoning in ethics education. First, it misplaces the main educational interest of 'models of moral reasoning' in ethics education. Second, it underestimates 'not knowing the right thing to do' as a factor contributing to unethical behavior. The details of these points will now be elaborated in turn.

MODELS OF ETHICAL DELIBERATION: FRAMEWORKS, NOT RECIPES

Depending on how one understands the point of 'teaching reasoning skills' in ethics, teaching reasoning skills is compatible with the basic assumptions of the new synthesis in moral psychology. It is if one regards the rules, steps or procedures that typically feature in models of moral deliberation as an analytic framework for breaking an impasse of uncertainty about an ethical problem—rather than as a kind of algorithm which, when applied to an ethical problem, produces a reliable moral judgment on which to base the ethically right course of action in the circumstances. The behavior ethics position appears to assume that the only valid rationale for any content in ethics education is that the content directly promotes ethical behavior. But ethical behavior is a complex thing. As behavioral ethicists are the first to point out, it is mediated by a myriad of social, contextual, and cognitive factors of which the individual agent's grasp is generally poor. A more realistic vocation for 'teaching reasoning skills,' then, is merely to improve learners' chances of making a thoughtful, responsible and minimally biased stance when faced with novel ethical problems and complex, situated value conflicts in life, and especially the workplace—problems in relation to which, by definition, agents do not have any clear intuitions about what is the right thing to do. Social intuitionist accounts of moral judgment like Haidt's highlight the social functions of moral reasoning. But these models not only accommodate the epistemic function of moral reasoning, as mentioned earlier. Haidt (Haidt and Kesebir 2010) acknowledges that social situations where moral intuitions conflict and where well informed people disagree about an issue—i.e., conditions that parallel dilemma situations in professional settings (cf. Lerner and Tetlock 2003)—are precisely those which tend to activate the epistemic function of moral judgment.

From this viewpoint, the pedagogical role of the sorts of models of ethical deliberation that are in common use in ethics education (and which are maligned in behavioral ethics for being mis-educational) is not as much to depict real-world ethical reasoning as it is to provide an enabling analytic framework intended to help individuals move forward conceptually when faced with uncertainty about what they should do. Having been introduced to some of the typical features of the epistemic function of moral reasoning, it is hoped that, when faced with an ethical problem, learners will be more inclined to activate the kinds of cognitive reflexes constitutive of the epistemic function of moral reasoning (e.g., Do I have all the factual information I need to make a sound decision? Who is affected directly by the decision and how? Am I familiar with a situation that is comparable to this novel situation? If so, what lessons can be drawn from that comparison?) and deactivate the cognitive reflexes associated with the social functions of moral reasoning (e.g., What do other people think I should think about this issue? Which decision is most consistent with the kind of person I think I am? What reasons can I come up with to convince others to adopt my point of view? What stance on this issue and what arguments will make me appear intelligent and thoughtful to the people around?)

One could object that, whatever their pedagogical intentions are, the uptake of ethical deliberation frameworks is weak. Indeed, the limited research that exists on professionals' use of theoretical frameworks learned previously in didactic contexts to negotiate ethical problems in a work setting lends some credence to this assertion (see Drolet and Hudon 2014; Keefer and Ashley 2001). This charge could be laid, although against any technique that is taught in higher education, from coherent writing to drug prescription protocols. Whether the technique is applied correctly, effectively, or at all depends on factors that are outside the educator's control, in particular on the cultural environment of work. Hence it seems to involve a double standard to measure the instructional value of a technique taught in ethics primarily in relation to how widely it is used post formal instruction. In ethics, as in any other content area, what matters most is whether the technique is effective when it is used.

Furthermore, even if we grant that the only legitimate purpose for teaching 'reasoning skills' is as a means to promote ethical behavior, teaching about the subtle cognitive and environmental forces that drive ethical and unethical behavior may not be a more promising pedagogical response. There are reasons to think that we should not accept any more readily the claim that knowing about cognitive bias will make one less susceptible to them. Again, the research on this question speaks in favor of such skepticism. One study has shown that the principal consequence of being aware of cognitive biases is a greater propensity to think that, while others easily fall prey to cognitive biases, we ourselves are quite immune to them (Miller and Ratner 1998). Other research has shown an inverse relation between the cognitive load one is carrying and the capacity to avoid forms of cognitive bias of which one is fully aware (Sanna et al. 2002). In other words, by increasing an individual's cognitive load, a factor like a stressful work environment negates the positive 'debiasing' benefits that might have been gained from learning about judgment bias. In sum, the debiasing literature gives us a reason to be concerned about the limits of instruction about bias as a prophylactic against the influence of bias on ethical thinking and hence as a means of promoting ethical behavior (for a review see Kenyon and Beaulac, 2014).

TEACHING ABOUT THE COMPONENTS OF RATIONAL THOUGHT

A second limitation of the behavioral ethics argument concerns the argument's assumption that learners do not need any special instruction in moral reasoning. This claim is based on the prevailing view in behavioral ethics that learners are for the most part "good people" (Ariely 2012) who want to "do the right thing" (Bazerman and Tenbrunsel 2011). From this point of view, the main obstacles to ethical behavior are the cognitive "blind spots," to use Bazerman and Tenbrunsel's (2011) label, which prevent people from acting in ways that are consistent with their generally honest ethical values. And this is why teaching about them, not coaching in ethical reasoning, should be central to ethics education.

One of the reasons why this position is so *prima facie* compelling is because, clearly, the ability to understand the cognitive limits of an ethical blind spot—what is blinding about a blind spot, in other words—turns on the ability to think clearly or 'rationally' in the meritorious sense of the word. You cannot recognize biased thinking unless you can appreciate what it means to think in a way that is relatively bias-free. This is why, presumably, the consistent advice we find in the behavioral ethics literature for how to avoid cognitive biases and reduce the influence of situational factors on ethical judgment is to activate so-called 'System 2' cognition. This advice refers to a standard distinction in the cognitive sciences of morality between two basic modes of cognition. Again, System 1 is fast, lazy, heuristic, intuitive, and less reliable. System 2, by contrast, is thinking which is slow, effortful, conscious, methodological, and more reliable. The advice comes down to: "slow down and think about it!"

To see why following this advice is in and of itself a poor defense against cognitive bias, consider the following problem.

Jack is looking at Anne, but Anne is looking at George. Jack is married, but George is not. Is a married person looking at an unmarried person?

A) Yes
B) No
C) Cannot be determined

To try to find the answer you slowed down, you thought about the parameters of the problem carefully, and most likely came to the conclusion that the answer is "C": the problem does not provide us with enough information to know whether a married person is looking at an unmarried person. Because you used 'System 2 thinking,' you are probably also very confident that you got the answer right.

But you are wrong. You got the wrong answer because you failed to deploy "disjunctive reasoning" (see Bruner et al. 1956), reasoning that considers all the possibilities—concretely, if Anne is married and if Anne is unmarried. Now that you have received this simple bit of coaching, you will be able to see fairly easily that, in the problem, a married person will be looking at an unmarried person if Anne is married and if she is unmarried.

As this demonstration shows, getting the right answer has little to do with the speed or deliberativeness of the cognitive processing involved and much to do with the quality of the cognitive processing. This is why, if we are looking for advice on how to avert the pitfalls of ethical thinking, that the cognitive sciences of morality have so effectively exposed. We need to look beyond the distinction between two different cognitive modes, System 1 versus System 2, that one can opt to engage in when approaching a problem. Instead, we should look to a set of qualitative distinctions within System 2. These differentiate between rational thinking in the descriptive sense of mere deliberation (rational as opposed to non-rational) and rational thinking that leads us toward the right answers and away from the wrong ones. The second sort leads us toward better rather than worse solutions to a practical problem.

These are distinctions which, in a general sense, form the foundation of informal logical and critical thinking as sub-fields of philosophy but which have also been investigated in cognitive psychology under various headings. David Perkins, for instance, uses the term 'mindware' (i.e., learnable algorithm-like procedures stored in memory and which can be retrieved when needed), which he distinguishes from 'contaminated mindware' or 'mindware gaps.' For his part, Keith Stanovich has developed an inventory of the "components of rationality" (Stanovich 2011) which, like Haidt's Social Intuitionist Model of moral judgment, constitutes a synthesis of a dense history of psychometric research on cognitive strategies and skills which, collectively, define good decision making. The inventory divides rational thinking into a set of major dimensions, such as "probabilistic thinking," "objective reasoning styles," and "absence of irrelevant context effects in decision making" which are conceptualized specifically as patterns, habits, or styles of thought that counter the effects of cognitive biases, situational influences, and other common sources of errors in reasoning.

Particularly in light of the emerging evidence on the limitations of debiasing through direct instruction (see the discussion of this point noted earlier), Stanovich's "components of rational thought" offer a promising direction for the renewal of "teaching moral reasoning" in ethics education. First, they are grounded in the same basic body of cognitive science research that has given rise to the cognitive sciences of morality paradigm, including behavioral ethics. Yet, second, the components of rational thought also overlap significantly with the kind of 'good ethical thinking' skills that are already commonly encouraged in textbooks on applied and professional ethics and by instructors of ethics courses, albeit with one important difference: they have been operationalized and measured in extensive empirical research. Finally, from an educational standpoint, it is significant that the use of Stanovich's "components of rational thought" has been shown to be largely independent of intelligence, at least as intelligence is traditionally conceived (e.g., IQ). This means that they can be taught effectively to learners with diverse basic cognitive abilities (Stanovich and West 2008) and indeed learning about them has been shown to have a positive impact on the ability to avoid cognitive biases (Stanovich 2011).

Notwithstanding the reservations expressed in this section about the behavioral ethics proposal to largely substitute, in ethics, the traditional "teaching of ethical reasoning" with instruction in our ethical 'blind spots,' we wholeheartedly applaud the leading role that behavioral ethics has played in renewing the discussion about the teaching and learning priorities and in underlining the educational value of learning about cognitive bias, situational influences on ethical behavior, and the multiple roles of ethical reasoning in social life. Typical of research on bias and situational functioning is to show that the overwhelming majority of participants succumbed to non-conscious influences on ethical judgment. These kinds of findings are impressive and should make us stop and think seriously about how much conscious control we have over our ethical decision and what this means for teaching ethics. What we have urged in this section, however, is that just as much if not more can be learned about how to wrest control back from these influences by attending carefully to the cognitive skills possessed by the small minority of research participants who did not succumb to these biases.

RESPONSIVE EARLY CHILDCARE: A NEW FOUNDATION FOR ATTACHMENT PARENTING IN DEVELOPMENTAL NEUROSCIENCE

In education and early childcare as well, the media, popular science, and some neuroscientists have heralded the promises of 'brain-based' education and the revolutionary promises of more scientific and objective understandings of learning and developmental processes (Gura 2005; Meltzoff 2009; Organisation for Economic Co-Operation and Development 2002; Racine, Bar-Ilan and Illes 2006). Although the hope for evidence-based and scientifically informed education and childcare practices has merit, the eagerness to translate basic neuroscience research to the educational setting raises important practical epistemological and ethical questions.

Respecting Levels of Evidence and the Nature of Neuroscience Evidence

Reflecting a strong interest in developmental science among the public and in the media (Thomson and Nelson 2001), a body of literature has emerged in recent years to draw practical conclusions about childcare from the new field of affective and social neuroscience. Along with frequent child-caregiver physical contact, nursing on demand, late weaning, and co-sleeping, "responsiveness," "responsive parenting" or "responsive early childcare" is an abiding element in a package of early childcare practices advocated in this literature for its positive impact on the development of the infant's "social brain" (Gerhardt 2004; Leach 2010; Newton 2008; Schore 2003; Sunderland 2006). Responsive childcare, by helping to maintain low levels of stress hormones in the infant's brain, is alleged to be conducive to the 'normal,' 'healthy,' or 'optimal' development of the neurological systems involved in stress regulation.

This argument is discernible, for instance, in Lupien and colleagues' review on the effects of stress on the brain (Lupien et al. 2009). Humans, they state, give birth to relatively immature young, and the larger part of neuroendocrine maturation, including the development of the stress-response system, occurs *ex utero*. They claim that because of human babies' extreme physical vulnerability, they may have a species-specific predisposition to anticipate the threat posed by being left unattended by an adult and to become psychologically stressed in the absence of constant care. One intervention that they identify as being an especially salient means of limiting the activation of the stress response in infants is "sensitive and supporting care." They argue that "it is now time to turn our attention to the potential positive impact of early intervention on brain development" (Lupien et al. 2009, 442). A simpler form of the neuroscience and responsive parenting argument appears in the popular parenting writer Penelope Leach's book, the *Essential First Year* (Leach 2010). Leach claims that neuroscience research has shown that when babies are left alone to cry for long periods, the level of the stress hormone cortisol in their brains rises and that repeated exposure to high levels of cortisol causes permanent negative alterations to the neurological systems involved in stress management. Parents must understand that babies cry when they are left alone for a reason. Responsive childcare, Leach concludes, favors the development of a nervous system that reacts appropriately to life's stresses and may protect children against the risk of neuropsychological conditions, such as anxiety and depression later in life.

The new knowledge that neuroscience promises to contribute to our understanding of the influence of early experiences on psychosocial development are insights into the biological mechanisms by which early experiences might "get under the skin" (Hyman 2009). The scientific study of the influence of a child's early experience on its behavior and dispositions as an adult has long taken for granted that any personological traits attributable to early experiences have a biological substrate, in particular in the body's neuro-endocrine system (Kagan 1998). Meta-analysis of research on the relationship between responsive parenting and child health and development show clear links between early care and various aspects of child health and development (including language, cognitive as well as psychosocial development). Such considerations are already operating as a point of reference for the justification of public health interventions aimed at promoting responsive parenting in developing regions and elsewhere (Eschel et al. 2006). The neuroscience research on the effects of early stress on the stress-response system can be read as not only triangulating with this conclusion. It also suggests a powerful explanation at the biological level for the association between an absence of responsive early childcare and poor behavioral and cognitive outcomes: the effects of early life stressors on key neurological systems account for the observed negative developmental sequel (Fenton et al. 2009; Lupien et al. 2009).

Nevertheless, the work of discerning the practical significance of neuroscience research on the effects of early environmental stress on the stress-response system poses significant interpretive challenges for both non-expert interpreters and the experts/scientists doing the research themselves. For example, the basic biological research tends to operationalize "negative developmental effects" in terms of measures that do not easily map onto meaningful concepts for non-scientists. Parents and caregivers are interested in knowing socially meaningful effects, such as 'secure,' 'calm,' 'happy,' etc. Whereas researchers try to assess "pathophysiological changes" by measuring the effects on phenomena such as growth rates (weight and height), cognitive performance (learning impairments), "reduced hippocampal volume," "behavioral disturbances," and "basal HPA [hypothalamic-pituitary-adrenal] axis activity" (Dawson et al. 2000; Lupien et al. 2009). Furthermore, the question of what is meant by a "well regulated stress-response system" tends to be glossed over in the neuroscience of parenting literature with the assumption that "psychosocial problems" themselves constitute evidence of a disregulated stress-response system. The view that there is a single universally 'healthy' or 'normal' stress-response system for humans, however, is hard to square with another key concept in developmental neuroscience, i.e., 'brain plasticity.' The stress-response system, like other neurological systems, undergoes structural changes in response to its environment such that the 'adaptiveness' of a neurological system is a function of the environment in which that system operates. A stressful environment of early life, for instance, will tend to favor the emergence of a stress-response system that is adaptive in a stressful life environment, but which may be maladaptive in low-stress environments. Meta-analyses (Dawson et al. 2000; Lupien et al. 2009) indicate stress affects various measures of development and of brain systems involved in cognition and associated with mental health. Yet the heterogeneous research sources create a more complex picture on which such claims rest. For example, some experiences associated with high cortisol levels (i.e., attending all-day daycare) appear not to be a risk factor for the emergence of developmental problems; some stressful experiences—especially very stressful ones—do not always lead to raised cortisol levels; and some evidence suggests that the effects of certain stressful experiences on stress-regulatory systems are reversible, not permanent.

Thus, in spite of the importance of developmental neuroscience, there is a need to take into account its limitations, especially with respect to the nature of neuroscience concepts being investigated and the level of evidence acquired about them.

Applicability of Basic Neuroscience Research to the Context of Education

A second issue concerns the applicability of neuroscience evidence to the ordinary life of parenting and education. The biological research concerned with investigating the influence of stress on specific neuro-endocrinal pathways reviewed earlier is experimentally contrived and highly technical. A significant portion of it is also animal-based and typically involves subjecting newborn rodents and primates to severe maternal deprivation: prolonged or "repeated, unpredictable separation from the mother, unpredictable maternal feedings, or spontaneous maternal abusive behavior" (Lupien et al. 2009). That is to say, hypotheses about the effects of stress on the developing brain are in this body of research addressed negatively, with the key neuroscience research tending to look not at the beneficial effects of responsive infant care, but at the negative effects of abuse and neglect (McEwen 2002). Typical relevant human studies identify potentially stressful conditions (e.g., all-day daycare, being cared for by a clinically depressed mother), measure the effects of these conditions on cortisol levels, and can extrapolate the developmental effects of high cortisol on the children's activity of the hypothalamic-pituitary-adrenal (HPA) axis or other pathway. The underlying biological model of the effects of exposure to high levels of cortisol on the body's stress-regulatory system is, again, derived from animal studies (Lupien et al. 2009).

Two related epistemic limitations stand out. The first is that responsive parenting is not a factor studied *per se* in the research linking severe abuse and neglect to poor developmental outcomes. When the implications of this research for parenting practice and policy are considered, the responsive parenting construct plays the role of an interpretive lens through which to assess the research's significance. Second, even if one brackets the complexities identified earlier about generalizing across types of stressful situations, the operative comparison between the circumstance of children (including human infants) on the one hand, and animals exposed to extreme conditions of deprivation, neglect, and abuse, on the other, seems doubtful. The question is how well conclusions in an experimental lab situation apply to comparatively typical parenting: can the effects of social abuse and neglect on the mammalian stress-response system so readily apply to the situations of human infants exposed to varying degrees of "unresponsive early childcare" within average contemporary family environments in developed countries that are otherwise reasonably predictable, caring, safe, and healthy?

Possible Negative Implications of Neuroscience on Education and Parenting

As a number of writers have pointed out, when it comes to translational research on child development, epistemological and ethical issues are tightly interlinked (Bruer 1998; Shonkoff 2000; Thomson and Nelson 2001). The rhetorical appeal of neuroscience justifications for educational interventions and family policy is not innocuous hype. First, policy or practice proposals, which are poorly grounded epistemologically, risk diverting resources away from more effective strategies for promoting child welfare and positive development (Bruer 1998; Chugani 1998; Hinton 2002). A historical example of the impact of the seductive allure of neuroscience explanations on child policy was the former Georgia State governor Zell Miller's provision of several million dollars in the 1998 state budget to fund the purchase and delivery of a recording of classical music to families of all newborn children. The policy, now widely criticized, was based on a hasty interpretation of neuroscience research on the benefits of exposure to classical music on cognitive development, or the so-called "Mozart effect" (Rauscher et al. 1993). Second, the way that neuroscience research findings are interpreted, presented, and their policy implications drawn out becomes an ethical issue when parents and educators are sold dubious or even harmful interventions (e.g., "brain-based" educational DVDs for toddlers [Insel and Young 2001]) and when simple neurological explanatory accounts of complex social problems (e.g., the effects of exposure to violence in the media on violent behavior [Shonkoff 2000]) come to gain widespread public credibility.

If the correlational behavioral-cognitive research on the benefits of responsive parenting to child health and development are reasonably solid, one might reason, the tenuousness of the neuroscience-based argument for responsive parenting is of little consequence from a policy and practice perspective. If we already know that responsive parenting practices improves various aspects of child health and well-being, it may seem to make little difference why these practices gain favor in the eyes of parents and policy makers. At worst, future research on the effects of early stress on brain development will give the lie to the currently hypothetical link between 'unresponsive' early childcare and psychological health. In this eventuality, parental choice or family policy wrongly based on neuroscience evidence would have nevertheless contributed to improving the quality of early childcare by helping to make responsive parenting practices more widespread in the population. However, the validity of the specific neuroscience argument for responsive parenting is ethically salient, because it raises the stakes of individual parents' choices about whether or not to adopt responsive parenting practices. By casting the choice as being highly consequential for their children's future health and well-being, the neuroscience argument can fuel unwarranted parental distress and anxiety.

The potential distressing consequences of the neuroscience argument stem partly from the fact that it depends on the basic theoretical apparatus of critical periods found in developmental neuroscience. Seen through this framework and in light of human infants' dependency during this unique period of neurological development, the claim that caregivers' interventions have a wide-ranging, significant, and possibly irreversible impact on children's psychosocial development may seem established *a priori*. Against the background of critical periods, it is imminently foreseeable that parents and offshore translators of neuroscience research will perceive the choice of whether to adopt the practices associated with 'responsive parenting' as having significant consequences for their children's future health and well-being. Yet, as noted earlier, reliably assessing the effect of stress on the developing brain is a complex affair. Numerous critical studies on the translation of neuroscience to education and early childcare have documented how the theoretical framework of critical periods is misapplied to domains other than the ones in which the framework was initially conceived (i.e., in the development of the sensory system and language acquisition) (Bruer 1998; Organisation for Economic Co-Operation and Development 2002; Thompson and Nelson 2001). Typical points of misunderstanding include (i) overlooking the evidence that critical periods may be exceptional, not typical, in brain development and (ii) that there is not a single 'right kind' of environmental input that each neurological system 'needs' in order to develop normally.' Rather, because the environmental input plays the role of steering the maturation process by fine-tuning neurological systems to the organism's specific environment, the range of 'expectant' environmental input for any organism is extremely wide. This is particularly so for socially complex, culture-bearing, and ecologically adaptable mammals such as humans. The claims repeated in the offshore literature on the neuroscience of parenting—that insufficiently responsive early childcare is potentially 'toxic' to the brain and that 'responsive parenting' constitutes a protective factor against disabling psycho-developmental disorders such as autism-spectrum disorders, anxiety, depression, and ADHD—are then at best apt to generate unwarranted anxiety in parents. But the consequences of overestimating the neuroscience-based link between responsive parenting and healthy brain development are especially pernicious for the parents with children suffering from severe developmental disorders. They may come to believe that if only they had been more 'responsive'—if during the child's infancy they had eschewed the extinction method of sleep training and opted instead for co-sleeping—that their child would today be healthy and normal. Although further research on the specific real-world effects of the critical period framework on parental behavior is needed, tangible behavioral and psychological effects appear to follow from deterministic neuroscience explanations (Vohs and Schooler 2008).

Public Trust in Developmental Neuroscience and Responsible Translation of Research

It appears that one of the reasons why the neuroscience of stress effects on brain development has attracted the interest of parenting science writers is because this research seems to provide new and scientifically credible grounds for prescribing 'responsive parenting.' As background, the concept of responsive childcare in contemporary discourse on parenting is largely a legacy of Attachment Theory (Barrett 2006). However, the marriage of neuroscience explanations and parenting advice literature in attempts to advocate responsive early childcare on the basis of evidence on stress and brain development poses evidential challenges. Often, neuroscience evidence is suggested to have more 'reality' than what is revealed by common sense or by social sciences and the humanities (Racine et al. 2005; Racine et al. 2010). Neurorealism therefore describes a form of naïve realism propelled by public fascination for contemporary neuroscience. A general rhetorical appeal of neuroscience-based explanations has been observed both in studies of media coverage of neuroscience (Racine et al. 2005; Racine et al. 2010) and in research in social psychology on how non-experts evaluate the evidential strength of neuroscience explanations (McCabe and Castel 2008; Weisberg et al. 2008). In the context of neuroeducation, there is a suspicion that developmental science is manipulated to promote particular personal views about good parenting (Barrett 2006).

Jack Shonkoff has argued that, in this context, effective translation of the results of research on child development to the realm of policy and practice requires that careful attention be paid to the distinction between established knowledge, reasonable hypotheses, and unwarranted or irresponsible assertions in the field of investigation (Shonkoff 2000). It is the very nature of scientific knowledge about human development, he reminds us, to be provisional and limited. Mirroring more recent calls for translational prudence in the neuroethics literature and commitment to integrity and accountability (Fenton et al. 2009; Illes and Racine 2005; Rosen et al. 2002; Wolpe et al. 2005), Shonkoff advocates a cautious approach to policy not only because it enhances developmental science's potential contribution to the advancement of human health and well-being but also because, without it, public trust in psychological science's role in developing sound child and family policy risks being undermined. By fueling the growth of public skepticism and cynicism toward the possibility of reliable or well-established knowledge in child development, imprudent interpretations of child development research weaken developmental science's potential to enhance human health and well-being (Shonkoff 2000).

More generally, the translation of neuroscience to the domain of education calls for an appreciation of the multi-faceted interactions between educational practice, neuroscience, and societal expectations. A fair appreciation of the ethical challenges demands sensitivity to such complex issues as the epistemological underpinnings of neuroscience research in this area (e.g., use of animal models of learning and development), the social and policy consequences of early translation of research (e.g., the sound use of neuroscience evidence to confirm or discredit educational practices), and the role that (sometimes tacit) values play in informing decisions made by neuroscientists, policy makers, and parents in this translational effort (e.g., the implicit prioritization of efficiency, competitiveness, and increased productivity and performance). In sum, neuroscientists and other stakeholders confronted by the promises of neuroscience in education and parenting face a range of decisions and challenges in determining the epistemological credibility of neuroscience-based explanations as well as acting upon them in responsible and value-sensitive ways.

CONCLUSION

In this chapter, we reviewed two cases in neuroeducation knowledge transfer: behavioral ethics and responsive parenting. First, we examined claims to the effect that behavioral ethics challenges the role of 'traditional' ethics teaching, which stresses moral reasoning skills. Studies in the cognitive of morality would lead to the deprioritizing of moral reasoning in favor of greater awareness to the psychological and social determinants of moral judgments and moral reasoning. We argued that this common interpretation is debatable because (i) the emphasis on the debiasing of moral judgment has so far proven to be a limited strategy (awareness of biases does not lead to the uptake of ethical behavior) and (ii) remediation of biases may rely partly on System 2 skills (e.g., recognition of biases induced by System 1 relies on System 2 cognition, for instance, to develop skills of less biased thinking). In the second part of the chapter, we explored how the case of responsive parenting illustrates the types of practical ethical questions associated with the use of neuroscience in education and parenting literature. We drew attention to the epistemological and public understanding dimensions of these ethical challenges, notably when it comes to assessing the applicability of basic neuroscience research to the context of education and communicating the findings (and implications) of basic research to the public.

The contributions of cognitive science and neuroscience to education are tremendous. As these contributions redefine ethics education—their application raises ethical challenges in their own right—this entire area of investigation will represent an important and stimulating task for interdisciplinary scholarship.

ACKNOWLEDGMENTS

The authors would like to thank Natalie Zizzo for editorial support. E. R. acknowledges support of a FRQ-S career award as well as support from a grant of the Social Sciences and Humanities Research Council of Canada.

REFERENCES

Ariely, D. 2008. *Predictably Irrational: The Hidden Forces that Shape Our Decisions*. New York: Harper Perennial.
Ariely, D. 2012. *The (Honest) Truth About Dishonesty*. New York: HarperCollins.
Barrett, H. 2006. *Attachment and the Perils of Parenting*. London: National Family and Parenting Institute.
Bazerman, M.H., and A.E. Tenbrunsel. 2011. *Blind Spots*. Princeton, NJ: Princeton University Press.
Ben, D.J., and H.K. McConnell. 1970. "Testing the Self-Perception Explanation of Dissonance Phenomena: On the Salience of Premanipulation Attitudes." *Journal of Personality and Social Psychology* 14: 23–31.
Blasi, A. 1980. "Bridging Moral Cognition and Moral Action: A Critical Review of the Literature." *Psychological Bulletin* 88: 1–45.
Bowie, N.E. 2003. "The Role of Ethics in Professional Education." In *A Companion to the Philosophy of Education*, edited by R. Curren, 617–626. Malden, MA: Blackwell.
Bruer, J.T. 1998. "The Brain and Child Development: Time for Some Critical Thinking." *Public Health Reports* 113 (5): 388–398.
Bruner, J., J.J. Goodnow, and A. Gorge. 1956. *A Study of Thinking*. New York: Wiley & Sons.
Bull, B. 1993. "Ethics in the Preservice Curriculum." In *Ethics for Professionals in Education*, edited by K.A. Strike and P.L. Ternasky, 69–83. New York: Teachers College Press.
Chugani, H.T. 1998. "Neuroscience and Public Policy." *Public Health Reports* 113 (6): 480–481.
Darley, J.M., and C.D. Batson. 1973. "'From Jerusalem to Jericho': A Study of Situational and Dispositional Variables in Helping Behavior." *Journal of Personality and Social Psychology* 27 (1): 100–108.
Dawson, G., Ashman, S.B., and Carver, L.J. 2000. "The Role of Early Experience in Shaping Behavioral and Brain Development and Its Implications for Social Policy." *Development and Psychopathology* 12 (4): 695–712.
De Cremer, D., and A.E. Tenbrunsel, eds. 2012. *Behavioral Business Ethics: Shaping an Emerging Field*. New York: Routledge.
Drolet, M.-J., and A. Hudon. 2014. "Theoretical Frameworks Used to Discuss Ethical Issues in Private Physiotherapy Practice and Proposal of a New Ethical Tool." *Medicine, Health Care and Philosophy* 18: 51–62.

Eschel, N., B. Daelmans, M. Cabral de Mello, and J. Martines. 2006. "Responsive Parenting: Interventions and Outcomes." *World Health Organization Bulletin* 83 (12): 991–998.

Fenton, A., L. Meynell, and F. Baylis. 2009. "Responsibility and Speculation: On Possible Applications of Pediatric fMRI." *American Journal of Bioethics* 9 (1): W1–W2.

Gerhardt, S. 2004. *Why Love Matters*. London: Routledge.

Gura, T. 2005. "Educational Research: Big Plans for Little Brains." *Nature* 435 (7046): 1156–1158.

Haidt, J. 2001. "The Emotional Dog and Its Rational Tail: A Social Intuitionist Approach to Moral Judgment." *Psychological Review* 108 (4): 814–834.

Haidt, J., and S. Kesebir. 2010. "Morality." In *Handbook of Social Psychology, 5th Edition*, edited by S. Fiske, D. Gilbert, and G. Lindzey, 797–832. Hoboken, NJ: Wiley.

Hinton, V.J. 2002. "Ethics of Neuroimaging in Pediatric Development." *Brain and Cognition* 50 (3): 455–468.

Howe, K.R. 1986. "A Conceptual Basis for Ethics in Teacher Education." *Journal of Teacher Education* 37 (3): 5–12.

Hyman, S.E. 2009. "How Diversity Gets Under the Skin." *Nature Neuroscience* 12 (3): 241–243.

Illes, J., and E. Racine. 2005. "Imaging or Imagining? A Neuroethics Challenge Informed by Genetics." *American Journal of Bioethics* 5 (2): 5–18.

Insel, T.R., and L.J. Young. 2001. "The Neurobiology of Attachment." *Nature Reviews Neuroscience* 2: 129–136.

Kagan, J. 1998. *Three Seductive Ideas*. Cambridge, MA: Harvard University Press.

Keefer, M.W. 2013. "Understanding Morality from an Evolutionary Perspective: Challenges and Opportunities." *Educational Theory* 63 (2): 113–131.

Keefer, M., and K.D. Ashley. 2001. "Case-Based Approaches to Professional Ethics: A Systematic Comparison of Students' and Ethicists' Moral Reasoning." *Journal of Moral Education* 30 (4): 377–398.

Kenyon, T., and G. Beaulac. 2014. "Critical Thinking Education and Debiasing." *Informal Logic* 34 (4): 341–363.

Knobe, J., and S. Nichols, eds. 2008. *Experimental Philosophy*. New York: Oxford University Press.

Leach, P. 2010. *The Essential First Year*. New York: DK Publishing.

Lerner, J.S., and P.E. Tetlock. 2003. "Bridging Individual, Interpersonal, and Institutional Approaches to Judgment and Decision Making: The Impact of Accountability on Cognitive Bias." In *Emerging Perspectives on Judgment and Decision Research*, edited by S.L. Schneider and J. Shanteau, 431–457. New York: Cambridge University Press.

Levin, B. 2004. "Making Research Matter More." *Education Policy Analysis Archives* 22 (56): 1–20.

Lupien, S., B.S. McEwen, M.R. Gunnmar, and C. Heim. 2009. "Effects of Stress Throughout the Lifespan on the Brain, Behaviour and Cognition." *Nature* 10: 434–445.

McCabe, D.P. and A.D. Castel. 2008. "Seeing Is Believing: The Effect of Brain Images on Judgments of Scientific Reasoning." *Cognition* 107 (1): 343–352.

McEwen, B. 2002. *The End of Stress As We Know It*. Washington, DC: Dana Press.

Meltzoff, A.N., P.K. Kuhl, J. Movellan, and T.J. Sejnowski. 2009. "Foundations for a New Science of Learning." *Science* 325 (5938): 284–288.

Miller, D.T., and R.K. Ratner. 1998. "The Disparity Between the Actual and Assumed Power of Self-Interest." *Journal of Personal and Social Psychology* 74: 53–62.

Newton, R.P. 2008. *The Attachment Connection*. Oakland, CA: New Harbinger Publications.

Nisbett, R.E., and T.D. Wilson. 1977. "Telling More Than We Can Know: Verbal Reports on Mental Processes." *Psychological Review* 84 (3): 231–259.

Organisation for Economic Co-Operation and Development (OECD). 2002. *Understanding the Brain: Toward a New Learning Science.* Vol. 1. Paris: OECD Publications.

Racine, E., O. Bar-Ilan, and J. Illes. 2005. "fMRI in the Public Eye." *Nature Reviews Neuroscience* 6 (2): 159–164.

Racine, E., O. Bar-Ilan, and J. Illes. 2006. "Brain Imaging: A Decade of Coverage in the Print Media." *Science Communication* 28 (1): 122–142.

Racine, E., S. Waldman, J. Rosenberg, and J. Illes. 2010. "Contemporary Neuroscience in the Media." *Social Science and Medicine* 71 (4): 725–733.

Rauscher, F.H., G.L. Shaw, and K.N. Ky. 1993. "Music and Spatial Task Performance." *Nature* 365 (6447): 611.

Rest, J.R. 1986. "An Overview of the Psychology of Morality." In *Moral Development: Advances in Research and Theory*, edited by J. Rest, 1–27. New York: Praeger.

Rosen, A.C., A. Pearl, and J.A. Yeasavage. 2002. "Ethical, and Practical Issues in Applying Functional Imaging to the Clinical Management of Alzheimer's Disease." *Brain and Cognition* 50 (3): 498–519.

Sanna, L., S. Stocker, and N. Schwarz. 2002. "When Debiasing Backfires: Accessible Content and Accessibility Experiences in Debiasing Hindsight." *Journal of Experimental Psychology: Learning, Memory, and Cognition* 28 (3): 497–502.

Schore, A. 2003. *Affect Dysregulation and Disorders of the Self.* New York: Norton.

Shonkoff, J.P. 2000. "Science, Policy, and Practice." *Child Development* 71 (1): 181–187.

Stanovich, K. 2011. *Rationality and the Reflective Mind.* New York: Oxford University Press.

Stanovich, K., and R.F. West. 2008. "On the Relative Independence of Thinking Biases and Cognitive Ability." *Journal of Personality and Social Psychology* 94 (4): 672–695.

Sunderland, M. 2006. *The Science of Parenting.* New York: DK Publishing.

Thompson, R.A., and C.A. Nelson. 2001. "Developmental Science and the Media." *American Psychologist* 56 (1): 5–15.

Vohs, K.D., and Schooler, J.W. 2008. "The Value of Believing in Free Will: Encouraging a Belief in Determinism Increases Cheating." *Psychological Science* 19 (1): 49–54.

Weisberg, D.S., F.C. Keil, J. Goodstein, E. Rawson, and J.R. Gray. 2008. "The Seductive Allure of Neuroscience Explanations." *Journal of Cognitive Neuroscience* 20 (3): 470–477.

Wolpe, P. R., Foster, K. R., & Langleben, D. D. 2005. "Emerging Neurotechnologies for Lie-Detection: Promises and Perils." *The American Journal of Bioethics* 5 (2), 39–49. http://doi.org/10.1080/15265160590923367

Zimbardo, P. G. 1971. *Stanford Prison Experiment.* Stanford, CA: Stanford University.

5 Neuroscience, Neuropragmatism, and Commercialism[1]

Deron Boyles

REDUCTIONISM AND COMMERCIALIZATION OF NEUROSCIENCE IN EDUCATION

As Tibor Solymosi recently pointed out, there appear to be 'neurophiles' who are proclaiming neuroscience so wonderfully revolutionary as to make it on par with steam engines, electricity, and iPads (Carlson 2011; Solymosi 2011a). On this view, we only stand to benefit from the work of neuroscientists who unlock the puzzles of the human brain. Zack Lynch proclaims, "'neurosociety's'. . . arrival is both inevitable and already in progress . . . . It will be nothing less than the birth of a new civilization" (Lynch and Laursen 2009, 11). Once we piece together how alleles, synapses, and frontal cortexes function, in other words, we can solve the mysteries Tom Wolfe once noted as "the riddle of the human mind and the riddle of what happens to the human mind when it comes to know itself absolutely" (Tom Wolfe, quoted in Frank 2009).[2]

Neuroscience is also prominently in the news of late, not altogether unproblematically. Eben Alexander, a neurosurgeon, recently published his book, *Proof of Heaven: A Neurosurgeon's Journey into the Afterlife*. In it, he makes the leap from inactive synapses to consciousness to claim that heaven exists. Naomi Wolf's book, provocatively titled *Vagina*, also makes neuroscientific claims about dopamine being a 'feminist' neurotransmitter. Fox news, and other media outlets, ran a story of the Harvard study that used a functional magnetic resonance imaging scanner to show that people would rather talk about themselves than talk about other people. The Science Channel features a show titled "Hack My Brain," in which the host, Todd Sampson, devotes three months to neuroscientific practices so he will prove that he is smarter as a result (Genzlinger 2014).

For education, 'Mind-Brain Education' (MBE) advocates are already publishing research that trumpets what brain functions are most important for success in school, how to identify the parts of the brain 'responsible' for those functions, and what models and strategies exist for 'maximizing' brain control for increased success in learning (see, for example,

Noble et al. 2005; see also Abadzi 2006; Yeap 1989).[3] The language used is, I argue, highly symbolic. MBE advocates, such as Tom Vander Ark, draw attention to what they call the 'conclusions' MBE provides. Among Vander Ark's list of twelve conclusions are the following three:

- Emotions direct students' learning processes, helping them gravitate toward positive situations and away from negative ones.
- Education should give students opportunities to practice setting goals, tracking progress toward them, adjusting strategies along the way, and assessing outcomes.
- Education can support the development of emotional regulation skills, and this should be a priority, as emotional regulation skills strongly predict academic achievement.

(Vander Ark 2012)

The conclusions are instructive: students prefer positive situations over negative ones. When Vander Ark writes that "education should give students opportunities," and then "track," "adjust strategies," and "assess outcomes," he's writing within the context of advancing what MBE advocates call 'student-centered learning.' But we can rightly ask: what is so student centered about an amorphous 'education' that should 'give,' 'track,' 'adjust,' and 'assess?' It appears that the power imbued to 'education' (which I suspect is code for teacher authority or control) undermines the agency in the idea of student-centered inquiry. When he writes about developing "emotional regulation skills" and their link to "academic achievement," he helps us understand that MBE is about particular forms of cognition colored almost solely by behaviorism (Hinton et al. 2012).[4] These 'skills' are what are valued because, in the view of MBE, they predict. Even if true, where are the students in all of this?

I argue, akin to Richard Quantz, that the foregoing ideas represent a kind 'puzzlemastering,' appealing to an ideal that reflects what John Dewey criticized as the quest for certainty (Dewey 1929a; Quantz with O'Conner and Magolda 2011). My concern here is that the puzzlemaster approach to inquiry is one where the pieces of puzzles are tried and tried until the puzzle appears to fit together and is complete. Our job as humans, as our job as teachers and students, is to fit pre-existing blocks into their respective holes (or 'discover' how the pieces of the puzzle fit together). Accordingly, the 'answers' to neuroscientific questions already exist. We simply need to find them through methods of, say, functional magnetic resonance imaging or, arguably more problematic, commercial 'brain-training' programs. Neuroscience is not unique in this sort of reductionism, but what is unique is the relatively recent trend in philosophy to use John Dewey to rescue neuroscience from such reductionism and reconstruct neuroscientific inquiry as a form of pragmatism aimed toward integrated and transactive inquiry: neuropragmatism (Shook 2011).[5]

Dewey's reconstruction borrowed from Darwin's effort to navigate and explain the shifting world of 'body' that was historically set against the permanent world of 'mind.' As Solymosi puts it,

> Reconstruction . . . brings the problems of philosophy back down to earth. No longer should philosophers be distracted by questions divorced from the lived and living world. Instead of trying to escape such a world by finding some metaphysical or epistemological principle that holds always and forever, pragmatism seeks to turn the attention and energy of philosophers to the less permanent and less stable world of humans in nature. The redirection of effort is central to Dewey's main tools of reconstruction: situatedness, continuity, and experience as organic-environmental transactions.
>
> (Solymosi 2011a, 156)[6]

This chapter provides historical background to substantiate the claim that neuroscience in education is currently largely divorced from philosophy and history, preferring to focus absorbedly on microbiology, nanotechnology, and cognitive psychology. Commercial applications, such as Lumosity, Fit Brains, and Cognifit, exploit such foci for financial gain.[7] While biological, cognitive, and technical elements may be necessary conditions for positive growth in humanity, they are not sufficient. What is needed is a form of pragmatism—neuropragmatism—to counter reductionism and commercialism and provide warranted justification for reimagining human potential. My claim is not that neuropragmatism is 'the' answer to the conundrum of scientism and commercial exploitation, but a legitimate adaptation and extension of classical pragmatism and neopragmatism that meets the specifics and the spirit of Deweyan inquiry—and one that has serious implications for teaching, learning, and schooling.

CLASSICAL PRAGMATISM, NEOPRAGMATISM, AND NEUROPRAGMATISM: A BRIEF OVERVIEW

At risk of oversimplification, the development of classical pragmatism from Dewey's time to now reveals important shifts in thinking that allow us to imagine neuropragmatism. What I intend in this section of the chapter is to lay out, briefly, the key elements of classical pragmatism and neopragmatism in order to show how neuropragmatism is thinkable. Classical pragmatism was, positively, an outgrown of Darwin and, negatively, a reaction against analytic philosophy. I view Dewey's mature thought as transactional realism and believe, with David Hildebrand, that neopragmatists such as Richard Rorty and Hilary Putnam, while offering significant interpretations of pragmatism, get key parts of Dewey's metaphysics and epistemology wrong (Hildebrand 2003). This is important for the larger topic, because emphasizing the centrality of facts versus the implosion of the fact/value dualism matters to the causal, primal, correlative, and integrative arguments involving brain, mind, and inquiry.

What Rorty and Putnam advanced was arguably anti-scientific, where science is understood in Dewey's terms as integrative and cohesive inquiry between and among theory and application. Dewey argued that "what 'science' means is simply the most authentic knowledge of nature, man [sic], and society that is possible at any given time by means of the methods and techniques then and there available" (Dewey 2008, 258). The core of the Rorty–Putnam debates over science, essentially pitting realism against antirealism, centered on linguistics, at least for Rorty. As Rorty noted, "I linguisticize . . . in order to read [philosophers] as prophets of the utopia in which all metaphysical problems have been dissolved, and religion and science have yielded their place to poetry" (Rorty 1995, 35). Rorty interprets Dewey's logic, his theory of inquiry, as merely a method.[8] He's wrong.

Dewey calls science

> the perfected outcome of learning—its consummation. What is known, in a given case, is what is sure, certain, settled, disposed of; that which we think *with* rather than that which we think about. In its honorable sense, knowledge is distinguished from opinion, guesswork, speculation, and mere tradition.
>
> (Dewey 1944, 188)

Significantly, Dewey adds, "But experience makes us aware that there is a difference between intellectual certainty of *subject matter* and *our* certainty" (Dewey 1944, 188). His point is to caution us on two fronts. First, we should not take science to be such a universalized worldview—nor a reified (overgeneralized) method—that we forget context. Second, we should not throw out a naturalistic empiricist interpretation of science-in-common-life. Yes, Dewey wants us to get away from superstition and mere opinion. So do neuroscientists. Yes, Dewey wants us to employ scientific method. So do neuroscientists. The difference is that Dewey goes on to make an important stipulation:

> On the other hand, the fact that science marks the perfecting of knowing in highly specialized conditions of technique renders its results, taken by themselves, remote from ordinary experience—a quality of aloofness that is properly designated by the term abstract.
>
> (Dewey 1944, 189–190)

In other words, science as laboratory experiment yields 'scientific' results, but the connection between science and the context of everyday life is where Dewey wants science to go—and *not* via the imposition of science *onto* everyday life.

Putnam, contrary to Rorty's relativist extension of pragmatism, takes classical pragmatism's merging of truth and verification, i.e., inquiry, as a move away from what he saw as an important goal: the 'tenselessly' true. Putnam's neopragmatism wants to find a middle ground between metaphysical realism—objectivity and correspondent truth—and the total rejection of truth. He does this, in short, by providing 'idealized justification.' In his book *Reality with a Human Face*, Putnam navigates shared territory with Rorty:

> [I am] willing to think of reference as internal to "texts" (or theories), *provided* we recognize that there are better and worse "texts." "Better and "worse" may themselves depend on our historical situation and our purposes; there is no notion of a God's-Eye View of Truth here. But the notion of a right (or at least "better") answer to a question is subject to two constraints: (1) *Rightness is not subjective.* What is better and worse to say about most questions of real human concern is not just a matter of *opinion* . . . . (2) *Rightness and justification* . . . . My own view is that truth is to be identified with idealized justification, rather than with justification-on-present-evidence. "Truth" in this sense is as context sensitive as *we are.*
>
> (Putnam 1990, 114–115)

This extended quote provides at least two insights. First, in his effort to block the slide to relativism, Putnam inserts his tool of 'idealized justification.' For a classical pragmatist, the move is confusing, if not unnecessary altogether. As Hildebrand notes, "as long as inquiry is done with care, there is no reason that 'present evidence' could not provide a satisfactory answer—one we might even call 'better' or 'right'" (Hildebrand 2003, 134). If correspondence theories of truth are to be rejected, as any pragmatist would have to maintain, why bother with what is arguably a mitigated correspondence theory? I suspect that Putnam's debates with Rorty made him overzealous in his rejection of relativism—but Dewey was not a relativist, he was a fallibilist. Providing warrant for claims to 'truth' is part and parcel of his theory of inquiry. Although potentially temporal, facts are still facts, until they no longer are. We 'know' that if we step off a ladder, we will fall at a rate of 32.2 feet per second squared. While true, and knowable, such a truth is not universal, as it is possible that gravity (as a rate of acceleration) may change by .001 ft/s^2 (or some other variation) in a thousand or a million years. Consider Dewey's clarification:

> The 'truth' of any present proposition is, by definition, subject to the outcome of continued inquiries; *its* 'truth,' if the word must be used, is provisional; as *near* the truth as inquiry has *as yet* come, a matter determined *not* by a guess at some future belief but by the care and pains with which inquiry has been conducted up to the present time.
>
> (Dewey 1985, 57)

Second, Putnam hints at a central epistemological problem within the nexus of disciplines in the Mind-Brain Education (MBE) movement. That is, when Putnam asserts that truth "is as context sensitive as *we are*" (Putnam 1990, 115), he is trying to distinguish his theory of truth as very distinct from Rorty, but also distinct from Dewey. He is delineating his epistemology. Where Dewey understands 'pure' and 'applied' science as interdependent, Putnam sees Dewey as separating science from ethics. Regarding Dewey's *Logic: The Theory of Inquiry*, Putnam writes,

> What Dewey's argument does show is that there is a certain overlap between scientific values and ethical values; but even where they overlap, these values remain different. Scientific values are not simply instrumental . . . but they are relativized to a context—the context of knowledge acquisition—and knowledge acquisition itself is something that can be criticized ethically.
>
> (Putnam 1994, 174)

Putnam is making a categorical mistake in that while he rightly subjects science to ethical examination, he seems to think that Dewey would have seen scientific values set in contrast to ethical or aesthetic ones. For Dewey, the contrast is part of the problem. While Putnam is no positivist, the effort to separate scientific values from other values mistakes what Dewey vigorously championed as the continuity between and among scientific and ethical inquiry.

We have, then, the merging of the fact/value dualism in order to establish what counts as knowledge in scientific inquiry. This is an important bridge to neuroscientific research and what counts as research in education in the twenty-first century. In short, the neopragmatists are helpful, even when they are wrong, for they provide arguments that enable us to more clearly understand classical pragmatism and its potential for becoming neuropragmatism. Where Rorty relativized to language and poetry, Putnam tried to hold to a weak correspondence theory of truth and a robust understanding of knowledge as the 'end product' of inquiry. Neuroscientists working in education are far more likely to cohere with Putnam's accounts, even if they do not use the language of neopragmatism. What, then, are the terms they use and what are the metaphysical and epistemological assumptions they make when they define neuroscience and neuroscientific inquiry in application to education?

SKETCHING NEUROSCIENCE, NEUROPSYCHOLOGY, AND MIND-BRAIN EDUCATION: COMMERCIAL SUBTEXT?

For the sake of brevity, I am using a collection of essays from neuroscientists and 'educational neuroscientists' to represent the general—and not wholly unified—field of neuroscience applied to schooling. While there are some clear differences among the scientists, there are many similarities that, by using their own definitions about what they do and why they think neuroscience is so important for education, I can capture an accurate reflection of the field of neuroscience in education. There are promises and perils, of course, but the goal in this section of the chapter is to correctly represent the field in order to raise questions about how it might be aided (or rescued) by the relatively new area of neuropragmatism.

So what is neuroscience? Neuroscience is the study of the anatomy, physiology, biochemistry, and/or molecular biology of nerves and nervous system tissue. Some of the focus of neuroscience is on understanding the evolution of the organ. From archipallium or reptilian brains to neomammalian ones, some neuroscientists try to understand the development of the brain over many thousands of years.[9] Other neuroscientists are interested in the 'micro' elements that make up the brain, such as axon terminals, dendritic spines, and myelin sheaths. This sort of study is about the elements that make up the brain and provide its functionality. The primary question here is, "How does the brain work?" Relatedly, other neuroscientists focus on issues such as brain trauma, autism, and dyslexia. Overwhelmingly empirical, neuroscience is the grounding some psychologists use to develop 'models' to address issues such as attention deficit disorders and behavior disorders. The links to pedagogy should be apparent. If not, a quick review of the increasing number of centers or institutes that focus on neuroscience reveals a clear bent toward psychology and, by some extension, pedagogy.

Georgetown University's Center for the Study of Learning (CSL) is typical of institutes and centers that focus on neuroscience and education. It claims to

> conduct research that will shed light on the causes and effects of learning disorders, so that better programs for diagnosis and treatment can be developed. CSL's researchers have identified some of the important neurophysiological mechanisms of reading acquisition, disorders of reading and its remediation. Our mission is to use neuroscience research to help identify avenues for effective education and remediation for a variety of cognitive skills.
>
> (Center for the Study of Learning)

At Simon Fraser University, Stephen Campbell runs an educational neuroscience laboratory called ENGRAMMETRON. His goal is to "bring to bear as much observational control of the learning process as possible" (Campbell 2011, 13). He does this by using electroencephalograms (EEGs), electrocardiograms (EKGs), electrooculograms (EOGs), and electromylograms (EMGs). In much of the justification for his work, he highlights the centrality of rigor and science as the basis for solving learning problems.

Campbell's concern for rigor is shared by Kathryn Patten, also at Simon Fraser. Her assertion is that the "neuromyths that have crept into pedagogy must be replaced by an applied neuroscience, primarily concerned with educational practice both informed by educational neuroscience *and* informing research in neuroscience and neuropsychology . . . [i.e.] neuropedagogy" (Patten 2011, 87).[10] Patten's project is linking empirical science to practical issues in classrooms. One of the founders of neuropedagogy, Kurt Fischer, apparently shares her concern. His work at Harvard, since at least the 1990s, established course work that became known as Mind-Brain Education (MBE). MBE is, according to Zachary Stein and Kurt Fischer, "poised to usher in a new era in both the science of learning and scientifically based educational reforms" (Stein and Fischer 2011, 57). This is reminiscent of Zachary Lynch's exclamation from the beginning of this chapter that neuroscience (and, by extension, MBE) is "nothing less than the birth of a new civilization." My suspicion is that both areas see a lucrative commercial industry resulting from such enthusiasm, a point illustrated throughout this chapter.

While Stein and Fischer concede that there are significant complexities facing the 'new field,'[11] they nonetheless advance a particular form of research and a particular view of science that necessarily qualifies what it means to learn. Repeatedly, terms such as 'rigorous science,' 'research grounded in science,' and the oft-cited acronym STEM (Science, Technology, Engineering, and Mathematics) reinforce a particular vision of what the field can do to help children in schools—whether they are labeled as atypical or not. Cognitive psychology *qua* cognitive neuroscience provides the foundation for much of the work in this field, but another element also exists: money. At the Southwest Center for Mind, Brain, and Education at the University of Texas, Arlington, the pitch for studying MBE goes as follows:

> Imagine participating in a program that could change the face of education while advancing your career. Mind, Brain, and Education (MBE)—an emerging field exploring the biology and mental activity of learning—does just that by helping educators understand the internal factors involved in the learning process.
>
> (Southwest Center for Mind, Brain, and Education)

Careerism is pitched, and in part also linked, to the not-so-subtle assumption that there is only one learning process: 'the learning process.' Like Vander Ark earlier, the common theme of work, skills tied to jobs, competitiveness, commercial implications etc., too frequently get mentioned without critique and without any sense that there might be more to human existence than employability, hierarchical comparisons, entrenched notions of what constitutes proper behavior, and how commercialized 'training programs' will lead to a more competitive brain advantage.

Linking this back to neopragmatism and neuroscience in education, Mind-Brain Educators (MBEs) want nothing to do with Rorty. 'Poetry' may be nice, but it informs the 'neuromyths' that MBEs are concerned is a central problem in education. We should get away from speculative ideas about what works in schools and develop models that are scientifically proven to work. I am reminded of Gert Biesta's essay in *Educational Theory* titled "Why What Works Won't Work." Biesta points out how the imposition of scientific data collecting reduces the democratic potential of teaching and learning, among other things (Biesta 2007). In this sense, Putnam's neopragmatism, while not the same as what MBEs argue, is similar in a key regard and emphasis: pure versus practical knowledge/scientific facts versus ethical values. Where Putnam sees a dichotomy, so do MBEs. Both regard truth as a findable 'end.' Both place more privilege on scientific fact than on values. Both elevate expertise over ordinary experience. Like Rorty's premature announcement that epistemology is dead, Putnam and MBEs appear to err in embracing (false) dualisms.

Dewey is important here because, as Jim Garrison notes, affect and cognition are part and parcel of being human (Garrison 2008). Larry Hickman writes, "Dewey simply bypassed the chasm this [science vs ethics] debate has opened. He proposed that the two sides—the one that emphasizes facts and the one that emphasizes values—are at bottom connected as *phases* or *moments* within inquiry" (Hickman 2007, 158). Where neuroscience attempts to identify clusters of neurons, neuropragmatists, following Dewey, seek to understand the transactional continuity of the cluster of neurons in a brain in a nervous system in an organism in an environment—all of which *change*. Implications for teaching and learning are outlined in the section that follows, but, in brief, run parallel: identifying student 'learning styles' or 'proving' 'what works' or identifying 'best practices' become isolated 'strategies' that discount teachers and students because the contexts of both groups are marginalized or ignored in favor of (over) generalizability of what are deemed or vaunted as 'scientific facts.' Neuropragmatism does not reject science; it understands that science and neuroscience are valuable elements within a larger theory of inquiry. Schools should be seen and understood, on the neuropragmatist view, as spaces for transactional inquiry wherein students and teachers in varying classrooms investigate the variety of problems that reflect their interests within and surrounding their school, town, state, country, globe, etc. In short, we should be more wary about 'programs,' 'protocols,' and 'inventories' (perhaps especially their commercial implications) and, instead, privilege pragmatic generativity over scientistic and psychologistic assumptive imposition.[12]

NEUROPRAGMATISM AND EDUCATION

Given that neuropragmatism is defined by multi-layered and multi-faceted inquiry that requires mind and body, such as human will and dopamine, in transactional relationship with changing contexts, how might neuropragmatism best be illustrated? Far from novel, I nonetheless use food as the illustration of evolutionary utility that grows and changes over time due to social and cultural development. Where food is initially seen, reductively, as a basic biological requirement, it morphs in meaning and grows in scale and importance. The corollary for schools is basic content, whether reading, writing, or ciphering. Yet, for the neuropragmatist, content, like food, is mistakenly understood in its most rudimentary way. I first consider food and then contemplate possible connections to school, as a means of both clarifying and applying neuropragmatism to education—and, thus, rescuing the most useful elements of neuroscientific inquiry while also problematizing MBE.

In strict evolutionary terms, sustenance is a requirement for existence. Food is necessary to be and continue being. Species adapt, or become extinct, given the ecological reality or context in which they eat (or starve). The immediacy of food, as with a rabbit or deer chewing on whatever it can find, is part of the evolutionary narrative. With humans, however, food becomes more than sustenance, more than merely evolutionary biological processes of ingesting and digesting. Still evolutionary, food is selected. Food is prepared. Food is cooked. Food is used for celebrations and sacrifices. Food is eaten in social and ecological contexts that necessarily merge the biology and sociology of human being and human becoming.[13]

In this connected, not reductionistic and dualistic understanding of food and human growth, we see the primacy of inquiry. Solymosi explains that

> [t]hrough inquiry—at first as trial-and-error, later as experimental science—digestion and cognition are extended beyond the gut and the brain, respectively, into the environment. Seen as systems of environmental transaction, digestion and cognition gain significance as they are able to contribute to growth. The evolution of cooking and agriculture illustrate how something that happens (metabolic processes) becomes selected for in more effective ways to the point at which the selection is not simply natural but artificial as well, i.e., done for desired reasons, or, ends-in-view as Dewey would put it.
>
> (Solymosi 2011b, 362)

All of this is simply to restate the 'nested' nature of conjoined mind/body with (and within) environment. Neurotransmitters and alleles in the brain, brains in heads of humans, humans in family and social spheres, sociality contextualized ecologically, environments in flux, and all of this in continuity and transaction distinguishes neuropragmatism from traditional neuroscience and MBE. Where the latter two isolate, neuropragmatism enjoins. Even when traditional neuroscience rejects Cartesian materialism, there still is primacy placed on laboratory observations to show or prove what must be done in spaces and places far away from the laboratory.

Friedrich Nietzsche wrote that science has been our way of "putting an end to the complete confusion in which things exist, by hypotheses that 'explain' everything—so it has come from the intellect's dislike of chaos" (Nietzsche 1967, 324). This dislike of chaos, for Nietzsche, explains why "mechanistic" interpretations of our world "stand victorious," and why "no science believes it can achieve progress and success except with the aid of mechanistic procedures" (Nietzsche 1967, 332). I think Nietzsche alludes to an important component of the scientific imaginary: the need to "tame chance," a phrase I borrow from Ian Hacking's study of the use of statistics in Western societies (Hacking 1990).

Before providing a reading of this need to tame chance in the scientific imaginary, I want to situate the narrative of MBE within larger political forces that make it possible and which it in turn makes possible, namely the imperatives of what can be termed the 'informational society.'[14] If science is, as Horkheimer indicated, one of humanity's "productive powers" (Horkheimer 1932, 227), then we should ask, what exactly does it *produce*? It produces scientific knowledge about the world, of course. But perhaps not *of course*, for if the premise is correct that the creation and manipulation of information is a key aspect of our political landscape, then we must rethink such knowledge as having a particularly salient role to play. As Ben Baez and I have argued elsewhere, science produces a world of 'data,' which (a) allows that world to be 'tamed,' and (b) converts it into 'information' for easy administration. I explore this line of reasoning in order to further substantiate the problem with scientism that, in my view, informs why we are faced with an increase in MBE-like prescriptions and commercial applications that appear to privilege certainty over chance in education. First, the taming of the world, then its "informationization" (Baez and Boyles 2009).

TAMING EDUCATION

The need to tame chance probably comes from the natural sciences, characterized by a "widespread instinctive conviction in the existence of an *Order of Things*, and, in particular, of an *Order of Nature*" (Whitehead 1925, 11). This order is hidden and our task is to uncover it. We must control for indeterminacy in order to uncover the secrets of nature. What is interesting about the need to tame chance is that it comes concomitantly with the belief that our world is actually governed by chance. Hacking explains that the most decisive conceptual event of the modern era has been the discovery that the world is not deterministic; causality, or the idea that the past necessarily determines what happens next, was toppled, and a space was cleared for chance. Coinciding with the evolution of the belief in chance also came the practice of the enumeration of people and their habits by state bureaucracies. That is, society became statistical.

Statistics were originally data collected by state bureaucrats to aid them in carrying out the affairs of government. These bureaucrats derived their statistics from censuses, cadastral surveys, tax rolls, public health records, crime figures, and other sources, and they allowed its readers not only to summarize facts but also to discover social truths (Anderson 2003, 9). These two events, the belief in indeterminacy and the enumeration of people, brought into being laws, analogous with those of nature but pertaining to people, expressed in terms of probability. These laws carry with them the connotations of normalcy and of deviations from the norm (Hacking 1990, 1). These laws, in other words, create 'normal people,' defined as such if they conform to the central tendency of such laws, while those at the extremes are pathological or neuromythological (Hacking 1990, 2).

The idea of the 'normal,' as Hacking explains, has always been part of a pair: its opposite is the pathological. For a short time, its domain was chiefly medical, but then it moved into the sphere of everything: people, behavior, states of affairs, diplomatic relations, molecules—all these may be normal or abnormal. The word *normal* became indispensable because it created a way to be "objective" about human beings (Hacking 1990, 160). In a sense, the concept of the normal tames the indeterminable human 'beast.' The magic of the word is that we can use it to say two things at once: how things are and how they ought to be. The normal stands indifferently for what is typical, the unenthusiastic objective average, but also for what has been and for what needs to be. That is why the benign and sterile-sounding word 'normal' has become one of the most powerful ideological tools of our time (Hacking 1990, 169).

The taming of chance, coinciding with the creation of a 'society of statistics,' made up people: the normal, the pathological, the educated, the poor, and so on. Population studies, with their classifying practices, put people into categories (Hacking 1986). With the pervasive classification taking place in schools, we might inquire, how are people made up? When and how, for instance, did the 'gifted,' 'ADHD,' 'intelligent,' 'at risk,' 'high achiever,' and, for that matter, the 'leader,' 'teacher,' and 'educated citizen' come into being? Hacking proposes that in thinking about "making up people" two vectors of analyses might be useful: the vector of labeling, pressing from above by a community of experts who create a 'reality' that people make their own; and the vector of the autonomous behavior of the person so labeled, which presses from below, creating a reality every expert must face (Hacking 1986, 234).

All this is not simply a matter of creating people by the sciences or social sciences. From their statistics could also be developed statistical laws, which did not need theory, only numbers. One need only collect more numbers and regularities (and anomalies) would appear. The more numbers one has, the more inductions one can make (Hacking 1990, 62–63). These laws did not matter just for their own sake; they dictated freedom and constraint. 'Statistical fatalism,' therefore, was born, according to which if a statistical law was applied to a group of people, then the freedom of individuals in that group could be constrained (Hacking 1990, 121). In this way, institutionalized violence is made 'scientific.' Yet the scientist, now powered by the magic of numbers, cannot be held responsible for such violence, since she could appear to be simply and neutrally explaining human behavior through 'laws of nature.' The scientist is apolitical, and thus not subject to political control, since she is simply developing laws from numbers and other kinds of data. She can say, "the truth is in the numbers, not in the scientist."

To see events, people, and brains as 'data,' however, whether quantitative or qualitative, required a radical break in how the world was ordered. As Thomas Popkewitz explains, it required both: (1) the objectification of the individual, so that the inner characteristics of the person could be known as data and used for change—the individual, that is, became an 'empirical fact' that could be observed and made an object of knowledge, irrespective of the feelings and values of the observer and (2) the re-inscription of the data into positive strategies by which groups and individuals would become agents of change (Popkewitz 1997, 19). The social world, and its individuals, could now be made into 'things' that could be ordered systematically and taxonomically within a functional system that was administrable: schools (Popkewitz 1997, 19).

The problem of modern science, natural and social, is to make observable that which was previously hidden so as to make it subject to administration. To do this, scientists must fix space in time, so that the former becomes understandable in terms of, and only in terms of, the latter—people, schools, and events develop and change *in time*—and this is important since time could be measured in a linear, sequential way. This need to tame chance seems irresistible. Let someone propose an anti-statistical idea to reflect individuality or to resist creating probabilities of the universe, and the next generation effortlessly co-opts it so that it becomes part of the standard statistical machinery of information and control (Hacking 1990, 141). Precise measurement controls for indeterminacy, and so the task of the neuroscientist is to develop precise measures in a world that resists it, and precisely because this world is understood as resisting precision, more and more sophisticated mechanisms are necessary to tame it.

We may now read MBE or any attempt at establishing neuroscience for education as a very significant political act in the administration of individuals. Given the indeterminacy of the world, the enumeration of people, and the needs of administration, we can now create a neuroscientist who will carry a very powerful and very particular function in this world. This education neuroscientist will come into the school precisely because schools resist statistical laws. Indeed, this resistance is not only the problem the neuroscientist seeks to solve, but it is also the very reason why she was invited into the school in the first place; its resistance is a spark for more measurement and precision: 'what works!' The invocation of a culture of neuroscience in education, therefore, has to be understood as part of this mechanism of taming chance and the 'statistical fatalism,' or scientific violence, to which it inevitably leads. The neuroscientist and professional development consultants are enthusiastically invited into a realm of indeterminacy, the public school, in order to measure it, establish its laws, commercialize it, make up its people, and, in short, *tame* it.

INFORMATIONIZATION OF EDUCATION

There is another aspect of the taming of chance that warrants discussion: The taming of chance permits the transformation of knowledge into information. The measurement and precision taming chance requires allows for the transformation of all that was previously imprecise, indeterminable, and unknowable into 'data.' Jean-François Lyotard wrote that the nature of knowledge in the postmodern age has undergone (and is undergoing) dramatic change, largely as a result of the proliferation of information-processing machines. 'Knowledge' is being transformed into 'quantities of information,' easily translatable into databases, easily used by anyone with a computer, and easily exchanged and sold. This 'informationization' of knowledge also transforms relations between and among myriad institutions and individuals, all of which are being converted into 'data' that can be stored in a database. So knowledge must now fit new channels and become operational only if learning is translated into quantities of information (Lyotard 1984/1979, 4).

We should ask ourselves how much of what 'education' now means can be represented by the figure of the 'database.' Institutions, individuals, and brains—everything and anything—can be converted into an information byte and stored in a database. Indeed, 'accountability,' a concept ubiquitous in education discourse, is unintelligible outside a system of databases, a system which gives us what we now call knowledge, which then is turned back on the system to spark conversions of new things into data.

Part of the problem with the federal government's privileging of brain-mapping is the type of data that is collected and reported in the What Works Clearinghouse (WWC). The WWC promotes informed education decisions through a set of easily accessible databases and user-friendly reports that provide 'education consumers' with ongoing, high quality review of the effectiveness of replicable educational interventions that intend to improve student outcomes (What Works Clearinghouse n.d.). It also puts forth guidelines for determining the validity of studies, privileging the randomized field trial. Consider this privileging of the randomized field trial, and the mechanistic logic of reporting them in its particular ways, as ideological, as dictating a narrow scientism for education research, neuroscience, and the commercial implications of MBE. It is that, surely, but it *may not be only that*. If knowledge must be transformed into information as required by the new channels of cultural and economic exchanges, then the experiment is not merely a scientific method, it is also a technology of informationization; that is, a technology for transforming knowledge into a database. MBE requires that particular forms of neuroscientific experiments be conducted in particular ways, results collected in particular ways, and reports given in particular ways, not only because this privileges a narrow vision of the neuroscientific knowledge applied to education but also because this will permit the easy reduction of educational knowledge into information bytes that anyone can use and manipulate for whatever purposes he or she wishes, since data are 'neutral'—anyone can use them. Indeed, I wonder whether the champions of MBE knew this all along, and their attempt to define an education science that was not reducible to the experiment of the type neuroscience requires was actually a way of legitimating the expertise of the scientists of a very specialized knowledge, one which particular subgroups within the scientific community, and only that community, can decipher, validate, and profit.

For how long will we be able to think of education outside of a system of databases? This 'informationization' of knowledge is not simply a *practical* matter. The information is not just useful for acting upon the individuals and institutions in education. The informationization is also an *epistemological* matter, for it will become what we can know, and an *ontological* matter, for it will become what *is* education. Moreover, this informationization of knowledge is also *technological and commercial* in that it makes all phenomena numerical, calculable, reproducible, and saleable (Thrift 2004, 584–585). This point will make even more sense if one heeds what Walter Benjamin indicated is one of the most significant forces shaping modernity: his understanding of modernity as reproducibility, where the reproduction of things becomes the end (Lechte 1994, 204). In other words, reproducibility, brought about by neuroscientific progress, becomes the logic of production so that the end of productive forces becomes solely the *reproduction* of objects. The originals are no longer valued as such; they are valued—commercially valued—to the extent they can be reproduced and sold. 'Best practices.' 'What works.' 'Proven methods.' What we lose is the uniqueness and authenticity of the object itself; we lose its value for itself and for the moment (Benjamin 1936). In reductive neuroscience, we lose the messiness of human transaction and mistakes made—and learned from—among authentic inquirers in (and out of) schools and classrooms. We open the door to commercial ventures that materially exploit such reductionism.

Instead of this kind of reductionism, neuropragmatism repositions laboratory work as vital, but only if transactionally emergent from ever-changing contextual realities. This is why, in 1927 (well before neuroscience was neuroscience), Dewey noted that "the question of the integration of mind-body in action is the most practical of all questions we can ask civilization" (Dewey 1988, 29–30). For schooling and issues of teaching and learning, the parallels are similar. The truism that students and teachers in classrooms are not divorced from the school and society they inhabit (or from the various topics of inquiry) becomes meaningful only when generative of their inquiry. If they are to be neuropragmatic in the Deweyan sense, schools integrate mind and brain, individual and group, context and interests in ways that do not privilege reductionism or certainty. This, it seems to me, is the biggest pitfall of MBE and most traditional schooling: subordinating and commercially exploiting teachers and students via 'best practices,' 'proven methods,' and 'brain-based pedagogy' that assume they already have the answer to the puzzle of human minds.

NOTES

1. A section of this chapter was presented at the Philosophy of Education Society meeting in Portland, Oregon, and published in the PES Yearbook. See Boyles 2013.
2. For the discerning reader, yes, the subtitles of both books are exactly the same.
3. Other recent work includes an entire edition of *Educational Philosophy and Theory* 43 (1) (2011) in which the various authors make their case for the legitimacy of the field of MBE. Many of the articles are thoughtful reflections and some raise significant questions, but none uses neuropragmatism or Dewey.
4. The 'editors' introduction' specifically notes that MBE is primarily in the 'cognitive and behavioral sciences.'
5. The work of Richard Dawkins, Daniel Dennett, and Paul and Patricia Churchland stands in contrast to the reductionism I am charging much of neuroscience with (particularly as it has been taken up for teaching and learning). For the scope of this chapter, however, I will not concentrate on their important work. See Churchland 1989, 2002; Dawkins 2003; Dennett 1996, 2005.
6. For a different historical context, see Weidenbaum 2008.
7. See, for example, www.lumosity.com/, www.fitbrains.com/, and https://www.cognifit.com/.
8. As Hildebrand notes, "Rorty is inspired . . . against science and toward literature" (Hildebrand 2003, 100). See also Eldridge 1998.
9. See, for example, Maclean 1991.
10. See also Della Salla and Anderson 2012.
11. Some of the issues identified include whether to follow a medical model (diagnoses) or whether there is a common lexicon for the field.
12. See Dewey 1929a.
13. This point is far from novel and is more thoroughly explored by the following: Dennett 1995; Popp 2007; Power and Schulkin 2009; Solymosi 2011b.
14. 'Informational society' refers broadly to a phenomenon in which the creation and manipulation of knowledge has become the basis for cultural, economic, and political activity. See generally Castells 1996.

REFERENCES

Abadzi, Helen. 2006. *Efficient Learning for the Poor: Insights from the Frontier of Cognitive Neuroscience*. Washington, DC: World Bank Publications.

Anderson, Lisa. 2003. *Pursuing Truth, Exercising Power: Social Science and Public Policy in the 21st Century*. New York: Columbia University Press.

Baez, Benjamin, and Deron Boyles. 2009. *The Politics of Inquiry: Education Research and the "Culture of Science."* Albany, NY: SUNY Press.

Benjamin, Walter. 1936. *The Work of Art in the Age of Mechanical Reproduction*. Los Angeles: UCLA School of Theater, Film, and Television, n.d. Retrieved from http://www.marxist.org/reference/subject/philosophy/works/ge/benjamin.htm.

Biesta, Gert. 2007. "Why 'What Works' Won't Work: Evidence-Based Practice and the Democratic Deficit in Educational Research." *Educational Theory* 57 (1): 1–22.

Boyles, Deron. 2013. "Brain Matters: An Argument for Neuropragmatism and Schooling." In *Philosophy of Education 2013*, edited by Cris Mayo, 403–411. Urbana, IL: Philosophy of Education Society-University of Illinois. Retrieved from http://ojs.ed.uiuc.edu/index.php/pes/article/viewFile/4036/1348.

Campbell, Stephen R. 2011. "Educational Neuroscience: Motivations, Methodology, and Implications." *Educational Philosophy and Theory* 43 (1): 7–16.

Carlson, Charles R. 2011. "John Dewey's Ecological Naturalism as a Critique of Genetic Reductionism." Paper presented at the Society for the Advancement of American Philosophy, March 2011.

Castells, Manuel. 1996. *The Rise of the Network Society.* Oxford: Blackwell Publishers.

Center for the Study of Learning. Georgetown University, Retrieved from http://csl.georgetown.edu/.

Churchland, Paul. 1989. *A Neurocomputational Perspective: The Nature of Mind and the Structure of Science.* Cambridge, MA: MIT Press.

Churchland, Patricia Smith. 2002. *Brain-Wise: Studies in Neurophilosophy.* Cambridge, MA: MIT Press.

Dawkins, Richard. 2003. *A Devil's Chaplin: Reflections on Hope, Lies, Science, and Love.* New York: Houghton Mifflin.

Della Sala, Sergio, and Mike Anderson, eds. 2012. *Neuroscience in Education: The Good, The Bad, and The Ugly.* Oxford: Oxford University Press.

Dennett, Daniel. 1995. *Darwin's Dangerous Idea: Evolution and the Meanings of Life.* New York: Simon & Schuster.

Dennett, Daniel. 1996. *Kinds of Minds: Toward an Understanding of Consciousness.* New York: Basic Books.

Dennett, Daniel. 2005. *Sweet Dreams.* Cambridge, MA: MIT Press.

Dewey, John. 1929a. *The Quest for Certainty.* New York: Minton, Balch & Company.

Dewey, John. 1929b. *Sources of a Science of Education.* New York: Horace Liveright.

Dewey, John. 1944. *Democracy and Education.* New York: The Free Press.

Dewey, John. 1985. *Human Nature and Conduct*, vol. 14 of *John Dewey: The Middle Works.* Carbondale, IL: Southern Illinois University Press.

Dewey, John. 1988. "Body and Mind." In *The Later Works of John Dewey*, vol. 3, edited by Jo Ann Boydson, 29–30. Carbondale, IL: Southern Illinois University Press.

Dewey, John. 2008. "The Determination of Ultimate Values or Aims through Antecedent or A Priori Speculation or Through Pragmatic or Empirical Inquiry." In *John Dewey: The Later Works, 1925–1953*, vol. 13, edited by Jo Ann Boydston, 255–270. Carbondale, IL: Southern Illinois University Press.

Eldridge, Michael. 1998. *Transforming Experience: John Dewey's Cultural Instrumentalism.* Nashville, TN: Vanderbilt University Press.

Frank, Lone. 2009. *Mindfield: How Brain Science Is Changing Our World.* Oxford: Oneworld.

Garrison, Jim. 2008. "A Pragmatist Approach to Emotional Expression and the Construction of Gender Identity." In *Reconstructing Democracy, Recontextualizing Dewey: Pragmatism and Interactive Constructivism in the Twenty-First Century*, edited by Jim Garrison, 157–184. Albany, NY: SUNY Press.

Genzlinger, Neil. 2014. "What Were They Thinking?" *The New York Times*, September 19, Sec. C2. Retrieved from http://www.nytimes.com/2014/09/19/arts/television/hack-my-brain-self-improvement-on-science-channel.html.

Hacking, Ian. 1986. "Making Up People." In *Reconstructing Individualism: Autonomy, Individuality, and the Self in Western Thought*, edited by Thomas C. Heller, Morton Sosna, and David E. Wellbery, 222–236. Stanford: Stanford University Press.

Hacking, Ian. 1990. *The Taming of Chance*. Cambridge, UK: Cambridge University Press.

Horkheimer, Max. 1932. "Notes on Science and the Crisis." In *Critical Theory: Selected Essays*, edited by M. O'Connell, 3–9. New York: Continuum Press, 1999.

Hickman, Larry. 2007. *Pragmatism and Post-Postmodernism: Lessons from John Dewey*. New York: Fordham University Press.

Hildebrand, David L. 2003. *Beyond Realism and Anti-Realism: John Dewey and the Neopragmatists*. Nashville, TN: Vanderbilt University Press.

Hinton, Christina, Kurt W. Fischer, and Catherine Glennon. 2012. "Mind, Brain, and Education." A Report for Jobs for the Future Project, March. Retrieved from http://www.studentsatthecenter.org/papers/mind-brain-and-education

Lechte, John. 1994. "Walter Benjamin." In his *Fifty Key Contemporary Thinkers: From Structuralism to Postmodernity*, 203–207. London and New York: Routledge.

Lynch, Zack, and Byron Laursen. 2009. *The Neuro Revolution: How Brain Science Is Changing Our World*. London: Macmillan.

Lyotard, Jean-François. 1984/1979. *The Postmodern Condition: A Report on Knowledge*, translated by Geoff Bennington and Brian Massumi. Minneapolis: University of Minnesota Press.

MacLean, Paul D. 1991. *Triune Brain in Evolution: Role in Paleocerebral Functions*. New York: Kluwer.

Nietzsche, Friedrich. 1967. *The Will to Power*, edited by Walter Kaufman, and translated by Walter Kaufman and R.J. Hollingdale. New York: Vintage Books.

Noble, Kimberly G., Nim Tottenham, and B.J. Casey. 2005. "Neuroscience Perspectives on Disparities in School Readiness and Cognitive Achievement." *The Future of Children* 15 (1): 71–89. doi:10.1353/foc.2005.0006.

Patten, Kathryn E. 2011. "The Somatic Appraisal Model of Affect: Paradigm for Educational Neuroscience and Neuropedagogy." *Educational Philosophy and Theory* 43 (1): 87–97.

Popkewitz, Thomas S. 1997. "A Changing Terrain of Knowledge and Power: A Social Epistemology of Educational Research." *Educational Researcher* 26 (9): 18–29.

Popp, Jerome. 2007. *Evolution's First Philosopher: John Dewey and the Continuity of Nature*. Albany, NY: SUNY Press.

Power, Michael L., and Jay Schulkin. 2009. *The Evolution of Obesity*. Baltimore, MD: The Johns Hopkins University Press.

Putnam, Hilary. 1990. *Realism with a Human Face*. Cambridge, MA: Harvard University Press.

Putnam, Hilary. 1994. *Words and Life*. Cambridge, MA: Harvard University Press.

Quantz, Richard A. with Terry O'Conner, and Peter Magolda. 2011. *Rituals and Student Identity in Education: Ritual Critique for a New Pedagogy*. New York: Palgrave Macmillan.

Rorty, Richard. 1995. "Response to Hartshorne." In *Rorty and Pragmatism: The Philosopher Responds to His Critics*, edited by Herman Saatkamp, 29–36. Nashville, TN: Vanderbilt University Press.

Shook, John R. 2011. "Conference on Neuroscience and Pragmatism: Productive Prospects." *Philosophy, Ethics, and Humanities in Medicine* 6 (14): 1–4.

Solymosi, Tibor. 2011a. "A Reconstruction of Freedom in the Age of Neuroscience: A View from Neuropragmatism." *Contemporary Pragmatism* 8 (1): 153–171.

Solymosi, Tibor. 2011b. "Neuropragmatism, Old and New." *Phenomenology and the Cognitive Sciences* 10 (3): 347–368.

Southwest Center for Mind, Brain, and Education. Retrieved from http://www.uta. edu/coehp/curricandinstruct/research-community/mind-brain/.

Stein, Zachary, and Kurt W. Fisher. 2011. "Directions for Mind, Brain, and Education: Methods, Models, and Morality." *Educational Philosophy and Theory* 43 (1): 56–66.

Thrift, Nigel. 2004. "Movement-Space: The Changing Domain of Thinking Resulting From the Development of New Kinds of Spatial Awareness." *Economy and Society* 33 (4): 582–604.

Vander Ark, Tom. 2012. "12 Findings on Mind, Brain & Education—Getting Smart by Tom Vander Ark—Brain Research, Edpolicy, Edreform, JFF | Getting Smart." March 18. Retrieved from http://gettingsmart.com/2012/03/12-findings-on-mind-brain-education/.

Weidenbaum, Jonathan. 2008. "The Philosopher and the Neuroscientist: Dewey, Harris, and the Nature of Religious Experiences." *The Journal of Liberal Religion* 8 (1): 1–14. Retrieved from http://berkeleycollege.academia.edu/ JonathanWeidenbaum/Papers/1435454/The_Philosopher_and_the_Neuroscientist_Dewey_Harris_and_the_Nature_of_Religious_Experiences

What Works Clearinghouse. *Who We Are.* Washington, DC: Institute for Education Sciences, n.d. Retrieved from http:www.whatworks.ed.gov/whoweare/overview. html

Whitehead, Alfred North. 1925. *Science and the Modern World.* New York: The New American Library.

Yeap, Lay Leng. 1989. "Hemisphericity and Student Achievement." *International Journal of Neuroscience* 48 (3–4): 225–232. doi:10.3109/00207458909002164.

6   Neoliberalism and the Neuronal Self
A Critical Perspective on Neuroscience's Application to Education

Clarence W. Joldersma

In the last few decades, neuroscience has entered the public arena, with a dizzying array of applications emerging, including criminal law, corporate organization, sports psychology, and meditation. One area of neuroscience research, brain plasticity, has especially caught the public imagination and is often central in discussions about policy change. Academic disciplines are being transformed by neuroscience, including not only biology and psychology but also philosophy, aesthetics, economics, and theology. The field of education too, especially its theories and practices of teaching and learning, is increasingly being framed in neuroscience terms. At the same time, neoliberalism has gained ascendency in the socio-political scene. As an ideology, neoliberalism has become a central discourse for envisioning economic and political life in many of our societies. It has intruded into many areas of our social life, reshaping what it means to be a citizen, worker, and consumer. It has constructed major inroads into educational policies and practices, reshaping not only curriculum and testing but more profoundly the very identities of students as learners. These twin developments call for a critical examination together.

This essay connects neuroscience and neoliberalism. The argument is that popular understandings of neuroscience can easily be co-opted into the political ideology of neoliberalism. The paper begins with a description of neoliberalism and shows how recent turns in educational discourse, especially that of lifelong learning, is aligned with neoliberalism. The paper then turns to a brief description of neuroscience, including specifically brain plasticity. It shows that the allure of brain images gives popular neuroscience an easy if overextended scientific authority. The paper then turns to the emerging discipline of critical neuroscience to uncover the way that neuroscience's scientific authority can be used to more effectively push forward a neoliberal agenda, also within education. Using Victoria Pitts-Taylor's conception of the neuronal self, the paper argues that neuroscience can give neoliberalism increased power through what Foucault calls governmentality. This enhances the already existing responsibility of the learner to continually care for the self and be on the ready for learning the new labor skills required by the market economy. The paper suggests that this increased responsibilization is a way of maintaining or enhancing class differences and social inequality.

NEOLIBERALISM AND EDUCATION

The political-economic vision of neoliberalism has become prominent in recent years (Steger and Roy 2010). At its simplest, it is a set of ideas about the relationships between individuals, government, and the economy (Harvey 2005; Saltman and Perselli 2007). Neoliberalism as a vision is one of reducing the size of government, especially with respect to public infrastructures and social safety-nets (Small 2011). It advocates bringing such public areas into the market as commercial products and transactions. These market-based approaches are transforming and privatizing public institutions, such as public housing, schooling, military support, health care, data collection, and prisons, to name a few. Neoliberalism is not against government but relegates it to safeguarding things such as the monetary system, private property (including capital), and the unfettered functioning of markets. At a deep level, it amounts to a kind of missionary faith in the role of the free market for all areas of life, unfettering capital accumulation in as many ways as possible (Braedley and Luxton 2010). As such, it can be viewed as a vision for human flourishing accomplished through liberating individual entrepreneurial freedom.

The neoliberal vision is not merely about moving to a purely market-based economy. It is also an *ethics* to guide human action (Harvey 2005). By ethics I mean the realm of 'the ought' that instills a felt responsibility, holding as normative certain behaviors and social practices. The idea of a person in this ethic is someone who functions as a competent, rationally self-interested agent. The ethics is the normative obligation to accept the risks of participating in market exchanges. A good citizen is someone who puts him or herself in the best position possible to be competitive in the economic market. The good individual will take personal responsibility for the consequences of his or her choices, accepting the possibility of being left behind in any free-market competition, and ultimately recognizing oneself as the author of one's own misfortune. In short, the ethics of neoliberalism is one of personal responsibility in an uncertain market.

Naming this a personal ethics might suggest that an individual is free to adopt this as an ethical paradigm. However, it is more accurate to describe its effect as something that is done to the individual which, in Michael Peters's words, is a "responsibilizing of the self" (Peters 2001, 58). He argues that neoliberal ethics is constructed by the larger political context. Using Thatcher's Britain as the example, he points out that the state deliberately and effectively reengineered British culture toward the ethics of the entrepreneurial self, centralizing the characteristic of self-reliance (see also Brown and Baker 2012; Peters 2012). Policies included linking welfare to employment, moving toward individualized employment contracts, and shifting tax burdens away from corporations to individual wage earners. Peters argues that this was not only a reduction of the size of government but also, and more importantly, a matter of moral regulation (Peters 2001, 59). Through its policy moves, the state was excusing itself from its moral responsibilities as a modern welfare state, while simultaneously enacting greater social control through emphasizing the individual moral responsibilities of self-reliance, self-help, and self-empowerment. This amounts to employing state power through the use of *moral* self-descriptors. Historically situated economic and political forces regulate citizens to become responsible participants in the market (Ferguson 2010). The individual citizen receives a series of market-like arrangements as moral duties. The person is being responsibilized.

Peters points out that this is a form of what Foucault calls governmentality (Peters 2007). The term refers to the way human conduct is organized to govern populations, where governance happens through the individual's self-organizing capacities (Cromby and Willis 2013; Olssen 2008; N.S. Rose and Miller 2010). Governmentality works through the strategies and techniques that shape the conduct and attitudes of the individuals by acting on their wills, environments, and circumstances. When neoliberalism's vision is enacted through governmentality, its conception of what constitutes a good person is embodied in the techniques and strategies used to discipline individuals in order to re-envision themselves. The vision of the self as free, entrepreneurial, competitive, and economically rational is employed to govern the population (Hamann 2009). Peters argues neoliberalism's vision embedded in governmentality is a new ideological discourse, centrally composed of terms such as "excellence," "technological literacy," "skills training," "performance," and "enterprise" (Peters 2001, 66). These deliberately compete with the social democratic discourse of equality and the political redress of economic imbalances. At root, this is a new *ethical* vision of what it means to be human. The discourse functions as ethical presuppositions that reshape the individual's thinking about what it means to be a normal person. Peters's argument is that the idea of "the self-limiting state" creates "an intensification of an economy of moral regulation" (2001, 67). The emphasis on ethical self-organization and self-restraint is a deliberately constructed change. Through such techniques, the neoliberal-saturated governmentality responsibilizes the self in a particular ethical direction.

Much of current formal schooling enacts such responsibilizing. Although the narrative at neoliberalism's core is about the economy, education is one of its main vehicles (Doherty 2007; Peters 2001). An older vision of education is increasingly being supplanted by a neoliberal one, which sees education's primary purpose as acquiring skills for the new economy (Vassallo 2014). The discourse of the neoliberal vision is the language of self-regulated learning and accountability for their own successes and failures, namely, students as self-governing individuals. Language to describe justifiable school knowledge is recast as economically relevant skills and information (Connell 2013;

Down 2009; Rizvi 2013). In this educational discourse, important student skills include becoming competitive and autonomous, transforming the self into a responsible subject who fits well into the neoliberal workplace (Wilkins 2012). In the neoliberal educational vision, the purpose of learning is the production of human capital, namely, of "managing oneself to be adaptable, flexible, innovative, and a good problem solver" (Vassallo 2014, 158). When the neoliberal vision begins to govern a nation's education, it attempts to "make sure schools produce compliant, ideologically indoctrinated, procapitalist, effective workers" (Kumar and Hill 2009, 21). Responsible learning mirrors the responsible worker. To apply Peters's words, this is responsibilizing the learning self.

The neoliberal vision reduces what counts as good education. Equating it to self-regulated learning effectively narrows the discourse of education to one of learning (Biesta 2010, 2014). At the same time, the learning discourse expands education longitudinally with the phrase *lifelong learning*. The phrase in its mundane sense merely indicates the fact that all people can and do learn throughout their lives, not merely at the beginning or in school. But in much educational literature, the phrase 'lifelong learning' has gained a more specific meaning. Although some have used it to name a potentially emancipatory dynamic in education (Deakin Crick and Joldersma 2007; Joldersma and Deakin Crick 2010), its dominant use is associated with neoliberal discourse. For example, the European Union uses this phrase to name the knowledge, skills, and competencies associated with employability (Mitchell 2006). As such, lifelong learning signals a solution to the changing economic situations by focusing on knowledge and skills for employment (Uggla 2008).

The effects of enacting a neoliberal vision in education are not uniform within society. Rather, wealthier classes benefit from its influence, while poorer classes are harmed (Tienken 2013). Educational sociologist Dave Hill argues that the neoliberal vision in education reestablishes and strengthens social class distinctions. When enacted in schools, Hill argues, neoliberal policies

> are aimed at restoring schools (and further education and universities) to what dominant elites—the capitalist class—perceive to be their 'traditional role' of producing passive worker/citizens with just enough skills to render themselves useful to the demands of capital.
>
> (2009, 119)

Hill points out that the arrangements benefit those with capital in part through making the working class more dependent and passive. A neoliberal vision of a healthy economy includes a standing labor pool, one that is flexible in its ability to retool quickly in changing labor environments, something that dovetails with the educational discourse of lifelong learning (Halliday 2003; Tuschling and Engemann 2006). The discourse of neoliberalism, including particularly that of lifelong learning, signals the requirements for a working-class individual's coping strategy in an uncertain economy.

NEUROSCIENCE AND PLASTICITY

It might be entirely coincidental that neuroscience has gained prominence during the rise of neoliberalism. But a couple of factors bring them together. For one, neuroscience as a science seems to have authority unparalleled in society, not even genetics can compete (Choudhury and Sanchez-Allred 2014). For another, neuroscience has an equally unparalleled popularity, which some have critically called "neuromania" (Legrenzi et al. 2011). Neuroscience's perceived authority and popularity has given its discoveries great cache in reconfiguring the popular imaginary, easily translated into claims about everyday living. Much of this has centered on the brain. Increasingly, understanding the brain has been invoked as important for different areas of life—law, crime, education, music, and so on. It is increasingly thought that to understand complex social behaviors, we need to understand the underlying brain processes. On this view, the brain is made to carry the burden of a wide variety of social, moral, and behavioral concerns. The brain is increasingly becoming the site of morality and politics, transforming social concerns into brain-based ones. This naturalizes moral and social norms (Stadler 2011).

Recent neuroscience has focused on brain plasticity. Plasticity refers to the brain's capacity to be modified in its interaction with the environment (Huttenlocher 2009). Although the notion of neuroplasticity has been around for over a century, only in the last decades has it emerged as a major theme to understand the brain. Previously, it was thought that once developed, the neurons of the brain were permanent and could not be replaced or repaired, and hence the brain's wiring was set for the duration of its life. Only early in a child's life was the brain thought able to generate new neurons and connections. It was believed that regions of the brain were 'locked in' to particular tasks after certain developmental phases, with clear boundaries marking the various governance roles. But recent studies have shown that this picture was too simple. Newer research shows that new neuronal changes can be generated in the adult brain, far later than the critical periods previously thought (Baroncelli et al. 2009; Spolidoro et al. 2009). Research on the learning process shows that the brain indeed continues to be modified in response to experiences. New techniques allow scientists to look at a wide variety of experiences in examining how the adult brain is structurally transformed by its environment. These formative studies helped change how the adult brain is viewed, away from being a fixed entity, toward something susceptible to changes caused by everyday activities and restructured by learning (Holman and de Villers-Sidani 2014). Moreover, plasticity research is also discovering how to deliberately enhance brain plasticity, including physical exercise

(Hötting and Röder 2013) and mental workouts (Slagter et al. 2011), creating possible strategies for deliberately maintaining or enhancing one's brain. The narrative of the degenerating brain is being challenged by these discoveries, replaced by the idea that the aging brain can reorganize and adapt (Holman and de Villers-Sidani 2014).

Discoveries about brain plasticity are made possible by exciting new methods. These are centrally non-invasive brain imaging techniques that show brain plasticity under environmental change (Chein and Schneider 2005; Kelly and Garavan 2005; Ungerleider et al. 2002; Zatorre et al. 2012). Current techniques include electrophysiology (spreading a set of electrodes on various scalp locations), which records the brain's electrical activity; positron-emission tomography (PET); and single-photon emission computer tomography (SPECT), which measures blood flow in local regions of the brain and thus records indirectly energy consumption of local brain areas; magnetic resonance imaging (MRI), which scans the brain with a powerful magnetic field to measure blood-oxygen levels; and functional magnetic resonance imaging (fMRI), which does the same but can measure the difference between resting and active brain states. Although most of these require elaborate laboratory conditions, they do not need the brain to be opened up and thus are considered non-invasive. The results of non-invasive scans are typically displayed as colored photographs of the brain, with differently colored regions signifying differences in brain activity above or below a baseline.

Brain images are the result of a complex process, including scrupulous experimental design, decisions about what constitutes normal and abnormal, rigorous control over other aspects of the subject's actions during the experiment, artificial constructions required for measuring brain activity, equilibration of the raw data to match other brain measurements from other subjects, turning the numerical data into presentable brain images, and matching variations in quantities with a color scheme overlain onto a contour map of the brain area. Each of these steps requires assumptions, not only about anatomy and physiology but also about human nature (Dumit 2011). Further, techniques such as fMRI require artificial stillness inside a machine, thereby narrowing the human experience to an artificially simple sliver. In particular, fMRI technology has a fairly rough resolution in its ability to measure subtle mental effects. Although fMRI can only measure large-scale changes of millions of neurons at once over seconds, mental life might be nuanced at the single or merely multiple neuron level and in milliseconds. And because the signals are weak, there may well be a lot of noise captured in fMRI results, and the compensation for this is typically many repetitions of the task, which are then made into composite pictures (Raz 2011). They constitute proxy markers for cognitive and mental functions, including changes in blood flow and magnetic fields. To produce these seemingly simple pictures of localized brain activity requires complex, interdisciplinary data gathering and mathematical manipulation. The images are the result of a great deal of processing and synthesizing.

This also goes for images of brain plasticity. Many caution that attempting to image brain plasticity itself has conceptual and methodological issues (Dumit 2011; Manzotti and Moderato 2010; Poldrack 2000, 2010, 2011; S. Rose 2011). Brain plasticity does not refer to a single kind of process. Rather, the notion of brain plasticity "is an immensely fuzzy entity" (Holman and de Villers-Sidani 2014, 1); it is multivalent, meaning different things depending on the context and reference. There are multiple levels of plasticity, ranging from changes at the molecular level through changes in proteins, to changes at the cellular level through modifications of synapses and generation of neurons, to changes in whole bundles of neurons (millions) in response to environmental input (Poldrack 2000). Neuroimaging at best is an indirect measure of such changes precisely because plasticity is multivalent. Different levels of changes have different sorts of lifespans, ranging from milliseconds to much slower transformations. As a result, there is neither one way to study neuroplasticity nor one simple way to depict it. Brain images are underdetermined by the data from which they arise, which means that conclusions drawn from such images may or may not be valid. Certainly, strong claims about causality cannot be easily established (Poldrack 2000).

The pictures selected for publication don't reveal their complex history of production. The technical side is hidden in the seemingly direct pictures. As a result, in the popular imaginary, the glossy images are often interpreted as simple stand-ins for specific neural activity. The images suggest the seemingly straightforward narrative of showing where in the brain a person is undertaking some sort of what we call mental activity. The glossy photos are alluring, urging us to believe that the scan images are straightforward illustrations, like taking a snapshot at a sports event (S. Rose 2011). The visual character of the image contributes to its seeming transparency. But such appeals to brain images are potentially misleading and dangerous. Neuroscience-backed claims about visual evidence for specific mental activities are often over-extensions of the data. Yet, despite this complexity, the idea of plasticity in our social imaginary tends to simplify it to the idea that the brain has the capacity to reorganize and alter itself as a result of input from its environment. And the brain images are called upon in scientific support. The visual character of brain images gives authority and popularity to plasticity research. Their seeming transparency makes it seem like plasticity is simple and claims made straightforward. Yet neuroscience-backed claims about visual evidence for brain plasticity, and especially for practical implications, are often over-extensions and simplifications of the data.

CRITICAL NEUROSCIENCE AND THE NEURONAL SELF

The critique of neuroscience needs to go beyond criticisms of imaging methods to issues of conceptualization and ideology. Critical neuroscience is an emerging sub-discipline pioneered by Jan Slaby and Suparna Choudhury designed to uncover social-political interests that might frame neuroscience research (Choudhury et al. 2009). To be sure, research in neuroscience is not narrowly partisan nor deliberately hijacked by political interests but constitutes genuine science with valid methods and sound conclusions (Bickle 2013). However, this doesn't mean that neuroscience is immune to influence by such interests. Although neuroscience can rightly be accepted as factual, critical neuroscience attempts to make explicit that factual significance arises from sets of preconceptions that are themselves situated in political contexts. Slaby and Choudhury uncover the way that factual claims and observations are framed by normative judgments—that socially situated interpretations orient certain observed differences as significant. They argue that neuroscientific research is "shot through with our projections, and give rise to 'facts,' worldviews and policies that may collude with social and political orders" (Slaby and Choudhury 2011, 36). Conversely, they point out, political interests can find allies in neuroscience. By employing neuroscience's authority and popularity, neoliberalism can readily naturalize its narrow and class-differentiated idea of human capital. Neuroscience's focus on the brain can give increased legitimacy to neoliberalism by naturalizing its social-economic categories of inequality (N.S. Rose and Abi-Rached 2013).

The authority and popularity of brain plasticity is central in this. Brain plasticity has become central in the popular imaginary in many areas of life, including education, psychotherapy, parenting, social work, and criminal rehabilitation (Choudhury and Sanchez-Allred 2014). This popularity is not socially or politically neutral, for it not only highlights certain things such as individual brain plasticity, but it also hides other things such as inequitable social structures. The discourse of plasticity can easily become a substitute for the discourse focused on inequitable economic political forces. That is, brain plasticity can easily become a competing discourse, framing problematic political and economic differences as natural and internal. This then reframes questions about social inequality as issues about the individual brain in its natural environment. To be sure, brain plasticity is a genuine scientific discovery and has rightly helped us transcend the genetic determinism of previous eras. But its popularity outstrips this insight, and we are entering what some are calling the "plastic era" (Choudhury and Sanchez-Allred 2014, 107), one of naturalizing the political discourse via the notion of plasticity.

The 'plastic era' is framed by two related assumptions. On the one hand is the assumption that an individual's behavior changes because there is some change in that person's neural organization. On the other hand is the assumption that if the environment changes the brain's organization, it will change the behavior of the individual, because it is governed by that aspect of the brain (Kolb et al. 2003). Underlying the two assumptions is the idea that the brain is the key to understanding what it means to be human. In particular, the two parts suggest that there is a single line of causality associated with plasticity, going from environment to the brain and from the brain to human behavior. From here it is but a short step to making the brain central to personhood (O'Connor and Joffe 2013; Pickersgill et al. 2011; Vidal 2009).

Victoria Pitts-Taylor's idea of the neuronal self helps bring this together. She argues that brain plasticity is central to the portrayal of neuroscientific findings in the popular media. She remarks,

> Plasticity appears to challenge biological reductionism by providing room for the environment in brain development and functioning, thus opening up a bridge between the hard and social sciences, and between views of the mind/self as natural and hard-wired and those of it as nurtured and socially shaped.
>
> (Pitts-Taylor 2010, 636–637)

Whereas before it appeared that science was clear in affirming that the brain was permanently wired in particular ways based on the individual's genetic composition and expression, recent neuroscience challenges this reductionism. There is now the idea of lifelong brain plasticity. Her deeper insight, however, is that this focus gives power and credence to a *political* discourse around the brain's plasticity. The bridging between the social and natural sciences via plasticity allows political interests to employ naturalized categories for political action (Dunagan 2010). It allows the construction of social obligations for individual action directed toward natural processes, namely, maintaining or enhancing one's brain. And this can then more easily be employed differentially, as a way for dominant groups to keep working-class individuals aligned with the demands of capital accumulation.

Pitts-Taylor holds that the scientific discovery of brain plasticity has been transformed in the popular imaginary by economic and political notions. In particular, she concludes that "popular uses of neuroscientific theories of brain plasticity are saturated with a neoliberal vision of the subject" (Pitts-Taylor 2010, 635). Her point is that in popular usage, neural plasticity has been employed, on the authority and popularity of neuroscience, to frame humans as permanently open to enhancement and modification, ready to change as the economic circumstances warrant. The discovery of brain plasticity is easily used by neoliberalism to create in the popular imaginary a heightened self-image of personal responsibility, especially for the working classes. Neuroscience research can wittingly or unwittingly buttress neoliberal political ideologies of individualizing and naturalizing social responsibility, something that has caught on in the popular social imaginary. The neoliberal discourse can use plasticity to call for deliberate enhancement of learning and mental performance, as well as deliberate avoidance of various risks connected to the brain, including aging (Pitts-Taylor 2010, 639). In this neoliberal vision, the brain has become central to self-hood and to responsible citizenship. Pitts-Taylor gathers this view under the rubric of the *neuronal self*; namely, a form of self-identity involving self-regulation and self-enhancement via responsibilities toward one's brain. The neuronal self is the idea that what it means to be a self is centrally related to being a brain and being responsible for that brain because of its plasticity.

Although Pitts-Taylor's argument does not address the differential effect of this idea within society, it is not difficult to imagine that the idea of the neuronal self can easily be employed in the production and regulation of working classes. It is a ready construct for maintaining if not enhancing social class divisions and inequality.

EDUCATION, NEOLIBERALISM, AND THE NEURONAL SELF

It is important to develop a critical awareness of how the neoliberal notion of the person as the neuronal self can shape how to think about human agency and responsibility in education, especially when schooling is narrowed to economically relevant skills within working-class areas. In particular, the neoliberal discourse of lifelong learning dovetails well with the notion of the neuronal self. Thus it is but a small step to co-opt brain plasticity for the neoliberal governmentality of responsibilizing the learning self.

Basic research on brain plasticity has been rapidly commodified and brought into the marketplace as commercial products, many for education. There are now an array of products that promise brain enhancement through the purchase of their programs, many of which are geared toward educators. Holman and Villers-Sidani identify several: "Lumosity (Lumos Labs), Brain HQ (Posit Neuroscience), Cogmed (Pearson), CogniFit (CogniFit), Happy-Neuron (HAPPYneuron), Dakim Brain Fitness (Dakim), Fit Brains (Vivity Labs), and NeuroActive (Brain Center International)" (Holman and de Villers-Sidani 2014, 4). These products are commercial programs that rely on the authority and popularity of neuroscientific discoveries associated with brain plasticity. The programs evoke metaphors, such as developing strong brains, brain fitness, and healthier brains. Educators can readily understand and absorb these metaphors borrowed from the realm of body fitness. The claims of such programs are that they enhance the learning brain through certain activities just as the body is improved through particular exercise regimes.

The commercial success of such products relies on the neoliberal discourse of the neuronal self. The sales rhetoric for the products implicitly creates obligations for potential customers. Learners become obligated to avail themselves of these products to boost their lifelong learning. And educators and schools become obligated to buy and make use of them in the classroom to cultivate more effectively learning and thinking skills. But for individuals to feel obligated to purchase them, they need first to buy into the idea of the duty of individual self-regulation and self-enhancement via responsibilities toward one's brain. As Pitts-Taylor says, "the popular discourse on plasticity firmly situates the subject in a normative, neoliberal ethic of personal self-care and responsibility linked to modifying the body" (Pitts-Taylor 2010, 639). The discourse of plasticity associated with commercial products in effect places an ethical requirement onto the individual. Earlier we saw how the language of lifelong learning was central to the neoliberal vision, especially for the working classes. The discourse of plasticity adds a layer to that neoliberal ideology by painting the neuronal self as responsible for the brain's health and learning. Under the authority and popularity of neuroscience, the discourse of plasticity adds a depth layer to responsibilizing the subject. The idea of the neuronal self frames the power relations in society and effectively regulates the individual's behavior.

Accepting that one is a neuronal self makes it easy to accept that it is one's ethical duty to manage one's brain, including availing oneself of the technologies that can do so. Pitts-Taylor calls these "micro-political technologies of health" because they encompass all those techniques and products that help define and achieve certain states of health and learning. At a deep level, this enacts an ethical vision. Pitts-Taylor states, "Neoliberalism replaces an ethic of state care with an emphasis on individual responsibility and market fundamentalism" (Pitts-Taylor 2010, 639). By placing brain health and educational policies in the marketplace, especially working-class citizens are framed to view themselves as individuals ethically responsible to ensure their own learning and wellness. This simultaneously ensures that those individuals are ethically obligated to become a consumer of commercially offered brain health care and learning. Micro-political technologies of health are embedded in commerical products for brain-based learning. The metaphors sustaining these products are biovalues borrowed from bodily exercise, including the importance of having a healthy, strong brain and staying young and fit. However, the new biovalues for the brain are not merely natural or biological. Rather, they are social and political, moving the identity of individual, in particular as a learner, toward being a neuronal self. As a result, rather than seeing education or health care as a public good and a function of public justice, the neoliberal discourse of the neuronal self frames care for one's brain health and learning as the ethical responsibility of the individual. It is a personal duty rather than an intrinsic right. The neuronal self aligns with the general vision of the individual's duty toward lifelong learning. Responsibility toward one's brain is a duty precisely because of one's responsibilities to the changing job scene in the market economy. This is "a moral and ethical imperative to healthful action" (Holman and de Villers-Sidani 2014, 9). The ethics associated with the neuronal self hides the role of social structures and factors in learning and it hides the responsibility of society and state for education. Instead, it points all the responsibilities for learning inward and downward, into the interior of the individual person and downward to the brain.

When the meaning of being human is framed in neuronal terms, learning is easily reframed in terms of brain health and disease. The micro-political technologies of the brain change not only conceptions of biological "brain fitness" but also the concept of brain normalcy (N.S. Rose 2001; see also N. S. Rose 2014). What at one time might have been regarded as normal differences in ability to learn are increasingly framed as abnormal brain states requiring intervention. The commercial products using brain plasticity effectively normalize certain states of brain health and pathologize others, marking some as healthy and others as diseased. Seeing one's identity as a neuronal self easily aligns what counts as normal with commercial interests, increasing the pressure to enhance learning and stave off the atrophy of learning by purchasing its products. When a learning difference is diagnosed as abnormal, it pushes for new ways to intervene and remediate. This creates ethical pressure on individuals to regulate themselves and to augment that regulation with available commercial products. The narrowing of normalcy increasingly makes the brain into an object of consumer products, toward purchased care for neurons (Pitts-Taylor 2010, 640). In the educational realm, the neuronal self thus opens itself up to its commercialization. Maintaining the normalcy of the brain is entangled with the political interests of the market economy. The working classes are opened up further to the upward accumulation of capital.

Pitts-Taylor's analysis uncovers the neoliberal discourse embedded in plasticity rhetoric. Although plasticity is often articulated in terms of individual freedom and opportunity, it can be interpreted through Foucault's idea of governmentality, where the brain is the target for governing citizens (N. S. Rose and Abi-Rached 2014). In particular, the discourse of plasticity opens up individuals to techniques of self-directed and self-initiated enhancement of the brain as well as risk avoidance, for the sake of the economy. This dovetails well with the governmentality of lifelong learning (Olssen 2008). As we have seen, the rhetoric and policies around lifelong learning are forms of governmentality because they tap into the self-regulating capacities of individual citizens and workers. The discourse of the neuronal self similarly shapes the conduct of individuals, while hiding its economically charged political origins, making it appear individual instead. The discourse of the neuronal self enacts governmentality by making it appear natural to engineer one's own biological brain life, because of the authority and popularity of neuroscience. In this the individual's identity is transformed toward making the brain central to self-hood and to ethical responsibility.

This brings us back to the idea of responsibilization in education. As stated previously, this is the technique of making students feel free and yet responsible for their actions and outcomes (Biebricher 2011). Responsibilization has been happening through shifts in social conventions, reinterpretations of normativity, exhortations about ethical behaviors, and enacting new legislation and policies. Educationally, this has been happening through the politically engineered shift to lifelong learning (Fejes 2008). The discourse of lifelong learning shifted responsibility for coping with change onto the individual student, where the individual becomes ethically responsible for gaining new knowledge and skills as the market economy shifts its demands. As Biesta points out, the means of control is not overt coercion, but rather a naturalizing of what counts as proper motivation, legitimate knowledge, and worthwhile learning (Biesta 2008). Such responsibilization is an attempt to ensure an individual student's conduct aligns with the interests and performance of the political economy. As such, responsibilization in education can be viewed as a form of social control (Halliday 2003; Tuschling and Engemann 2006). The discourse of brain plasticity heightens this neoliberal discourse of student responsibility. Responsibilization through the discourse of brain plasticity adds a layer of enforcement to neoliberal governmentality by making individual students feel they are ethically responsible for their own brains.

CONCLUSION

Much of formal schooling today is ripe for the influence of neuroscience. Especially in areas of poverty and chronic underemployment, schools are under increasing pressure to measure up to the narrow standards of excellence and accountability. At the same time, especially inner-city education is under increasing attack by political and business leaders as being wasteful, inefficient, and ineffective. The allure of neuroscience to buttress the image and practice of school, thus, is extremely tempting. Especially those in working-class areas are ripe for 'saving' through neuroscience. Although neoliberal discourse is for an entire economy, a central worry should be that a society's most vulnerable school population may be the most likely affected by neuroscience's co-option into the neoliberal vision.

Students will be obligated to maintain their brains for their learning. And the rhetoric of lifelong learning means that students will have a lifelong responsibility to be ready to initiate their own retooling in the changing economy over their labor career. Rather than merely being responsible for one's learning, the idea of the learner as a neuronal self is that centrally one's identity is connected to being a brain. Thus one's responsibility for learning shifts toward one's brain in addition to obligations concerning one's overt learning actions. The responsibility associated with the neuronal self via brain plasticity makes more effective the way that lifelong learning can regulate the population. Care for one's learning brain, central to lifelong learning, enhances the effectiveness of social control for political and economic interests because it naturalizes the learning process further. In sum, the neuronal self is an important instrument of governmentality, for through it working-class students are trained to act on new principles of conduct, thereby responsibilizing themselves even more. The alignment of the authority and popularity of neuroscience with neoliberalism gives its application to education easy scientific cover for neoliberalism's economic political agenda of social inequality.

REFERENCES

Baroncelli, L., C. Braschi, M. Spolidoro, T. Begenisic, A. Sale, and L. Maffei. 2009. "Nurturing Brain Plasticity: Impact of Environmental Enrichment." *Cell Death & Differentiation* 17 (7): 1092–1103.

Bickle, John, ed. 2013. *The Oxford Handbook of Philosophy and Neuroscience.* New York: Oxford University Press.

Biebricher, Thomas. 2011. "(Ir-)Responsibilization, Genetics and Neuroscience." *European Journal of Social Theory* 14 (4): 469–488. doi:10.1177/1368431011417933.

Biesta, Gert J.J. 2008. "Encountering Foucault in Lifelong Learning." In *Foucault and Lifelong Learning: Governing the Subject*, edited by András Fejes and Kathy Nicoll, 193–205. London and New York: Routledge.

Biesta, Gert J.J. 2010. *Good Education in an Age of Measurement: Ethics, Politics, Democracy.* Boulder, CO: Paradigm Publishers.

Biesta, Gert J.J. 2014. *The Beautiful Risk of Education.* Boulder, CO: Paradigm.

Braedley, Susan, and Meg Luxton, eds. 2010. *Neoliberalism and Everyday Life.* Montreal-Kingston: McGill-Queen's Press.

Brown, B.J., and Sally Baker. 2012. *Responsible Citizens: Individuals, Health, and Policy Under Neoliberalism.* London: Anthem Press.

Chein, Jason M., and Walter Schneider. 2005. "Neuroimaging Studies of Practice-Related Change: fMRI and Meta-Analytic Evidence of a Domain-General Control Network for Learning." *Cognitive Brain Research* 25 (3): 607–623. doi:10.1016/j.cogbrainres.2005.08.013.

Choudhury, Suparna, Saskia Kathi Nagel, and Jan Slaby. 2009. "Critical Neuroscience: Linking Neuroscience and Society through Critical Practice." *BioSocieties* 4 (1): 61–77. doi:10.1017/S1745855209006437.

Choudhury, Suparna, and Alberto Sanchez-Allred. 2014. "To Speak for Human Nature: Cosmopolitics, Critique and the Neurosciences." *BioSocieties* 9 (1): 104–109. doi:10.1057/biosoc.2013.44.

Connell, Raewyn. 2013. "The Neoliberal Cascade and Education: An Essay on the Market Agenda and Its Consequences." *Critical Studies in Education* 54 (2): 99–112. doi:10.1080/17508487.2013.776990.

Cromby, John, and Martin E.H. Willis. 2013. "Nudging Into Subjectification: Governmentality and Psychometrics." *Critical Social Policy*, 34 (2): 241–259. Online First October 15, 2013. doi:10.1177/0261018313500868.

Deakin Crick, Ruth, and Clarence W. Joldersma. 2007. "Habermas, Lifelong Learning and Citizenship Education." *Studies in Philosophy and Education* 26 (2): 77–95.

Doherty, Robert A. 2007. "Education, Neoliberalism and the Consumer Citizen: After the Golden Age of Egalitarian Reform." *Critical Studies in Education* 48 (2): 269–288. doi:10.1080/17508480701494275.

Down, Barry. 2009. "Schooling, Productivity and the Enterprising Self: Beyond Market Values." *Critical Studies in Education* 50 (1): 51–64. doi:10.1080/17508480802526652.

Dumit, Joseph. 2011. "Critically Producing Brain Images of Mind." In *Critical Neuroscience: A Handbook of the Social and Cultural Contexts of Neuroscience*, edited by Suparna Choudhury and Jan Slaby, 195–225. Hoboken, NJ: Wiley-Blackwell.

Dunagan, Jake F. 2010. "Politics for the Neurocentric Age." *Journal of Futures Studies* 15 (2): 51–70.

Fejes, András. 2008. "Historicizing the Lifelong Learner: Governmentality and Neoliberal Rule." In *Foucault and Lifelong Learning: Governing the Subject*, edited by András Fejes and Kathy Nicoll, 87–100. London and New York: Routledge.

Ferguson, James. 2010. "The Uses of Neoliberalism." *Antipode* 41 (January): 166–184. doi:10.1111/j.1467–8330.2009.00721.x.

Halliday, John. 2003. "Who Wants to Learn Forever? Hyperbole and Difficulty with Lifelong Learning." *Studies in Philosophy and Education* 22 (3–4): 195–210. doi:10.1023/A:1022865103813.

Hamann, Trent H. 2009. "Neoliberalism, Governmentality, and Ethics." *Foucault Studies* 7 (February): 37–59.

Harvey, David. 2005. *A Brief History of Neoliberalism.* Oxford: Oxford University Press.

Hill, Dave. 2009. "Class, Capital and Education in This Neoliberal and Neoconservative Period." In *Revolutionizing Pedagogy: Education for Social Justice Within and Beyond Global Neo-Liberalism*, edited by Sheila Macrine, Peter McLaren, and Dave Hill, 119–144. London and New York: Palgrave Macmillan.

Holman, Constance, and Etienne de Villers-Sidani. 2014. "Indestructible Plastic: The Neuroscience of the New Aging Brain." *Frontiers in Human Neuroscience* 8: 1–15 (April). doi:10.3389/fnhum.2014.00219.

Hötting, Kirsten, and Brigitte Röder. 2013. "Beneficial Effects of Physical Exercise on Neuroplasticity and Cognition." *Neuroscience & Biobehavioral Reviews* 37 (9, Part B): 2243–2257. doi:10.1016/j.neubiorev.2013.04.005.

Huttenlocher, Peter R. 2009. *Neural Plasticity.* Cambridge, MA: Harvard University Press.

Joldersma, Clarence W., and Ruth Deakin Crick. 2010. "Citizenship, Discourse Ethics and an Emancipatory Model of Lifelong Learning." In *Habermas, Critical Theory and Education*, edited by Mark Murphy and Ted Fleming, 137–152. London: Routledge.

Kelly, A.M. Clare, and Hugh Garavan. 2005. "Human Functional Neuroimaging of Brain Changes Associated with Practice." *Cerebral Cortex* 15 (8): 1089–1102. doi:10.1093/cercor/bhi005.

Kolb, Bryan, Robbin Gibb, and Terry E. Robinson. 2003. "Brain Plasticity and Behavior." *Current Directions in Psychological Science* 12 (1): 1–5. doi:10.1111/1467–8721.01210.

Kumar, Ravi, and David Hill. 2009. "Neoliberalism and Its Impacts." In *Global Neoliberalism and Education and Its Consequences*, edited by David Hill and Ravi Kumar, 12–29. London: Routledge.

Legrenzi, Paolo, Carlo Umilta, and Frances Anderson. 2011. *Neuromania: On the Limits of Brain Science.* New York: Oxford University Press.

Manzotti, Riccardo, and Paolo Moderato. 2010. "Is Neuroscience Adequate as the Forthcoming 'mindscience'?." *Behavior and Philosophy* 38: 1–29.

Mitchell, Katharyne. 2006. "Neoliberal Governmentality in the European Union: Education, Training, and Technologies of Citizenship." *Environment and Planning D: Society and Space* 24 (3): 389–407. doi:10.1068/d1804.

O'Connor, C., and H. Joffe. 2013. "How Has Neuroscience Affected Lay Understandings of Personhood? A Review of the Evidence." *Public Understanding of Science* 22 (3): 254–268. doi:10.1177/0963662513476812.

Olssen, Mark. 2008. "Understanding the Mechanisms of Neoliberal Control: Lifelong Learning, Flexibility and Knowledge Capitalism." In *Foucault and Lifelong Learning: Governing the Subject*, edited by András Fejes and Kathy Nicoll, 34–47. London and New York: Routledge.

Peters, Michael A. 2001. "Education, Enterprise Culture and the Entrepreneurial Self: A Foucauldian Perspective." *The Journal of Educational Enquiry* 2 (2): 58–71.

Peters, Michael A. 2007. "Foucault, Biopolitics and the Birth of Neoliberalism." *Critical Studies in Education* 48 (2): 165–178. doi:10.1080/17508480701494218.

Peters, Michael A. 2012. "Neoliberalism, Education and the Crisis of Western Capitalism." *Policy Futures in Education* 10 (2): 134–141. doi:10.2304/pfie.2012.10.2.134.

Pickersgill, Martyn, Sarah Cunningham-Burley, and Paul Martin. 2011. "Constituting Neurologic Subjects: Neuroscience, Subjectivity and the Mundane Significance of the Brain." *Subjectivity* 4 (3): 346–365. doi:10.1057/sub.2011.10.

Pitts-Taylor, V. 2010. "The Plastic Brain: Neoliberalism and the Neuronal Self." *Health: An Interdisciplinary Journal for the Social Study of Health, Illness and Medicine* 14 (6): 635–652. doi:10.1177/1363459309360796.

Poldrack, Russell A. 2000. "Imaging Brain Plasticity: Conceptual and Methodological Issues—a Theoretical Review." *NeuroImage* 12 (1): 1–13. doi:10.1006/nimg.2000.0596.

Poldrack, Russell A. 2010. "Subtraction and Beyond: The Logic of Experimental Designs for Neuroimaging." In *Foundational Issues in Human Brain Mapping*, edited by Stephen Jose Hanson and Martin Bunzl, 147–160. Cambridge, MA: MIT Press.

Poldrack, Russell A. 2011. "Inferring Mental States From Neuroimaging Data: From Reverse Inference to Large-Scale Decoding." *Neuron* 72 (5): 692–697. doi:10.1016/j.neuron.2011.11.001.

Raz, Amir. 2011. "From Neuroimaging to Tea Leaves in the Bottom of a Cup." In *Critical Neuroscience: A Handbook of the Social and Cultural Contexts of Neuroscience*, edited by Suparna Choudhury and Jan Slaby, 265–272. Hoboken, NJ: John Wiley & Sons.

Rizvi, Fazal. 2013. *Globalization and Education*. London; New York: Routledge.

Rose, Nikolas S. 2001. "Normality and Pathology in a Biological Age." *Outlines: Critical Practice Studies* 3 (1): 19–33.

Rose, Nikolas S. 2014. "Governing Through the Brain: Neuropolitics, Neuroscience and Subjectivity." *Cambridge Anthropology* 32 (1): 3–23. doi:10.3167/ca.2014.320102.

Rose, Nikolas S., and Joelle M. Abi-Rached. 2013. *Neuro: The New Brain Sciences and the Management of the Mind*. Princeton, NJ: Princeton University Press.

Rose, Nikolas S., and Joelle M. Abi-Rached. 2014. "Governing through the Brain: Neuropolitics, Neuroscience and Subjectivity." *Cambridge Anthropology*, 32 (1), 3–23.

Rose, Nikolas S., and Peter Miller. 2010. "Political Power Beyond the State: Problematics of Government." *The British Journal of Sociology* 61 (January): 271–303. doi:10.1111/j.1468-4446.2009.01247.x.

Rose, Steven. 2011. "The Need for a Critical Neuroscience." In *Critical Neuroscience: A Handbook of the Social and Cultural Contexts of Neuroscience*, edited by Suparna Choudhury and Jan Slaby, 53–66. Hoboken, NJ: John Wiley & Sons.

Saltman, Kenneth J., and Victoria Perselli. 2007. "Review Symposium: A Brief History of Neoliberalism (David Harvey)." *Policy Futures in Education* 5 (2): 249–263. doi:10.2304/pfie.2007.5.2.249.

Slaby, Jan, and Suparna Choudhury. 2011. "Proposal for a Critical Neuroscience." In *Critical Neuroscience: A Handbook of the Social and Cultural Contexts of Neuroscience*, edited by Suparna Choudhury and Jan Slaby, 29–51. Hoboken, NJ: John Wiley & Sons.

Slagter, Heleen A., Richard J. Davidson, and Antoine Lutz. 2011. "Mental Training as a Tool in the Neuroscientific Study of Brain and Cognitive Plasticity." *Frontiers in Human Neuroscience* 5 (February): 1–12. doi:10.3389/fnhum.2011.00017.

Small, David. 2011. "Neo-Liberalism in Crisis? Educational Dimensions." *Policy Futures in Education* 9 (2): 258–266. doi:10.2304/pfie.2011.9.2.258.

Spolidoro, Maria, Alessandro Sale, Nicoletta Berardi, and Lamberto Maffei. 2009. "Plasticity in the Adult Brain: Lessons from the Visual System." *Experimental Brain Research* 192 (3): 335–341. doi:10.1007/s00221–008–1509–3.

Stadler, Max. 2011. "The Neuromance of Cerebral History." In *Critical Neuroscience: A Handbook of the Social and Cultural Contexts of Neuroscience*, edited by Suparna Choudhury and Jan Slaby, 135–158. Hoboken, NJ: John Wiley & Sons.

Steger, Manfred B., and Ravi K. Roy. 2010. *Neoliberalism: A Very Short Introduction*. Oxford: Oxford University Press.

Tienken, Christopher H. 2013. "Neoliberalism, Social Darwinism, and Consumerism Masquerading as School Reform." *Interchange* 43 (4): 295–316. doi:10.1007/s10780–013–9178-y.

Tuschling, Anna, and Christoph Engemann. 2006. "From Education to Lifelong Learning: The Emerging Regime of Learning in the European Union." *Educational Philosophy and Theory* 38 (4): 451–469. doi:10.1111/j.1469–5812.2006.00204.x.

Uggla, Bengt Kristensson. 2008. "Who Is the Lifelong Learner? Globalization, Lifelong Learning and Hermeneutics." *Studies in Philosophy and Education* 27 (4): 211–226. doi:10.1007/s11217–007–9074-y.

Ungerleider, Leslie G., Julien Doyon, and Avi Karni. 2002. "Imaging Brain Plasticity During Motor Skill Learning." *Neurobiology of Learning and Memory* 78 (3): 553–564. doi:10.1006/nlme.2002.4091.

Vassallo, Stephen. 2014. "The Entanglement of Thinking and Learning Skills in Neoliberal Discourse." In *Psychology in Education: Critical Theory-Practice*, edited by Tim Corcoran, 145–165. Rotterdam: Sense Publishers.

Vidal, Fernando. 2009. "Brainhood, Anthropological Figure of Modernity." *History of the Human Sciences* 22 (1): 5–36. doi:10.1177/0952695108099133.

Wilkins, Andrew. 2012. "The Spectre of Neoliberalism: Pedagogy, Gender and the Construction of Learner Identities." *Critical Studies in Education* 53 (2): 197–210. doi:10.1080/17508487.2012.672332.

Zatorre, Robert J., R. Douglas Fields, and Heidi Johansen-Berg. 2012. "Plasticity in Gray and White: Neuroimaging Changes in Brain Structure during Learning." *Nature Neuroscience* 15 (4): 528–536. doi:10.1038/nn.3045.

Part II

Thinking Philosophically with Neuroscience and Education

7 Cultivating Moral Values in an Age of Neuroscience

Derek Sankey and Minkang Kim

INTRODUCTION

The distinguished broadcaster and naturalist, David Attenborough, is show-casing the activities of two rather engaging capuchin monkeys (Linfield 2004). They have been brought in from their outside enclosure to participate in an experiment about cooperation, trust, fairness, and justice, although they no doubt think it is just another opportunity to enjoy some favorite treats. This time the treats are hazel nuts, but there is a problem. The nuts are in a sealed jar. One of the monkeys has the pot of nuts in his cage, while the other monkey has a flint in his cage that can be used to break open the jar. A small opening between the cages is large enough to pass the flint, but not enough to pass the jar. The more experienced monkey with the flint duly passes it to the other monkey who, rather clumsily, begins to use it to open the jar. Despite some impatience from the monkey looking on, the jar is eventually opened.

Now what will happen? Will the less experienced monkey seize all the nuts, or will he *share* them with the other monkey who *cooperated* to make them available? Can the monkey with the nuts be *trusted* to share them *fairly*, or will he eat the lot, justifying the claim of Richard Dawkins (1976) and his socio-biology associates that we are motivated by 'selfish genes?' In fact, he shares them equally; capuchin monkeys do this reliably. But why? How did they learn to do that, how are these 'moral values' cultivated in capuchin society? Or, are we going to say that these monkeys cannot, by definition, employ 'moral values'; their apparent sharing, trust, and sense of fairness must result from some other socio-behavioral factors and/or innate pre-programming?

JOURNEYING IN THE FOOTHILLS

It is not so long ago that it was thought that only human beings use tools, but capuchins instinctively know how to use the flint. In fact, since the observations by Jane Goodall in the 1960s of chimpanzees in the wild using tools, field studies have confirmed that many animals, including some species of birds, know how to make tools and use them. And, over the past twenty years or so, we have also come a long way in our understanding of animal brain biology; indeed, much of what we know about the human brain has been learned from other animals, right down to sea slugs (Aplysia) and fruit flies (Drosophila melanogaster) (Kandel 2006, 234). We can now better appreciate the continuity between species in both brain anatomy and brain function, but what about moral values? Certainly, Attenborough was happy to use the word 'fairness' in his video, but are moral terms such as cooperation, trust, fairness, and justice being applied appropriately in the case of monkeys? Don't moral values only belong to humans, as tool making was once considered an exclusively human ability? Because, if moral values *are* rooted in biology, this would seem to have quite important implications for our philosophical claims about the human self, including the moral self. Alternatively, could it be that, scientifically speaking, no animals, including human beings, actually exhibit moral values, even though they appear to? Perhaps all animals are pre-programmed and there is no such thing as freedom to choose, no free will.

In this chapter, we will be interweaving science and philosophy, believing with Alva Noë that "Philosophy flourishes in the midst of scientific research, not only because philosophical problems are in good measure empirical, but because scientific problems are in good measure philosophical" (Noë 2004, vii). As authors, we share a common interest in the origins and development of the human person or 'self.' One of us comes from Developmental Science, the other from Philosophy of Science. We are also both committed to dynamic systems theory (DST), with its central concept of emergent self-organization (Kim and Sankey 2009, Sankey and Kim 2013). This will come to the fore later in the chapter. Moreover, we both work within the context of education, which we see as a values-based endeavor; hence our interest in the cultivation of moral values in education and claims that this might be informed by neuroscience.

Primatologist Frans De Waal, who works with capuchins and apes, has recently noted that we seem to be obsessed by what we consider new and important about ourselves, but in doing so, he says, "we overlook the fundamentals" (De Waal 2009, 15). Instead, he argues, we should start our "thinking from the bottom up," from what we can discover about animals if we want to know how we reached the peaks of human civilization; the "peaks glimmer in the sun, but it is in the foothills that we find most of what drives us" (16). Neurophilosopher Patricia Churchland, in her 2011 book *Braintrust*, says much the same thing, as she traces the neurobiological origins of moral values by examining how the homeostatic imperative to 'care-for-self' was extended to 'care-for-others.' Our chapter will be operating very much within the 'foothills' of moral values development and its neurobiology, in the belief that this is where we can begin to gain some purchase on the origins of moral values and some of the fundamentals for cultivating moral values in education. We are not concerned with the summits of grand moral theory; instead, our focus is on what lays underneath, at a different descriptive level, the level of natural science, including neurobiology and what can be learned from creatures such as capuchin monkeys that preceded us in the story of life.

But in journeying through the foothills, we are also sounding a cautionary note, as we have in our approach to neuroscience in education over the years. In teaching human development and neuroscience to large numbers of students, we are all too aware that education is very prone to neuromyths; some based on a very loose extrapolation of sound scientific theory to unwarranted conclusions, others simply resulting from misinformation or misunderstanding. A recent sampling of some 420 undergraduate teacher education students in Sydney, Australia, revealed alarming levels of belief in neuromyths (Kim 2015), such as VAK (visual, auditory, and kinesthetic), the belief that children have a dominant learning style, although it was some comfort to note that the numbers correlated with similar studies of teachers in Europe (Dekker et al. 2012). We are cautious not to create additional neuromyths and thus maintain that the science must be sound and its interpretation and application to education must be valid and relevant. And we acknowledge that exercising caution may well constrain what can be said currently in applying neuroscience to education; there is much that we still need to learn about the brain.

Moreover, some of what we currently 'know' from brain imaging studies could turn out to be less convincing than supposed, if not false. That is the nature of science (Popper 1963), not least because of the *underdetermination of theory by evidence* (Quine and Ullian 1970), the notion that evidence could fit two or more incompatible theories, such that 'fit with evidence' cannot be a sufficient criterion for determining the 'truth' of any given theory. Extreme caution is needed in extrapolating from 'evidence' produced by brain imaging studies, especially when it seems to fit neatly into, and therefore appears to corroborate nicely, our existing beliefs.

Previously, for example, we have expressed concern that in a paper by Darcia Narvaez and Jenny Vaydich (2008), neuroscience was being used to support the so-called Four Components Model of moral functioning in a manner that seemed to us to be "somewhat contrived" (Kim and Sankey 2009). We would express similar caution in regard to a recent paper claiming that "current neuroscientific research supports a holistic approach to pedagogy which emphasises the cognitive, affective, moral and other dimensions of learning and the corresponding need to facilitate development in all of these dimensions for authentic learning to take place" (Mudge et al. 2014). We fully endorse this vision of education, irrespective of whether it is supported by neuroscience or not. But we are also aware that those with a very different theoretical framework could also claim neuroscientific support, for example, the Behaviorist camp with their mechanistic vision of education.

Neuroscientific discoveries can also frequently challenge our settled ideas of the human self and its morality. In what follows, we begin with the discovery by Benjamin Libet that the brain is active in advance of our conscious decision to act (Libet et al. 1983). This appears to undermine the claim that we are free to make moral choices. Our discussion of the Libet experiment will take us into issues of dualism and determinism. We will advocate a holistic notion of the moral self as both conscious and subconscious and a view of the brain as embodied and socially embedded. We will turn to dynamic systems (complexity) theory in an attempt to counter the prevailing view in neuroscience that denies moral choice. Hopefully, discussion of these issues in the first half of the chapter will help to set a platform for the discussion in the second half, where we consider two main issues: moral intuition and the biological origins of moral values. In regard to the latter, we will argue against reductionism, another prevailing view in neuroscience. Throughout the discussion, we will attempt to keep the concerns of educational practice in view.

HOW FREE IS CONSCIOUS FREE WILL?

It is common sense that we make conscious moral choices and act on them, but the Libet experiment provides evidence that our decision to act (which would include our decision to act morally) is taken by the brain prior to our conscious decision to act. Using electroencephalography (EEG), he found the temporal difference to be fractions of a second, but more recent experimental work using fMRI says that the brain's decision may be anything up to ten seconds in advance of the conscious decision to act (Soon et al. 2008). Either way, these results would seem to raise very severe questions about our normal everyday claims that we are responsible for our actions and without that there can be little sense in attempting to cultivate moral values—our actions, it is claimed, are predetermined and not the result of conscious choice. But is this research reliable? Why, for example, does EEG produce such a different result than fMRI? Is there a problem with the science or our interpretation of the evidence, and might there be a problem with the notion of determinism inherent in these claims?

John-Dylan Haynes and his team conducted the fMRI experiment in Germany (Soon et al. 2008). Commenting on the discrepancy between the EEG and fMRI results, Haynes argues that the Libet result, using EEG, is only recording late stages of motor planning in the Supplementary Motor Area (SMA) of the brain. By contrast, he claims that their research, using fMRI, allowed them to "investigate any potential long-term determinants of human intentions that preceded the conscious intention far beyond the few hundred milliseconds observed over the SMA" (Soon et al. 2008, 544). Both forms of the experiment are concerned with actions, but in a more recent paper, the fMRI team have extended their investigations to what they call "more abstract types of decisions" (Soon et al. 2013). Science will decide the technical issues, but if it is the case that our brain is making decisions in advance of our conscious awareness, surely that undermines our common-sense claims that we are in *control* of our thoughts and actions and therefore responsible for them. Or does it?

THE CONSCIOUS/SUBCONSCIOUS SELF
AND THE EMBODIED/EMBEDDED BRAIN

There are two important issues here; one is dualism, the other scientific determinism. In regard to the first, we suggest that these experiments only threaten our sense of *control* over our actions and thoughts if we adopt a dualistic separation between the conscious mind and subconscious brain and assume that what happens subconsciously is "error prone and hence in need of correction by rational deliberation" (Woodward and Allman 2007, 189). But why draw this demarcation between the "conscious and sub-conscious self" (Sankey 2006, 168). From the perspective of neurobiology, the brain is not separated from the body, enjoying a life of its own, any more than the heart is separated from the body. Rather, the brain is inherently embodied and, moreover, it is socially and environmentally embedded. The brain's primary function is homeostasis, maintaining metabolic balance within the organism in response to both internal and external fluctuations. In other words, the brain's main function *is* control, and those fluctuations include social and environmental changes on a moment-by-moment basis. It is our view that what happens subconsciously is very much part of the 'self,' including the regulation of heartbeat and breathing and the extraordinary working of the immune system. Thankfully, these are very much under the control of the brain, keeping us alive. Likewise, neuroscience has shown that much of our thinking and acting is conducted below the level of conscious awareness (Lakoff and Johnson 1999, 10), such that "we often do not know why we do the things we do" (Sankey 2006, 170). But that does not mean that there is no control, only that there is no *conscious* control.

A holistic notion of the conscious/subconscious self, and of the brain as inherently embodied and socially/environmentally embedded, would seem to have important implications for cultivating moral values in education. The kinds of classrooms we create, whether they are values-based learning environments or not, and the kinds of pedagogies we employ will impact students both consciously and subconsciously. And this will influence what these students do and how they grow and mature in terms of their core values and beliefs, both consciously and subconsciously, well into the future. Moreover, as teachers know all too well, this educational endeavor is occurring against a backdrop of other less healthy influences, including, for example, so-called Internet 'games' such as Grand Theft Auto V that promotes violence and exploitation (even murder) of women for entertainment. All of these influences (desirable and undesirable) impact young minds and the moral choices they make, both consciously and subconsciously, well into the future.

DETERMINISM AND PREDICTABILITY

Of course, this assumes that children and adults have freedom to choose, but this is precisely what determinists deny, and in neuroscience, "hard determinism still reigns" (Gazzaniga 2011, 127). Indeed, one implication of *cultivating moral values in an age of neuroscience* is that most neuroscientists, including those involved with the experiments reported earlier, presume a fully deterministic and predictable mechanistic universe. So what teachers and education policy makers hear about the brain is not philosophically neutral, it is based on the deterministic assumption that all current and future events, including the moral choices we make, are operating according to the laws of nature; they are causally necessitated by preceding events and are thus entirely predictable. The Libet experiment is nicely in agreement with philosophical determinism. The conscious experience we have of making moral choices is an illusion, determinists believe, it's a trick of the brain that gives the impression of making decisions and choices when in reality they are predetermined and can be predicted in advance. So, they assert, "we don't do what we want, rather we want what we do." Moreover, there is evidence that this illusion is highly productive, that we need it in order to oil our social relationships and act in prosocial ways with one another (Baumeister et al. 2009).

But is the physical world deterministic in the way that most neuroscientists believe? Here we are treading into controversial territory, but let's consider the notion of 'predictability' in science, a core assumption of 'Newtonian science' and its notion of a deterministic, mechanical universe—although Isaac Newton (1642–1727) himself did not fully subscribe to "the mechanical philosophy" (McGuire and Rattansi 1966). Pierre-Simon Laplace (1749–1827) stated the deterministic position most clearly when he claimed that, in principle, given the velocities and positions of all the particles in the universe at any given moment, he could calculate all that had happened in the past and all that would happen in the future. But could he? Does science have that degree of predictability, even in principle?

Doubts first began to surface in 1900, when Henri Poincaré was investigating the interaction of three astronomical bodies in space. What he discovered was that small imperfections in initial measurements could, over time, increase far beyond mathematical predictability. A similar issue was picked up many years later when, in 1972, meteorologist Edward Lorenz gave a presentation called *Predictability: Does the Flap of a Butterfly's Wings in Brazil Set Off a Tornado in Texas?* In other words, could the tiniest of fluctuations in initial weather conditions in one location escalate in totally unpredictable ways (although remaining within the laws of nature) to produce a catastrophic event in another and distant location? The answer is yes, and that has dire consequences for Newtonian predictability. It introduces us to the notion of *chaos* in nature, which doesn't necessarily imply that systems are acting randomly, only that they are unpredictable. It seems the world is inherently unpredictable, such that the deterministic notion of 'operating according to the laws of nature' has at least to be revised to accommodate unpredictability. And, we suggest, this loosening of the grip of hard determinism begins to provide space within the laws of nature to accommodate moral choice.

COMPLEXITY AND EMERGENT SELF-ORGANIZATION

All living structures are complex, emergent, self-organizing, dissipative systems operating far from the thermodynamic equilibrium (Prigogine 1997). The notion of *emergence* is not one you will find in much neuroscientific literature, although it was embraced by neuroscientist Michael Gazzaniga in his 2009 Gifford Lectures, published as a book in 2011 under the title *Who's in Charge*. Emergence occurs when

> micro-level complex systems that are far from equilibrium (thus allowing for the amplification of random events) self-organize (creative, self-generated, adaptability-seeking behavior) into new structures, with new properties that previously did not exist, to form a new level of organization on the macro level.
>
> (Gazzaniga 2011, 124)

The notion of 'a new level of organization' is crucial to understanding the concept of 'emergence.' It is our view that much confusion can be avoided when addressing issues of mind and brain, self-hood and consciousness once we understand emergence and the notion of different levels of organization. Consciousness is an 'emergent property'; our conscious deliberative minds "emerge from the immense complexity of human brains; that is what highly complex brains do" (Kim and Sankey 2010). Calling consciousness an emergent property does not explain it, much less does it explain it away, but it does locate it at the appropriate level of organization and description. Moreover, as we will discuss later, this has implications for the claim that mind-talk can be reduced to brain-talk, the doctrine of reductionism that is also a guiding belief of much neuroscience.

In a paper published in the *Journal of Moral Education* (Kim and Sankey 2009), we argued that moral development is emergent and self-organizing, that it is highly dynamic, variable, context-sensitive, and somewhat unpredictable. This is a dynamic systems approach, a potentially new paradigm in moral education to replace what we saw as the outmoded Kohlbergian and Neo-Kohlbergian cognitive, rationalist tradition that had been influential in education during the second half of the twentieth century. Part of the popularity of Kohlbergian theory was its rather predictable, onward and upward notion of development through predetermined moral stages, which seemed to have promising implications for classroom practice, where teachers design the curriculum and pedagogy in terms of the putative 'stages' and students' readiness for moral learning. However, in cultivating moral values, it is not sufficient to get the curriculum and pedagogy right. These are certainly necessary, but as teachers, we also need to attend to the background assumptions and theoretical framework and get these right, even though they may make the curriculum and pedagogical tasks more difficult. The claim that moral development is often highly dynamic, variable, context-sensitive, and somewhat unpredictable does not make the educational task of cultivating moral values easy. Rather it provides a model of moral development that is complex and always in flux, developmental but often not predictable—that is the educational challenge.

In the first half of this chapter, we have been attending to a number of background assumptions and theoretical considerations that we believe should inform the task of cultivating moral values. Hopefully it will also provide a platform for the discussion that follows. Before embarking, however, we had better briefly say what we mean by moral values. Taking ordinary language as our guide when, for example, people refer to Australian values, Christian values, or environmental values, they generally mean guiding principles, beliefs, sensitivities held and displayed by individuals or groups in respect to how they relate to and deal with others and the world. And, to repeat, these guiding principles, beliefs, sensitivities are held both consciously and subconsciously.

DOING WHAT COMES NATURALLY

Back to our capuchin monkeys—what is going on when they are displaying what at least appear to be moral values? Our basic suggestion is that they are displaying *emergent social behavior*, operating below the level of conscious awareness. In other words, capuchin moral values are a subset of highly complex social practices and relationships, using much the same neural systems in the brain. So quite literally, in cooperating and sharing, capuchins are doing what comes naturally in their particular social context. But given the aforementioned definition, does 'doing what comes naturally' strip the capuchin's actions of moral content? Is it possible that capuchins could be said to possess 'guiding principles, beliefs, and sensitivities,' or is their display of cooperation, trust, fairness, and justice simply apparent? We would caution against the latter conclusion. Experimental evidence suggests that capuchins have a strong sense of fairness and justice. De Waal describes an experiment in which capuchins were given pebbles as a token, which they exchanged for a cucumber slice. All was well as the monkeys bartered their tokens for up to twenty-five times, until the experimenters introduced inequity into the experiment. He explains:

> One monkey would still get cucumber, while its partner now enjoyed grapes, a favourite food. The advantaged monkey obviously had no

problem, but the one still working for cucumber would lose interest. Worse, seeing its partner with juicy grapes, this monkey would get agitated, hurl the pebbles out of the test chamber, sometimes even throwing those paltry cucumber slices. A food normally devoured with gusto had become distasteful.

(De Waal 2009, 187)

So these clever monkeys can sense injustice when it is against their own self-interest, but what if there is another monkey in need? In a different experiment, a monkey was offered a choice between two differently colored tokens, one token was 'selfish' the other 'prosocial.' If the monkey used the selfish token, it received a small piece of apple in exchange, but its partner received nothing. If the monkey exchanged the prosocial token, however, both monkeys were equally rewarded, at the same time. De Waal found "the stronger the tie with its partner, the more a monkey would pick the prosocial token," showing "monkeys favour sharing over solitary consumption" (113). Moreover, he adds, the experiment was highly repeatable and "could not be explained by fear of punishment, because in every pair the dominant monkey (the one who had least to fear) proved the more prosocial one" (113).

Thinking 'from the bottom up,' from capuchins to ourselves, there is much in these experiments that we can recognize. The perception of injustice, the angry emotional response in the face of injustice, the refusal to accept what we like if we feel that we ought to have a better deal, and the preference for prosocial sharing, especially with those closest to us. But, presumably, in capuchins, all of this is occurring below the level of conscious awareness and verbal language, although not body language. Of course, one can continue to insist that only human beings are capable of moral values, some might argue that this is because morality requires language. We find that claim controversial. From our viewpoint in the foothills, it is hard to resist the conclusion that at least the rudiments of morality can be found in non-linguistic creatures such as capuchins, as it can in apes, elephants, and dolphins that are considered to possess conscious awareness.

INTUITION AND THE TACIT DIMENSION

Earlier we noted that, as humans, we often do not know why we do what we do and for sound neurobiological reasons: it is irredeemably below conscious awareness. We should now add "when we do think we know, our reasoning is often post-event; a narrative we tell to explain and justify our actions, but not actual reasons or causes, these are quite literally out of mind" (Sankey 2011, 419). Nevertheless, that does not imply that the subconscious choices we make are necessarily arbitrary or necessarily made without reason, even if the reasons are out of mind. Moreover, as in capuchins, they are shaped by learning and experience, especially social experience.

Clearly there are overlaps in what we are saying with the notion of 'moral intuitions,' although we are anxious to tread carefully through that maze. We are not concerned whether our intuitions can be defended or justified one way or another or whether or how they correlate with normative moral judgments. Our interest is in the origins and neurobiology of moral intuitions and values. This puts us on a quite similar track to James Woodward and John Allman (2007) in regard to moral intuitions and to Patricia Churchland (2011) in her concern with the neurobiological origins of moral values. In this section, we will consider the contribution of Woodward and Allman and come to Churchland a little later.

Woodward and Allman note that, in the philosophical literature on moral intuitions, "there is no agreement about the proper role of appeals to intuition within moral argument, there is also (and relatedly) no consensus about the nature and character of intuition itself" (2007, 180). Nevertheless, a distinction is usually drawn between moral intuition and moral reasoning; intuitions occur quickly and automatically, whereas reasoning involves deliberate and thoughtful decision making. Although helpful for analysis, this distinction comes with four caveats. First, if thought and action are to be held together consistently, there is, and needs to be, considerable overlap between these two systems "working together and mutually supporting one another" (189). Second, intuitive judgments are not inherently inferior, in need of correction by rational deliberation, as we will see shortly. Third, there is no dedicated faculty in the brain devoted solely to moral intuition or moral cognition, rather they "derive from and are structured by our more general capacities for social cognition" (182). Fourth, in a properly functioning brain, reason and intuition are valanced by emotion (Damasio 1994), and "the neural areas involved in paradigmatic cases of moral intuition are also centrally involved in emotional processing" (Woodward and Allman 2007, 182).

Woodward and Allman "propose that moral intuitions are part of the larger set of social intuitions that guide us through complex, highly uncertain and rapidly changing social interactions" (2007, 186). The neurobiological systems include at least three recently evolved components in the brain: fronto-insular (FI), anterior cingulate cortex (ACC), and anterior orbito-frontal cortex (antOFC), plus more ancient associated subcortical structures "such as basal ganglia and amygdala, all of which have been implicated by many functional imaging and brain lesion studies" (186). FI and ACC contain a class of large bipolar cells, called von Economo neurons (VENs). Until very recently, it was believed that these were also of recent origin and that they "emerged since the divergence of hominoids from other primates" (Woodward and Allman 2007). However, it has since been discovered that VENs are also present in elephants and whales (Allman et al. 2011) and even macaque monkeys (Evrard et al. 2012). We await similar research on capuchins. It appears that "VENs and associated circuitry enable us to reduce complex social and cultural dimensions of decision-making into intuition, thus facilitating the rapid execution of decisions" (Woodward and Allman 2007, 188).

As an example of enlightened intuition, Woodward and Allman cite a case in which a highly experienced fireman in charge of a fire crew became aware that, in tackling a fire, something was not right, and he immediately evacuated the crew in time to avoid disaster; moments later, the floor of the building collapsed because of a hidden fire in the basement below. When interviewed later, he attributed his actions to a 'sixth sense'; but on further analysis, it became apparent that he was also attending to specific cues, including the feeling that the room was hotter than expected given the type of fire being tackled, and it was not responding, as expected, to the water being applied. Woodward and Allman conclude that what we are seeing in this case is the result of

> implicit learning on the basis of past experience which leads to a norma-
> tively appropriate 'intuition' but without extensive deliberative reason-
> ing and indeed with little awareness of the processes that generate the
> intuition or the cues on which it is based.
>
> (2007, 190)

Moral intuition displays similar characteristics. Notice that in this case there was not 'extensive deliberative reasoning,' but neither it was entirely absent. The fireman's actions were not unreasonable; he had reasons, even though at the moment of the decision they were not in his mind. They were implicit, 'working together and mutually supporting one another.' In the 1960s, scientist turned philosopher Michael Polanyi referred to this as *The Tacit Dimension* (1966/1983), and he argued passionately that this is not simply a feature of our social lives, it is also a feature of scientific discovery—the ability of great scientists to notice new patterns in phenomena and sense when these are significant in solving a given problem. Polanyi said, "we know more than we can tell." The important point about this, as illustrated in the example of the fireman, is that the inability to provide systematic justifications of our intuitions does not imply they are unreliable; they can be highly reliable and highly productive in our social and moral lives and in science.

Intuitive, tacit knowledge requires learning and cultivation. We don't come into the world with ready-made intuitions, although we are equipped for social and moral learning and what we have previously called a "pre-dilection to value" (Kim and Sankey 2009), the notion that human beings and indeed life itself naturally orientates toward what is beneficial for survival, what is good rather than harmful, pleasant rather than unpleasant. The fireman was able to sense imminent danger as a result of long and detailed learning and experience of similar fires, and he was driven by a strong predilection toward survival. Polanyi referred to this kind of implicit, tacit learning as connoisseurship. Wouldn't it be wonderful if, in schools, we started to help children and adolescents to develop their sense of moral connoisseurship? This needs time, hands-on experience, and rehearsal (repeated practice), but how much time is this normally given in schools? We will return to this in the concluding section of the chapter.

FROM CARE-FOR-SELF TO CARE-FOR-OTHERS

We have so far suggested that moral values in capuchins and humans emerge from broader social relationships and practices and that moral intuitions are part of the larger set of social intuitions. The question arises whether attention to the broader social context can take us back to the origins of moral values. Churchland believes it can. She says her aim is to "explain what is probably true about our social nature, and what that involves in terms of the neural platform for moral behaviour" (Churchland 1986, 3). She is entirely aware, as we are constantly made aware, that drawing on the biological sciences to understand morality will likely be met with the rebuke that we are making the fool's error of trying to derive an *ought* from an *is*—the deontic fallacy.

Churchland's response focuses on the historical origins of this dictum and the use of 'derive' in deductive logic. She then notes, "in a much broader sense of 'infer' than *derive*, you can infer (*figure out*) what you ought to do, drawing on knowledge, perception, emotions, and understanding, and balancing considerations against each other" (1986, 6). This is surely correct as a description of how we conduct our everyday lives and, Polanyi would add, it is also correct in the context of science. In addition, we emphasize yet again, our focus is not on moral 'oughts,' but rather on moral origins, and these can certainly be informed by the biological sciences. However, to be clear, we are emphatically not saying that the biological sciences can account for the whole of morality, far from it; that would be absurd. But we are saying that they can shine a light on the emergence of social and moral values, how these are interwoven, and how they provide a platform for more developed forms of human morality.

Churchland asks, "What does it mean for a system of neurons to care about or to value something?" (1986, 13). Her answer takes us to the neural circuitry for self-caring. She notes, "In all animals neural circuitry grounds self-care and well-being" (13). This homeostatic imperative to care-for-self, is an example of the *predilection to value*, mentioned earlier, that we believe grounds the whole of life on this planet and has done so since the dawn of time. Without it, no creature could survive. Even bacteria "discriminate between nutrients and toxins and take avoiding action when necessary" (Kim and Sankey 2009, 294). Notice however, that this claim does not put a "ghost in the machine, or if it does, it is the ghost of life itself" (Thelen and Smith 1994, 316).

Churchland's thesis is that "in mammals (and quite possibly social birds) the neuronal organisation whereby individuals see to their own well-being was modified to motivate new values—the well-being of certain others" and the "widening of other caring in social behaviour marks the emergence of what eventually flowers into morality" (1986, 14). This widening from self-caring to other-caring, first for offspring, then kin, and eventually outward to strangers is operating at one level of organization: the level of interpersonal social engagement. But, underlying that manifest level are electro-chemical neuronal, synaptic processes, including the neuropeptide oxytocin, a very ancient and 'simple' peptide (string of amino-acids) found in all vertebrates, which Churchland believes "is at the hub of the intricate network of mammalian adaptations for caring for others, anchoring the many different versions of sociality that are seen" (14).

So 'what eventually flowers into morality' is the product of the brain and its underlying electro-chemical processes. There is much that rewards careful study in the way Churchland works through this thesis, but the underlying claim is not new; it is the standard neuroscientific account. One is reminded, for example, of Francis Crick's (1995) so-called 'astonishing hypothesis' that "you, your joys and your sorrows, your memories and your ambitions, your sense of personal identity and free will, are in fact *no more than* the behavior of a vast assembly of nerve cells and their associated molecules" (3; emphasis added). But, again, the idea that the substrate of all that we are and do is the brain, 'its nerve cells and associated molecules,' is the standard neurobiological account. For us, this is not an issue; what is at issue in the ontological reductionist claim that the human self and its values is *no more than*, nothing but, neurobiology, cells, and molecules.

Reductionism is a mainstay of the analytical approach of all science, understanding the parts and the parts that constitute the parts, downward to the laws of physics. But, if complexity theorists are correct, if you reverse the process from the bottom upward, you will not get the macro story from the micro story. As Gazzaniga notes, "Reductionism in the physical sciences has been challenged by the principle of emergence. The whole system acquires qualitatively new properties that cannot be predicted from the simple addition of those of its individual components" (Gazzaniga 2011, 134). Something happens when going from one organizational level to the one above, called a phase-shift. So while the substrate of the human self and its moral values *is* the brain and its neurobiology, that is not the whole story at all. Included in the new story, going from the microbiological level to levels above, is the emergence of social and interpersonal interaction, including our sense of responsibility and freedom to choose in our dealings, one with another. For us, that includes Churchland's story of how the homeostatic imperative to care-for-self has emerged to provide the new organizational level of care-for-others.

Churchland uses the word 'emergence' on a number of occasions in her book, but she does not address the issue of reductionism, which is particularly noticeable given the strong assertion in her seminal work *Neurophilosophy* in favor of reductionism, insisting that "if reductionism is a hopeless cause, then it would be foolish to search for an explanation of mental states and processes in terms of brain states and processes" (Churchland 1986, 277). Gazzaniga notes, "emergence is mightily resisted by many neuroscientists" (Gazzaniga 2011, 135), because they fear it is letting a ghost into their deterministic machine. One senses this is also Churchland's concern, but Gazzaniga is calling for his fellow neuroscientist to think again. This is a recent and very encouraging development in the dialogue between neuroscience and philosophy that bodes well for the future, although it may take time to bring about this particular paradigm shift. On the front cover of Churchland's *Braintrust*, Gazzaniga says, "Churchland once again leads the way." Perhaps she does, although we are inclined to think she will do it more productively if she listens to what Gazzaniga is saying about most neuroscientists needing to change their minds about reductionism.

CONCLUSION

Neuroscience can both inform and misinform the educational task of cultivating moral values. Educators should view neuroscience with critical eyes. We have cautioned against proliferating neuromyths in education and the use of neuroscience to support pet theories in ways that can appear highly contrived. We have also taken neuroscience to task for its adherence to hard determinism and ontological reductionism. However, we have turned to neuroscience in our quest for the neurobiological origins of moral values and when exploring the nature of moral intuition.

We should note that we have deliberately sidestepped the currently popular (if not popularist) account of moral intuition provided by psychologist Jonathan Haidt, who advocates five fundamental domains of intuitions, operating as content-rich, modules-in-the-mind (Haidt 2012, 123). Haidt's sociobiological approach to intuition, including the dubious notion of modules-in-the-mind, is largely at odds with our approach (Kim 2014; Sankey and Kim 2013). Haidt is generally dismissive of moral reasoning and the notion of moral development, but our approach *is* developmental, concerned with moral learning, and we have emphasized the interweaving of reason and intuition, 'working together and mutually supporting one another.' Moreover, Churchland notes that in Haidt's account, "No factual support from molecular biology, neuroscience, or evolutionary biology is marshalled for his substantive claims about basic domains of intuitions" (Churchland 2011, 114).

Educationally, our emphasis is on cultivating moral *values*, so we are not concerned with instilling moral norms, teaching children to be good, or with relativistic values clarification. We have defined moral values in terms of 'guiding principles, beliefs and sensitivities,' and it is these we are saying need to be cultivated in education, both consciously and subconsciously, involving both reason and intuition. And we have conceived the educational task as enhancing moral 'connoisseurship.' In closing, we will take this idea a little further.

Our view is that moral judgment is always a form of connoisseurship, whether it involves reasoned deliberation and/or intuition and whether it occurs consciously or subconsciously. Biology ensures that we are born with the necessary equipment to care for and cooperate with others and, for capuchins, the learning that occurs as part of their complex social life is sufficient to produce basic capuchin moral values. As humans, we also develop a set of guiding principles and beliefs that form a remembered backdrop for our thoughts and actions. But what we think and what we do in any given situation results from a sense of what is best and what is not so good, what is right and not right. It is an act of tacit discernment that can be refined and cultivated through constant practice and rehearsal. A good connoisseur of wine is born with the necessary senses to discern the quality of different wines, but that is not enough. The skills of connoisseurship require learning and refinement. Notice, however, that connoisseurship does not necessarily require language; a good connoisseur can rank a selection of wines in order of quality without saying a word or thinking a word.

However, in education there has been a long-standing view that moral learning need not require dedicated curriculum time; rather, it can form part of the hidden or implicit curriculum. Our view suggests that, although this may be helpful, it is not sufficient. Moral intuitions may well be implicit, but they require explicit teaching and learning; they can't just be caught, they need to be taught, they need constant rehearsal. The fireman was primarily acting intuitively, but it resulted from intense training, hands-on experience, and constant rehearsal, precisely what we suggest is needed if we are to successfully cultivate moral values in each new generation. And the importance of rehearsal is emphasized in neuroscience in regard to the plasticity of learning and memory, where repetition in the firing of neuronal connections strengthens the connections, whereas those not strengthened by repetition become weakened or pruned.

However, there is another backdrop that is impacting the educational task. We not only live in an age of neuroscience, we also inhabit the age of computer technology, where young people are constantly engaged in rehearsing skills and 'values.' Neuroscientist Susan Greenfield has noted, "We may now be living in an unprecedented era where an increasing number of people are rehearsing and learning a new default mind-set for negotiating the world" (Greenfield 2014, 211). She says that computer games are "excellent vehicles for manipulating brain processing at a very basic level" (162). She is particularly concerned with the way games allow young people to rehearse what she calls a "decoupling between understanding someone's suffering and caring about it sufficiently to modify your actions" (195). But if computer games are a problem, perhaps they are also a potential solution—i.e., producing educational games that maintain a close coupling between empathizing with suffering and action. Thus Greenfield's concern about the efficacy of computer games in manipulating brains through rehearsal can become an important pedagogical strategy for cultivating moral values and enhancing moral connoisseurship in this age of neuroscience.

REFERENCES

Allman, John M., Nicole A. Tetreault, Atiya Y. Hakeem, Kebreten F. Manaye, Katerina Semendeferi, Joseph M. Erwin, S. Park, V. Goubert, and P. Hof. 2011. "The Von Economo Neurons in the Frontoinsular and Anterior Cingulate Cortex." *Annals of the New York Academy of Sciences* 1225: 59–71.

Baumeister, Roy, E.J. Masicampo, and C. Nathan DeWall. 2009. "Prosocial Benefits of Feeling Free: Disbelief in Free Will Increases Aggression and Reduces Helpfulness." *Personality and Social Psychology Bulletin* 35 (2): 260–268.

Churchland, Patricia. 1986. *Neurophilosophy: Toward a Unified Science of the Mind/Brain*. Cambridge, MA: Bradford Books/MIT Press.

Churchland, Patricia. 2011. *Braintrust: What Neuroscience Tells Us About Morality*. Princeton, NJ: Princeton University Press.

Crick, Francis. 1995. *The Astonishing Hypothesis: The Scientific Search for the Soul*. New York: Simon & Schuster.

Damasio, Antonio. (1994). *Descartes' Error: Emotion, Reason, and the Human Brain*. New York: Putnam Books.

Dawkins, Richard. 1976. *The Selfish Gene*. Oxford: Oxford University Press.

Dekker, Sanne, Nikki C. Lee, Paul Howard-Jones, and Jelle Jolles. 2012. "Neuromyths in Education: Prevalence and Predictors of Misconceptions among Teachers." *Frontiers in Psychology* 3: 429. Doe:10.3389/fpsyg.2012.00429

De Waal, Frans. 2009. *The Age of Empathy. Nature's Lessons for a Kinder Society*. New York: Harmony Books.

Evrard, Henry C., Thomas Forro, and Nikos K. Logothetis. 2012. "Von Economo Neurons in the Anterior Insula of the Macaque Monkey." *Neuron* 74 (3): 482–489.

Gazzaniga, Michael. 2011. *Who's in Charge? Free Will and the Science of the Brain*. New York: Harper Collins.

Greenfield, Susan. 2014. *Mind Change: How Digital Technologies Are Leaving Their Mark on Our Brains*. London: Random House.

Haidt, Jonathan. 2012. *The Righteous Mind: Why Good People are Divided by Politics and Religion*. New York: Pantheon.

Kandel, Eric. 2006. *In Search of Memory: The Emergence of a New Science of Mind*. New York: Norton.

Kim, Minkang. 2015. "Neuromyths and Pre-Service Teachers in Australia: Prevalence and Origins." Poster Presentation at the Inaugural International Convention of Psychological Science (ICPS), March 12–14, 2015, Amsterdam.

Kim, Minkang. 2014. "Cultivating Teachers' Morality and the Pedagogy of Emotional Rationality." *Australian Journal of Teacher Education* 38 (1): 12–26.

Kim, Minkang, and Derek Sankey. 2009. "Towards a Dynamic Systems Approach to Moral Development and Moral Education: A Response to the JME Special Issue, September 2008." *Journal of Moral Education* 38 (3): 283–299.

Kim, Minkang, and Derek Sankey. 2010. "The Dynamics of Emergent Self-Organisation: Reconceptualising Child Development in Teacher Education." *Australian Journal of Teacher Education* 35 (4): 79–98.

Lakoff, George, and Mark Johnson. 1999. *Philosophy in the Flesh: The Embodied Mind and its Challenge to Western Thoughts*. New York: Basic Books.

Libet, Benjamin, Curtis A. Gleason, Elwood W. Wright, and Dennis K. Pearl. 1983. "Time of Conscious Intention to Act in Relation to Onset of Cerebral Activity (Readiness-Potential): The Unconscious Initiation of a Freely Voluntary Act." *Brain* 107 (Pt 3): 623–642.

Linfield, M., Producer. 2004. *Capuchins: The Monkey Puzzle*. London: BBC One.

McGuire, J., and Rattansi P. 1966. "Newton and the 'Pipes of Pan.'" *Notes and Records of the Royal Society of London* 21 (2): 108–143.

Mudge, Peter, Daniel Fleming, and Terence Lovat. 2014. "The Potential Impact of the Neurosciences on Religious and Spiritual Education: Ramifying from the Impact on Values Education." *Journal of Beliefs & Values: Studies in Religion & Education* 35 (2): 144–154.

Narvaez, Darcia, and Jenny L. Vaydich. 2008. "Moral Development and Behaviour Under the Spotlight of the Neurobiological Sciences." *Journal of Moral Education* 37 (3): 289–312.

Noë, Alva. 2004. *Action in Perception*. Cambridge, MA: MIT Press.

Polanyi, Michael. 1966/1983. *The Tacit Dimension*. Gloucester, MA: Peter Smith.

Popper, Kark. 1963. *Conjectures and Refutations: The Growth of Scientific Knowledge*. London: Routledge and Kegan Paul.

Prigogine, Ilya. 1997. *The End of Certainty: Time, Chaos, and the New Laws of Nature*. New York: Free Press.

Quine, W.V.O., and J.S. Ullian. 1970. *The Web of Belief*. New York: Random House.

Sankey, Derek. 2006. "The Neuronal, Synaptic Self: Having Values and Making Choices." *Journal of Moral Education* 35 (2): 27–42.

Sankey, Derek. 2011. "Future Horizons: Moral Learning and the Socially Embedded Synaptic Self." *Journal of Moral Education* 40 (3): 417–425.

Sankey, Derek ,and Minkang Kim. 2013. "A Dynamic Systems Approach to Moral and Spiritual Development." In *The Routledge International Handbook of Education, Religion and Values*, edited by James Arthur and Terence Lovat, 182–193. Oxon, UK: Routledge.

Soon, Chun S., Marcel Brass, Hans-Jochen Heinze, and John-Dylan Haynes. 2008. "Unconscious Determinants of Free Decisions in the Human Brain." *Nature Neuroscience* 11 (5): 543–545.

Soon, Chun S., Anna H. He, Stefan Bode, and John-Dylan Haynes. 2013. "Predicting Free Choices for Abstract Intentions." *Proceedings of the National Academy of Sciences* 110 (15): 6217–6222.

Thelen, Esther, and Linda B. Smith. 1994. *A Dynamic Systems Approach to the Development of Cognition and Action*. Cambridge, MA: MIT Press.

Woodward, James, and John Allman. 2007. "Moral Intuition: Its Neural Substrates and Normative Significance." *Journal of Physiology—Paris* 101: 179–202.

8 Naturalizing Aesthetics
Moderate Formalism and Global Education[1]

Pradeep A. Dhillon

In thinking about representation, philosophers of art have grown increasingly skeptical of the theory of mimetic representation and have begun to rely almost exclusively on conventionalism. This theoretical turn of events poses a challenge to the growing need for cosmopolitan aesthetic education, one that seeks to educate toward appreciating artworks from cultures, traditions, and historical periods other than our own. Specifically, the particularistic theories that undergird much of contemporary art history and education restrict aesthetic education in the task of encouraging intellectual curiosity about, and engagement with, unfamiliar cultural practices. These theories all too often obscure our ability to recognize shared histories and cognitive abilities, thus barring possible avenues for educating toward global citizenship. I suggest that a re-consideration of the formalism that has defined much of modern art would be useful in several ways. It would help us discover natural and historical affinities among aesthetic vocabularies across cultural traditions and historical periods, and it would help us to break out of the impasses between mimesis and conventionalism and between universalism and relativism, which currently impede educational practice.

I suggest that we could turn with some profit to a moderate formalism as proposed by the philosopher Nick Zangwill, and also to recent developments in neuroscience, in order to develop a way of educating students toward reading images more generally and toward reading images across cultures, historical periods, and various domains of knowledge, including various branches of the sciences, geography, and so on (Dhillon 2013; Zangwill 2001). In this paper, I will focus on the implications that such a turn would have for global education and, more specifically, for the related issues of curatorial practices and the writing of art history. These issues largely shape the ways in which we encounter art in both formal and non-formal educational texts.

As has often been pointed out, much of philosophical aesthetics following Hegel collapsed the field of aesthetics into the philosophy of art. However, earlier philosophers such as Alexander Baumgarten and Immanuel Kant maintained a distinction between aesthetics and art (Dhillon 2009). To hold this distinction is to blur the divide between art images and other images, including scientific ones. That is, what are taken to be images within the domain we call 'art' should be considered a subset within the domain of images in general (Elkins 2001). More recently, neuroscientists such as V. R. Ramachandran, Semir Zeki, Margaret Livingstone, and others have taken the lead in attempting to naturalize theories of aesthetics, thus further blurring the distinction between art and science (Ramachandran and Hirstein 1999).

Zangwill's moderate formalism seeks to characterize his theory in terms of aesthetic/non-aesthetic *determination*. If something has aesthetic properties, he argues, it is in virtue of those properties' supervenience on certain non-aesthetic properties. But, we might well ask, which non-aesthetic properties are potentially aesthetically relevant? I propose, drawing on developments in the neuroscience of vision, and in line with what Zeki calls neuro-aesthetics, that formal properties—lines, shapes, and colors—might be biologically determined, and I suggest that a focus on these properties leads one back to moderate formalism in the appreciation of artworks. This return to moderate formalism, I would argue, helps us not only answer the question of which non-aesthetic properties might be aesthetically relevant, but it also enables us to engage with artworks from cultures and historical periods other than our own.

In a recent debate on how important science is for understanding art, Roger Seamon and William Seeley agree on one fundamental point. Seeley describes their point of agreement as follows:

> I agree with (nearly) everything that Roger Seamon says about the general relationship between art and science. If I understand it correctly, the claim is that an understanding of the science of art is not necessary for an understanding of art, and what science does have to add isn't of much use in understanding the expressive and evaluative practices of artists and consumers.
>
> (2011)

Expressing a conventionalist approach to the appreciation and evaluation of artworks, Seeley goes on to say,

> Here all one needs to do is dive in and learn the conventions constitutive of the artistic practices of his or her community. One might ask art historians and critics to help get started, they are after all the experts who really know about the ways these conventions sort out. But it's unlikely a psychologist could help.
>
> (2013)

It is on this final point that my disagreement with these philosophers turns. I question the almost dogmatic reliance on conventionalism that drives most aesthetic discourse and therefore limits our appreciation of the productive role that science can play in our considerations of aesthetic and artistic merit. John Hyman (2010), the philosopher who has offered the most strenuous critique of neuro-aesthetics to date, remains sympathetic to the potential value of science to the understanding of art, albeit not of the variety served up by either Ramachandran or Zeki. Anticipating the charge of reductionism that might be leveled against the use of science in understanding art, Hyman says, "I do not believe that modern science drains enchantment from the world. In my view, explaining complex phenomena in terms of simple mechanisms, or explaining a variety of phenomena in terms of a single mechanism, is a good thing" (2010, 262). Hyman remains skeptical, however, as to the particulars that such an epistemological approach would yield. In his words,

> Neuroscience can explain some features of some paintings. For example, some of the color effects of impressionist paintings are explained by lateral inhibition. But the idea that there is a neurological theory of art in prospect is utterly implausible, in my view.
>
> (Hyman 2010, 262)

In other words, philosophers are intrigued by the possibilities offered by the recent turn to the sciences, particularly biology, neuroscience, and psychology, for establishing aesthetic merit, but these philosophers are not clear as to exactly what form such a possibility would take (Konenici 2012). This view is one that I share. I hold that science can assist in the evaluation and appreciation of artworks as long as we do not, like Zeki and Ramachandran, seek to provide a comprehensive theory of art. Rather, we can turn to science, particularly neuroscience, in order to address specific issues and problems in aesthetics. Thus, for example, we could turn to neuroscience when adjudicating between specific philosophical theories such as theories of pictorial depiction (Dhillon 2006).

In this paper, I argue that we can turn with profit to science in the evaluation of previously un-encountered artworks when we cannot rely on learned conventions to help engage these artworks. The artworks to which I refer are those that belong to a culture, or are from a time, with which we are relatively unfamiliar. My new approach, which relies on images from Western, Indian, and East African modern art, is not reductive, but rather is productive in the spirit of the Kantian sublime. My research makes us aware of our limits and yet guides us toward a felt sense of the cognitive structures that all humans share, even as we reflect on the dizzying array of images present in the world. Such reflection yields respect for the creative endeavors of peoples everywhere, even as it inspires admiration for our human capacities. In Kant's words, as he contrasts the pleasure in the beautiful and the sublime, "The satisfaction of the sublime does not so much contain positive pleasure as it does admiration or respect, i.e., it deserves to be called negative pleasure" (Kant [1790] 2001, 129). Optimistically speaking, the presentation of artworks from unfamiliar cultures should create aesthetic possibilities for educating students toward the global democratic ethos that is required of us today (Lyotard 1994).

The concept of the Kantian sublime in relation to engagement with artworks from different cultures and time periods takes us beyond Western/ non-Western dichotomies and art-historical discourses of contestation to make possible art histories and museum practices that could promote new— and more just—conversations among and about artworks from around the world. It is important to note that while this essay draws on examples from art worlds of national and global significance, this approach also serves to break down the dichotomies between high and low art and between *art* images and images more generally, and it illuminates the relationships among images from different historical periods within a single tradition (Elkins 2001).

In making the case for the value of naturalizing the reading of images, particularly those from other cultures and times, I first turn to the concept of 'supervenience,' which I construe as relating particular non-aesthetic states of affairs to those bearing aesthetic attributes. More specifically, we can rely on philosopher Marcia Mueldzer Eaton's discussion of supervenience, in order to ask:

1. What is the relation between ascribing aesthetic properties to something and ascribing non-aesthetic properties to that thing?
2. How are aesthetic properties related to non-aesthetic properties?
3. How are non-aesthetic properties used to justify aesthetic judgments?
4. How can one show that aesthetic properties are real?
5. How can judgments that are subjective play a role in objective language games?

(Eaton 1994)

The second and fifth questions lie at the heart of this essay. Neuroscience provides us with a fairly satisfactory answer to the second question, and this answer, in turn, guides us toward productive possibilities for thinking about the last question in non-conventionalist ways at the world- and trans-historical levels.

I follow Zangwill in taking formal aesthetic properties as supervening on arrangements of non-aesthetic properties such as lines, shapes, and colors. I take non-formal properties, by contrast, to be those determined by the history and context of the work of art. In other words, formal properties in an artwork are entirely determined by narrow non-aesthetic properties, whereas non-formal aesthetic properties are largely determined by broad non-aesthetic properties.

In the extreme formalist view, all of an artwork's properties that bear aesthetic value are formal, and they are narrowly determined. In the anti-formalist position, however, none of the value-bearing properties of an artwork are formal, and they are all broadly determined. Finally, in moderate formalism, some aesthetic properties are formal, while others are not. In other words, there is good reason to criticize Clive Bell and Roger Fry, who strenuously argued for privileging formal properties over all other aspects of an artwork, for ignoring representation in painting and playing down the social and historical importance of specific paintings. Bell and Fry were wrong, from the moderate formalist's point of view, in claiming that to appreciate a work of art, we need to bring with us nothing but a sense of form and color and knowledge of three-dimensional space—the artwork's formal properties. Bell and Fry were right, however, to note the importance of form, which has admittedly fallen by the wayside under the increasing influence of conventionalist approaches. It is in the context of this debate between strict formalism in art appreciation and education on the one hand and a rejection of formalism entirely on the other that the turn to a moderate formalism, particularly from a global perspective, promises a strong alternative.

When it comes to the appreciation of global, particularly modern, art, I argue that a moderate formalist approach goes a long way toward enabling us to write a fairer and more comprehensive art history (Dhillon 2014). Such an approach can be expected to impact museum curatorship, art scholarship, and education. Following this new approach, we would no longer display, view, and understand non-Western modern art solely in particularistic cultural and historical terms under the rubric of 'ethnic' art; rather, in keeping with these global times, we would take such art as robust, albeit local, expressions of art vocabularies that were developed no doubt in Europe but were taken up, and came to be realized, in interesting and creative ways around the world. Increasingly, taking such a view enables us to see with greater historical clarity the non-Western influences that are present in European art and architecture (Ives 2000). Furthermore, from a biological standpoint, taking a moderate formalist view of art enables us to see stable patterns of representation across cultural periods and historical traditions, thus allowing for alternative temporal and spatial aesthetic juxtapositions and deepening our understanding of representation. No doubt such aesthetic explorations would not provide the rich readings of artworks that more situated art histories can afford, but they would give us new ways of looking at familiar and unfamiliar artworks and would profitably challenge some basic assumptions regarding contemporary art historical discourse.

Historically, as in the context of India's struggle for independence from Britain, artists eagerly embraced European formalism, as it allowed them to produce artworks that carried the mark of a revolutionary nationalism as well as internationalism. As Amrita Sher-Gil—who was trained at the Ecole des Beaux-Artes in Paris and was in the 1930s a three-time winner of the gold medal at the Grand Salon—said upon her return to India in 1934,

> I am an individualist, evolving a new technique, which, though not necessarily Indian in the traditional sense of the word, will yet be fundamentally Indian in spirit. With the eternal significance of form and color

I interpret India and, principally, the life of the Indian poor on the plane that transcends that of mere sentimental interest.

> (Cited in Dalmia 2006, 200; see also Sundaram 1972)

In a similar vein, S. H. Raza, a member of the Progressive group seeking to break out of the British academic realism taught in the art schools in India prior to independence in 1947, said,

> The real common denominator for us (the progressives) was significant form. We were expressing ourselves differently, we had different visions during the early days, but what was common was a search for significant form—each in his own way, according to his own vision. In a painted work, howsoever different it may be, say, for example, Modigliani and Soutine, who both painted nudes, the approach, the vision is different, the sensibility is different, the way in which paint is applied is different and, of course, the temperament of the two artists is different. But the common denominator is form.
>
> (Dalmia and Hashmi 2007, 134)

The Progressives' focus on form allowed painter Jamini Roy, another member of the group, to seek inspiration in Bengali folk art, with its strong reliance on line and color. In Roy's modernist paintings, we certainly see him using this emphasis on form to locate himself as an artist within the international and revolutionary nationalist contexts, but we also see him using form to make common cause with the rural poor.

What we have here, in the production of an artwork that is both local and global, is a critical embrace of formalism—which is seen as universal—along with the particularity of the national and local subject matter that it is deployed to represent. Amrita Sher-Gil's claim, quoted earlier, goes beyond making historical connections between the modern art of Gauguin and van Gogh that influenced her work in Europe and in India. She makes the deeper, even universal connection when she speaks of the "eternal significance" of form and color. It is her awareness of form and color that lead her to famously exclaim, upon seeing the frescoes of Ajanta and Ellora in September 1934,

> Modern art has led me to the comprehension and appreciation of Indian painting and sculpture. It seems paradoxical but I know for certain that had we not come away to Europe, I should perhaps never have realized that a fresco from Ajanta or a small piece of sculpture in the Musee Guimet is worth more than a whole Renaissance.
>
> (Bethlanfalvy 2011)

No doubt Sher-Gil overstates her case, but her declaration nevertheless points to how formalism, the hallmark of modern art, can guide us in appreciating artworks that belong not only to different cultures but also to different historical periods. The critical spirit that informed her paintings breaks her away from a 'situated' art history to make possible one that can inform aesthetic judgments in a non-hegemonic manner, not only between cultures but also within traditions. In breaking away, she challenges dominant discursive regimes of viewing. These regimes are now more strongly present than ever before, given the influence of post-structural art theories, which focus on fine-grained historical and cultural descriptions to such an extent that it often becomes impossible even to raise questions about whether one can make aesthetic judgments about artworks that lie beyond the borders of the specific period and culture to which an artwork belongs. In the bid to build a theory that goes beyond such narrowly circumscribed locations of inquiry, it is important to make a distinction between aesthetics and art. The former bears epistemological entailments, and the latter is the object of inquiry. As I have discussed earlier, the two are certainly related, but they are not the same (Dhillon 2009).

Following Nick Zangwill, let us make a further distinction between *verdictive* and *substantive* judgments. We take verdictive judgments to be those judgments that allow us to say that certain artworks or objects are beautiful or ugly. That is, we make aesthetic judgments regarding their beauty or lack of it. Such judgments enable us to say whether artworks possess aesthetic merit or value. But we also judge artworks or other objects as being 'dainty' or 'dumpy,' in Austin's words, or 'graceful,' 'garish,' 'balanced,' 'warm,' 'passionate,' 'brooding,' 'awkward,' or 'sad.' These assessments are to be called *substantive* judgments. The role of substantive aesthetic descriptions is to pick out properties that determine aesthetic merit or beauty. In Zangwill's words, "They stand midway between the earth of non-aesthetic properties and the heaven of beauty." In other words, Zangwill strongly argues that aesthetic merit is supervenient on non-aesthetic properties (2001).

Some philosophers, such as Kendall Walton and Jerrold Levinson, hold that aesthetic merit is hardly, if at all, derived from narrow aesthetic properties; rather, aesthetic merit derives mainly from the broad properties of artworks within the context of the history of their production. For example, Byzantine and Roman mosaics do not differ in terms of their narrow aesthetic properties, but they do differ in terms of their broad historical properties. Arthur Danto, for example, taking a Hegelian line of argumentation goes so far as to insist that all peoples without an art history of the kind established within Europe, and the United States, since the eighteenth century are denied the notion of art entirely (Belting 2003). What Levinson and Walton miss, along with others who focus primarily on the broad properties of artworks, is the similarity of aesthetic experiences that artworks with shared non-aesthetic properties can afford. While such attention to broad aesthetic properties is certainly important, as post-structural theories have so adequately demonstrated, this focus on broad aesthetic properties does not negate the importance of narrow aesthetic properties. It merely indicates that aesthetic value is tied to narrow as well as broad aesthetic properties derived from historical and cultural contexts. The implication is that we need to broaden the base of the properties on which aesthetic merit supervenes.

On the metaphysical view, we take supervenience to be a relation between two families of properties. The supervenience claim is that if something has an aesthetic property, then that aesthetic property is based on some non-aesthetic property. Regarding the epistemic status of supervenience, we could say that it is pretty austere as a source of knowledge; nevertheless, it does carry some epistemological weight. First, if we know that something has a non-aesthetic property and also that it has some aesthetic property and that its having the aesthetic property supervenes upon its having the non-aesthetic property, given our knowledge that something else has the same non-aesthetic property, we can infer that the second object shares the same aesthetic property. Thus, for example, while Roman and Byzantine mosaics are different in terms of their broad aesthetic properties, they both afford us a similar aesthetic experience.

This line of argument provides warrant for the recent turn to neuroscience in aesthetics. The work of neuroscientists such as Semir Zeki reminds us that certain lines and colors (and their spatial relations) are more salient than others in the construction and appreciation of artworks; the salience of a given feature depends upon how it correlates with neurophysiological processes within the visual cortex. According to Zeki, the example of Mondrian correlates well with the findings of the scientists David Hubel and Torsten Wiesel in 1959. Mondrian insisted that art demonstrates constant truths concerning forms, and he eventually focused on the straight line and the specificity of its orientation within the pictorial plane as the most foundational of visual forms (Zeki 2000, 112). Hubel and Wiesel made the groundbreaking discovery that a large group of cells responded selectively to lines of specific orientation within the visual brain.

Although Zeki tells us that neuroscience is still far from definitively demonstrating how we build complex forms, it is fair to say that neuroscientists and artists have come to see lines and their orientation as the basic building blocks of visual processing and representation. In Zeki's (2000) words,

> What we can say with certainty is that, when we view one of Mondrian's abstract paintings in which the emphasis is on lines, or we view some of the paintings of Malevich, or Rozanova or Barnett Newman, large numbers of cells in charted visual areas of our brains will be activated and will be responding vigorously, provided a line of a given orientation falls on the part of the visual field that a cell with a preference for that orientation "looks at." . . . [Furthermore,] what is certain is that if such cells are lost by not being adequately visually nourished during the critical period or as consequence of lesions in the brain produced by

vascular or other damage, no experience, aesthetic or otherwise, of the work of Mondrian and others in which lines are emphasized, is possible.
(114–115)

While this correlation between specific artworks and neuroscientific findings does not provide us with an explanation for why a person would have an aesthetic experience, nor does it enable us to make systematic distinctions between artistic and non-artistic images, it does validate our turn to supervenience and moderate formalism in the appreciation of art. Taking these building blocks of form to be biologically determined leads us to possibilities of aesthetic appreciation that extend beyond artworks that belong to a specific historical period and culture.

In other words, these and other developments in cognitive neuroscience and visual neuro-processing go some way toward providing us with a clearer sense of the necessary epistemological dependencies that we seek. Just because we cannot yet point with precision to all the determinate relations between non-aesthetic and aesthetic properties does not mean that we must give up on the existence of such a relation and its consequences for aesthetic merit, even beauty. Furthermore, because these basic neural processes are shared, we could expect to find patterns of representation and affinities for such patterns across traditions.

However, as I have already pointed out, aesthetic formalism has fallen on hard times. At best, it receives unsympathetic discussion and swift rejection. At worst, it is the object of abuse and derision. Zangwill, as I have shown, defends formalism, but does so by articulating a moderate formalist view. Drawing on Kant's distinction between free beauty and dependent beauty, he characterizes formalism in terms of aesthetic/non-aesthetic *determination*. Kant's view is that dependent beauty involves a concept of an end or purpose, while free beauty does not. Although Kant is satisfied by this distinction between two kinds of beauty, it is not enough for us. In order for the argument to be compelling, the theory needs to be grounded in the materialist conditions of the body. If something has aesthetic properties, then it has them in virtue of the conjunction of non-aesthetic properties. But which non-aesthetic properties are aesthetically relevant? It is at this question that the issue of formalism, and by extension free beauty, should be located.

What, we might now ask, are non-formal aesthetic properties? It is not enough to say that a thing's non-formal aesthetic properties are aesthetic properties that are not determined by its narrow non-aesthetic properties and that are determined in part by facts about its history of production. The very question, 'What are non-formal aesthetic properties?' raises the worry that certain facts may be more relevant than others within a specific historical or cultural context. Contexts are both dense and indeterminate; in other words, contexts are dense in terms of content and have boundaries that are determined by the context of the question that is being asked. Yet when art historians and critics favor broad aesthetic properties, they neither specify the non-formal properties that warrant attention nor determine the boundaries of the context in question.

Perhaps it is because we have not yet asked these questions that we think that artworks are to be taken either in terms of formal properties alone or in terms of their broad cultural and historical properties. Recasting Kant's distinction between free and dependent beauty in light of this discussion of aesthetic properties, we no longer say that a thing is dependently beautiful because it executes some function in being beautiful. Rather, we say the thing is dependently beautiful because the thing constitutes the proper aesthetic representation for some aesthetic purpose. In this new view, a work of art has non-formal aesthetic properties because of the way the work realizes some historically given, non-aesthetic social, political, or moral function. Formal properties, on the other hand, do not depend on whether the thing has some non-aesthetic function. As neuroscience tells us, however, formal properties do serve to ground non-formal aesthetic properties. Thus the question we would need to address in future research is the following: what is the precise nature of the relationship between non-aesthetic formal properties and non-formal aesthetic properties?

To argue for a moderate formalism by turning to neuroscience is not to uncritically extrapolate from the modest but groundbreaking findings of neuroscientists. First, as a philosopher of education who is writing about global art, I am certainly not equipped with the knowledge to make such an argument. What I can do, however, is take the findings of which neuroscientists are certain and demonstrate how the findings might address issues that are central to the fields of philosophy of art and philosophical aesthetics. As neuroscientists themselves tell us, they are very far from explaining how basic visual processes combine to form larger visual units, much less can they tell us how those forms afford us aesthetic experiences. Furthermore, according to Zeki and other neuroscientists, the majority of experimental results in neuroscience, particularly in the case of electrophysiology, are highly controversial. This controversy is due to the inherent difficulty of brain experimentation (even more so when humans are involved), and the lack of a comprehensive neuroscientific theory to organize our scattered knowledge. Needless to say, any theory that emanates from or is supported by these tentative results ought to be considered as merely a speculative framework, remaining far from achieving the predictability of Popperian refutability that is usually required in other biology fields and in physics.

There are a few, very few, outstanding exceptions to the tentative nature of most neuroscientific findings, and they fall particularly in the realm of visual processing. Chief among these exceptions are Hodgkin–Huxley's classic work on the theory of the action potential (quite far from a theory of the mind), and Attick and Redlich's work (1992) on a first-principles derivation of the filter characteristic of retinal ganglion cells (in the periphery of the sensory system). The Receptive Field Theory on which so much of Zeki's discussion of art and neuroscience relies, as well as the theory's derivative, the Brain Modularity Theory, are not among these exceptions.[2] Nevertheless, theories of visual processing rely mostly on the exceptional experimental work of Hubel and Wiesel (1959), which shows that neurons in the primary visual cortex tend to respond strongly to very specific 'visual features' such as the presence of an edge or dash—our non-aesthetic properties—with a specific orientation in a specific location of the visual field (148). Hubel and Wiesel's findings opened the door to a number of subsequent experimental results that showed the existence of neurons that were adaptive for other, more abstract and complex visual features in different cortical areas, such as the selective response to faces anywhere in the receptive field in the infero-temporal cortex of primates. These results, in turn, led Huber and Wiesel to the conclusion that the different visual cortical areas have very specialized functions along an implicitly feed-forward pipeline of feature-extraction: first detect edges, then outlines, then color, then basic shapes, then more complex shapes, and so on until . . . well, somehow magic happens and we experience 'visual recognition.'

Here we must pause to address an additional level of complexity. Not only do we now know the 'primitives' or non-aesthetic properties on which aesthetic properties might supervene, but we also have some idea as to how non-aesthetic properties are implicated to form the complex visual representations that we call art. In other words, neuroscience gives us some insight into the ways in which different kinds of non-aesthetic properties are related to aesthetic properties, and neuroscience also gives us ways in which these aesthetic properties of a work are themselves often appropriate to other aesthetic properties of a work (and are intended to be). For example, the dependent aesthetic properties determined by a representation in a painting might fit snugly with the aesthetic properties determined by the two-dimensional design in which the representation is realized. That is, different narrow non-aesthetic properties can combine, where it is appropriate to the demands of broad aesthetic properties, to determine further aesthetic properties of the whole. Moderate formalism as articulated by Zangwill then pays attention to both narrow and broad properties, as well as to the relation between aesthetic and non-aesthetic properties. Relying as it does on the Kantian distinction between free beauty and dependent beauty, moderate formalism overcomes the extremes of both formalist and anti-formalist aesthetic theories.

The concept of moderate formalism has profound significance for discussions of critical approaches to museums, curatorship, museum education, and the use of aesthetics in global education more generally. At the very least, the turn to moderate formalism opens up possibilities for global art curatorial practices and for thinking of museums as sites of non-formal education. Thus, taking this approach, we might be motivated to bring together Cezanne's *Mont Sainte-Victoire* and an eighteenth-century Kangra painting from the Indian miniature tradition because they both use similar representational devices to signify distance on a two-dimensional pictorial space.

The psychologist and philosopher Maurice Merleau-Ponty was one of the earliest scholars to recognize the connection between our mental processes and art, relating art and science while keeping them distinct. For example, in his essay "Cezanne's Doubt," Merleau-Ponty (2007) discusses the contrast between lived perspective and geometric perspectivalism, arguing that Cezanne was an epistemologist because his paintings reflected an effort to know how we see and experience perspective and represent this knowledge on two-dimensional pictorial planes. As Merleau-Ponty shows, Cezanne anticipated the Gestalt psychologists in discovering, among other findings, that objects close at hand appear larger than those far away, that a circle seen obliquely oscillates around an ellipse, that a geometric outline is the limit to which an object recedes in depth, and that depth itself is inexhaustible. But if we look at Kangra paintings from the eighteenth century, we see similar visual strategies at play in the representation of distance and depth.

In his book *Writing Art History,* the philosopher and art critic David Carrier (2003) tells us that curatorial practices correspond with regimes of art history. Our existing curatorial practices, tightly linked as they are to the writing of art history, do not allow us to display *Mont Sainte-Victoire* and the Kangra painting together and marvel at the similarities of the patterns of representations in Impressionist paintings and the Kangra school of miniatures. Nor do they allow us to see that such strategies of pictorial depiction are also reflected in the works of the unschooled artist Grandma Moses, as, for example in her *Country Fair* (1950), as well as in a Tamilian child's painting of the 'troubles' in Sri Lanka in the 1990s. Seeing these stable forms of representation across cultures and historical periods inspires awe.

We might be just as likely to stand back in admiration and respect—to experience the Kantian sublime—at the resonance between the Tanzanian artist George Lilanga's *Ukifka Mjini Kila Mtu Na Lake* (1997) and Jackson Pollock's *Mural* (1943) when we engage them together at the level of similarity of form. Such curatorial practice would educate us into new ways of seeing and lead to recognition of our shared cognitive capacities as well as appreciation of our cultural differences. The practice would free us from having to choose between universalism and relativism, from having to decide between the local and the global, and from having to see stylistic borrowings in terms of originals and derivatives. Furthermore, such an appreciation could serve to encourage a lover of Western art to inquire into the broad historical properties of the work of non-Western artists such as, for example, George Lillanga. The approach would enable him or her to note that Lillanga's cartoon-like figures are the representations of the 'mshatani'—the devils that, in the view of the Makonde tribe of Tanzania, inhabit our mental and social worlds and entice us to moral misfortune. As for the Tanzanian artists, art publics, and cultural theorists, such juxtaposition would help them to situate their work in a manner that goes beyond narrow local and regional boundaries. Thus we could open up new, global educational spaces for intercultural and international communication. In other words, such juxtapositions should break down the distinction between self and other, interrupt the perpetuation of the cult of exoticism, and bring us face-to-face with our shared humanity. These juxtapositions should also pique our interest in the broad properties of an artwork that puzzle us and should encourage the study of distant others.

Curatorial practices that encourage such juxtapositions encourage new ways of seeing. That there is a need for such a turn to a historical—aesthetic—response to paintings is reflected in the recent efforts by many museums to provide such viewing possibilities by mounting exhibits based on themes rather than on art-historical relationships. For example, the curators of the Musée d'Orsay's exhibit *Nocturnes* explain that

> This display aims to shake up the sacrosanct classifications of traditional art history. In fact, in the centre of the Symbolist gallery, *Nocturnes* presents a dialogue between works of art that stylistic cross-referencing has usually kept apart. By bringing together in this way and without any contextualization, works that are, on the face of it, as dissimilar as Manet's *Clair de lune sur le port de Boulogne* (1893), and Alexander Harrison's *Solitude* (1893), for example, we hope to move outside the intellectual framework that determines the way we see art, in order to approach it more openly.
>
> (2012)

In other words, these exploratory museum displays educate us in new ways of seeing. These ways of seeing involve focusing on perception and on the formal properties of paintings rather than burying oneself under the weighty details of national and regional art histories. Such displays yield another important educational benefit: the simultaneous display of artworks from different cultures and traditions from the point of view of moderate formalism. Many of the rich artistic traditions around the world have yet to write their own art histories, because such writing has often been either entirely interrupted by colonial practices or marginalized and subordinated through related epistemological commitments. In other words, the new curatorial practices that I am suggesting here provide opportunities to link aesthetics to global justice in terms of cultural production and appreciation. This approach will facilitate the writing of a global art history that does not place traditions within a historical schema of cultural progress. Kant, calling for moral awareness and historical responsibility regarding "the burden of history" that we bear for future descendants, wrote,

> No doubt they [future generations] will value the history of the oldest times, of which the original documents would long have vanished, only from the point of view of what interests them, i.e. the positive and negative achievements of nations and governments in relation to

the cosmopolitan goal . . . and this may provide us with another small motive for attempting a philosophical history of this kind.

([1784] 1991 53)

One might argue that no matter how laudable the goal, such juxtaposition of artworks from around the world is feasible only when we are drawing on the holdings of a single museum, such as the d'Orsay—that it is far less possible when we must draw on the holdings of various museums around the world. Such an effort would indeed be challenging because of the enormous cost, in terms of time and money, of bringing paintings together to curate such an exhibit, not to mention the bewildering array of artworks to choose from within the global context. Nevertheless, such exhibits can certainly be mounted using the Internet and digital technology, and they can easily be displayed in smart classrooms. Because most major museums have quite sophisticated websites, it should also be relatively easy and inexpensive for museum educators and classroom teachers to curate virtual exhibitions that startle us into an awareness of our shared humanity and spark an interest in the norms that guide the lives of distant others. Admittedly, cost is not the only inhibitor to the mounting of such global exhibits. They are also difficult to curate because dominant art history demands that when such an exhibit is put together, the images must be drawn from artworks that are represented within specific art histories. As I have mentioned, many of these art histories have yet to be written. More importantly, museums and other agents in the art world have yet to develop the global art theories to undergird such curatorial practices (Dhillon 2014). Globalization demands a rethinking of the existing practices of scholarship, curation, and education.

In sum, while neuroscience is far from explaining why paintings move us to tears, it is quite up to the task of suggesting, philosophically, that we ought to return to a moderate formalism that is grounded in our biology. Such a development—a new way of reading images through naturalized aesthetics—suggests that we are at an exciting moment of developing a more level approach to aesthetic and art education, one that reminds us of our shared humanity even as we continue to appreciate the particularities that make for specific cultural practices and traditions. In adapting this new way of reading images, we can use aesthetics to create possibilities for educating toward a greater awareness of previously disparate worlds that are steadily being integrated into a global system.

NOTES

1. I wish to express gratitude to Ivan Gaskell, Vladimir Konecni, and Roman Frigg, who provided both encouragement and valuable criticisms at various stages of this paper.
2. I am grateful to an anonymous reviewer for these comments.

REFERENCES

Attick, Joseph J., and A. Norman Redlich. 1992. "What Does The Retina Know About Natural Scenes?" *Neural Computation* 4 (2): 196–210.

Belting, Hans. 2003. *Art History After Modernism*, translated by Hans Belting, Mitch Cohen, and Kenneth J. Northcott. Chicago: University of Chicago Press.

Bethlanfalvy, Geza. 2011. "Amrita Sher-Gil: A Painter of Two Continents." *The Hungarian Quarterly* LII 201: 87–98.

Carrier, David. 2003. *Writing About Visual Art*. New York: Allsworth Press.

Dalmia, Yashodhara. 2006. *Amrita Sher-Gil: A Life*. New Delhi: Penguin Press.

Dalmia, Yashodhara, and Salima Hashmi. 2007. *Memory, Metaphor, and Mutations: The Contemporary Art of India and Pakistan*. New Delhi: Oxford University Press.

Dhillon, Pradeep. 2006. "Pictorial Depiction: Letting Neuroscience Say Something to Nelson Goodman." Unpublished paper presented at the Conference *Beyond Mimesis and Convention: Representation in Art and Science*, June 22–23, 2006, London School of Economics, London, UK.

Dhillon, Pradeep. 2009. "Aesthetic Education." In *A Companion to Aesthetics* (Blackwell Companion to Aesthetics) (2nd ed.), edited by Stephen Davies, Kathleen Marie Higgins, Robert Hopkins, Robert Stecker, and David E. Cooper, 114–117. Oxford: Wiley-Blackwell.

Dhillon, Pradeep. 2013. "A Kantian Approach to Global Art History: The Case from Indian Modern Art." In The Many Faces of Beauty, edited by Vittorio Hösle, 302–326. Notre Dame, IN: University of Notre Dame Press.

Dhillon, Pradeep. 2014. "Thinking in Pictures: A Kantian Reading of Amrita Sher-Gil's Self-Portrait as Tahitian." In Women's Eye, Women's Hand: Making Modern Art and Architecture in India, edited by D.F. Ruggles, 163–183. New Delhi: Zuban Press.

Eaton, M.M. 1994. "The Intrinsic Non-Supervenient Nature of Aesthetic Properties." *The Journal of Aesthetics and Art Criticism* 52 (4): 383–397.

Elkins, James. 2001. *Domain of Images*. Ithaca, NY: Cornell University Press.

Hyman, John. 2010. "Art and Neuroscience." Reprinted. In *Beyond Mimesis and Convention: Representation in Art and Science*, edited by R.P. Frigg and M. Hunter. Boston Studies in the Philosophy of Science, 245–262. New York: Springer.

Hubel, David H., and Torsten N. Wiesel. 1959. "Receptive Fields of Single Neurons in the Cat's Striate Cortex." *Journal of Physiology* 148 (3): 574–591.

Ives, Colta. 2000. "Japonisme," in *Heilbrunn Timeline of Art History* New York: The Metropolitan Museum of Metropolitan Art. Retrieved from http://www.metmuseum.org/toah/hd/jpon/hd_jpon.html (October 2004).

Kant, Immanuel. [1784] 1991. *Kant: Political Writings*, edited by H.S Reis and translated by H.B. Nisbet. Cambridge, UK: Cambridge University Press.

Kant, Immanuel. [1790] 2001. *Critique of the Power of Judgment*, translated by Paul Guyer and Eric Mathews. Cambridge, UK: Cambridge University Press.

Konenici, Vladimir. 2012. "Empirical Psycho-Aesthetic and Her Sisters, Part 1: Substantive and Methodological Issues Part 1." *Journal of Aesthetic Education* 46 (4): 1–12.

Lyotard, Jean-Francois. 1994. *Lessons on the Analytic of the Sublime*. Stanford: Stanford University Press.

Merleau-Ponty, M. 2007. "Cezanne's Doubt." In *The Merleau-Ponty Reader*, edited by Ted Toadvine and Leonard Lawlor, 69–84. Evanston, IL: Northwestern University Press.

Ramachandran, Vilayanur R., and William Hirstein. 1999. "The Science of Art: A Neurological Theory of Aesthetic Experience." *Journal of Consciousness Studies* 6 (6/7): 15–51.

Seeley, William P. 2011. "The Science of Art Is as Relevant to the Philosophy of Art as Artistic Representations Are to Science: A Reply to Roger Seamon." *American Society for Aesthetics*. Retrieved from http://www.aesthetics-online.org/articles/index.php?articles_id=61.

Seeley, William P. 2013. "Art, Meaning, and Perception: A Question of Methods for a Cognitive Neuroscience of Art." *British Journal of Aesthetics* 53 (4): 443–460.

Sundaram, Vivan. 1972. *Amrita Sher-Gil: Essays*. New Delhi: Marg Publishers.

Zangwill, Nick. 2001. *The Metaphysics of Beauty*. Ithaca: Cornell University Press.

Zeki, Semir. 2000. *Inner Vision*. Oxford: Oxford University Press.

9 Exploding Brains
Beyond the Spontaneous Philosophy of Brain-Based Learning

Tyson E. Lewis

In the lecture titled "Philosophy and the Spontaneous Philosophy of the Scientist," Louis Althusser inquired into the relationship between philosophy and science. Without going into great detail concerning Althusser's overarching claims and without rehearsing the critiques of various aspects of his overall project, I want to summarize the nature of this particular philosophical intervention. For Althusser, the role of philosophy is to "draw lines of demarcation" (1990, 98–99) between science and certain ideological practices that block the development of scientific discovery. Such a gesture is, at its heart, neither pragmatic (although it could affect practices indirectly) nor theoretical (although it works on theoretical propositions), but rather political. To draw a line of demarcation is indeed to wage a political battle against a form of idealism that repeatedly inscribes itself in the spontaneous philosophy of scientists. Idealism in its many guises forms the theoretical background of science, exploiting the epistemological power of sciences to 'prove' eternal propositions concerning the Human, and attending to moral, ethical, and spiritual assumptions (one thinks here of the quest for the so-called 'God particle' as a contemporary example of such idealism playing itself out in the highest levels of physics). The myth of 'Humanity' as an eternal essence striving for spiritual enlightenment is naturalized through the work of scientists now enslaved to an idealist narrative.

In opposition to such idealism, Althusser suggests a turn to materialism. Only materialism lacks an exploitative relation to the sciences, and in this sense, is capable of safeguarding scientific practices from invasion by extra-scientific idealism. The transparent yet deadly effects of idealism act to corrode science's own materialist premises (replacing belief in material existence of objects as well as scientific objectivity with belief in subjective experience and questions of values and validation), leading to a tension that only manifests itself in moments of crisis. Philosophy is called upon by Althusser to transform the spontaneous philosophy of the scientists through materialist critique. The "alliance of scientists with materialist philosophy," summarizes Althusser, "brings to scientists the extra forces needed so to reinforce the materialist element as to dispel the religious-idealist illusions that dominated" (1990, 137) the spontaneous philosophies of scientists.

Several important points can be made about this alliance. First, philosophy does not speak the truth about science, but only protects it from extra-scientific invasions that exploit it. Second, it respects the work of science and doesn't try to intervene in any immediate way in its internal processes of knowledge production. Third, it calls for an ongoing struggle not only against idealism but also on behalf of the development of its own propositions.

It is interesting to compare this seminal statement on the alliance between materialist philosophy and science and Catherine Malabou's new materialist perspective on neuroscience. It would seem that while details might be different, the nature of the gesture remains largely intact. Philosophy for Malabou remains tightly bound with the sciences but offers the critical distance needed to draw a line between science's own materialism and an imported, extra-scientific intruder: the shadow of idealism. This struggle is now dominant in neuroscience research, and as I shall demonstrate, manifests itself most directly in relation to the question of neural 'plasticity.'

In what follows, I will trace Malabou's intervention into neuroscience in order to demonstrate the need for a materialist theory of the brain that, as Althusser might say, prevents certain forms of ideological/idealist appropriation of science. I will then argue that a similar intervention is needed in education. Briefly outlining some of the broad aspects of the emerging field of brain-based learning will allow me to conceptualize the underlying understanding of plasticity that informs not only the scientific research conducted but also educational applications and proposals. Drawing on Malabou, I argue that plasticity on this view is mired in a neoliberal concept of self-entrepreneurialism, continuous flexibility/adaptation, and economic efficiency that effectively undermines the broader scope of what we can do with our brains. What is needed here is a turn toward another notion of the plastic, one that emphasizes ruptures and events. But, as we shall see, this second notion of the plastic pushes us to the very limits of what can be considered education, literally exploding the very paradigms that are foundational for both a philosophy and science of education. In this sense, the violence demands its own question of educational ethics: if brains explode, should they?

EXPLODING BRAINS: MALABOU ON PLASTICITY

Much of Malabou's work concerns the concept of plasticity, both in the history of philosophy and in current neuoroscientific work on the brain (Malabou 2008; 2010; 2012). Reflecting on her own intellectual history, Malabou charts the emergence of plasticity through her engagement with Hegel, Heidegger, and Derrida. Indeed, plasticity forms the submerged concept running through these various philosophers. For Hegel, plasticity is the internal mobility of the system of logic, while for Heidegger, plasticity becomes the modification of *Dasein* within the world. Interestingly, Malabou finds within Derrida a resistance to plasticity that, on the surface, would seem to be the very essence of deconstruction. For Derrida, the formlessness of the trace speaks of its nonplastic nature, as does the formlessness of the messianic deferral. In order to theorize the plastic as such, Malabou began to realize that she needed to understand its metamorphic structure *on its own terms* as a structure that exists between (and is therefore not reducible to) her philosophical interlocutors. "This metamorphic structure," Malabou states, "did not belong entirely to the dialectic, destruction, or deconstruction, although it articulates all three of them" (p. 27). In other words, she began to appreciate the ontological plasticity of the plastic as an origin for dialectics, destruction, and deconstruction. Indeed, her major claim is that writing (in the form of codes, programming, trances, and information) is no longer the general organizational structure of the world. Rather, plasticity has come to prominence. This fact is perhaps most prevalent in cerebral plasticity and the capacity of synapses to modify their structure. Instead of code, the brain presents itself through cerebral images that are best described in relation to political metaphors (populations or assemblages) rather than as forms of writing. This insight then led Malabou from a critique of metaphysics and deconstruction to a critique of neuroscience as the central sphere to struggle over the meaning of plasticity today.

In neuroscience, Malabou finds two competing notions of the plastic. First, there is the sense of taking form (as in sculpture), and second, there is the notion of annihilation of form (as in an explosion). The plastic (flexible, adaptive) versus the plastique (destructive, violent). This distinction bears out political consequences. Contemporary neuroscience emphasizes the flexibility of brains, or the brain's ability to sculpt its own form through the development of habits. Far from an objective, neutral, and thus universal appraisal of the brain's most intimate functioning, Malabou points out that the conflation of plasticity with flexibility is a kind of "*neural ideology*" (2008, 11) that structures the field of neuroscience and that reflects the broader political and economic domains of neoliberalism. In this sense, philosophy must take aim at the spontaneous philosophy of the neuroscientist who is led astray by the overwhelming allure of neoliberal 'common sense' as it comes to constitute an emerging scientific field. For Malabou, the macro-politics of neoliberal flexible economies shapes the nano-politics of brain research, resulting in a model of brain activity that is docile rather than explosive. If the plastic notion of the brain has liberated us from certain false models, including the brain as central telephone exchange and as computer, it has also limited the freedom of the brain by constraining it to a flexible, de-centered, neural network metaphor that merely recapitulates the broader logic of neoliberalism. Indeed, neuroscience betrays its materialist roots when it naturalizes certain forms of capitalist exchange, which are decisively historical.

A key point of ideological convergence between the brain plasticity of the market is found in recent management literature that emphasizes flexibility, innovation, and de-centralized networks. In management guidelines, Malabou simultaneously finds (a) the socialization of cerebral language (the manager is a connector, the corporation a network) and (b) the cerebralization of sociological terminology (the brain is a population that maximizes efficiency and productivity). The self-creative, self-constituting aspects of brain plasticity mirror the ideal of the entrepreneurial self that is now the paradigm of the neoliberalist humanism, where freedom of the individual and the privileging of his or her creative powers of self-constitution are championed.

In addition to the socialization of cerebral language, the brain itself is politicized through a new kind of "psychological Darwinism" (2008, 65). On this account, the self is a translation of those neuronal configurations best adapted for survival and efficiency. The result is the biologization of a utilitarian philosophy that privileges useful synaptic connections for defining the self. The neoliberal governmentality of the self is so deeply internalized here that self-sufficiency, self-regulation, and self-management become the selective criteria for forming personality, and this personality is in turn granted a privileged place in the narrative of happiness, health, prosperity, and the quest for freedom.

Malabou thus takes up Althusser's challenge in order to draw a line between two philosophies found within the spontaneous philosophy of the neuroscientist. First, there is a sense in which the contemporary neuroscientific understanding of the brain resembles democracy. While not mentioning the political theory of Michael Hardt and Antonio Negri (2004), we can draw parallels between the flexible plasticity of the brain and larger democratic social movements that embody flexibility, mobility, networks, and swarm intelligence. But on the other hand, the very same neuroscience "produces, while taking its inspiration from, and extremely normalizing vision of democracy, in that it accords an overly central role to the absence of center, a too rigid prominence to flexibility, that is to say, to docility and obedience" (Malabou 2008, 53). This contradiction found within the heart of neuroscience leads Malabou to posit a provocative question: "Can the description of brain plasticity escape the insidious command of the New World Order?" (2008, 54). If neuroscience has produced a certain possibility for reimagining freedom, this freedom is equally constrained by the current of neoliberal ideology underpinning flexible plasticity. Where is there room in the brain for resistance . . . resistance to flexibility without reverting back to a rigid notion of the brain? Questions of the spontaneous philosophy of neuroscience thus spill over into political questions and vice versa.

The answer to such quandaries rests in the alternative notion of plasticity mentioned earlier: the plastique. Between neural networks and the conscious self, there lies an "indeterminate plasticity" (Malabou 2008, 69) that is potentially explosive and destructive. Returning to the brain, Malabou finds at its core a tension between formation and destruction. It is this tension that interrupts smooth flexibility with contingent, accidental, and abrupt neuronal ruptures that cannot necessarily be reincorporated into a unified sense of self. While the *creativity* of the self might very well find its place in the flexible plasticity of the brain, there is the question of *creation* below such networks in the insurgent events of disruption that explore and destroy and thereby open up new, unforeseen possibilities. On this view, moments of destruction are not simply negative and traumatic (although they might be). They are also points of creative resiliency and invention where the self emerges as transformed. Boldly stated, Malabou summarizes as follows: "*Creating resistance to neuronal ideology is what our brain wants, and what we want for it*" (2008, 77).

For Malabou, there is untapped potentiality within destruction for resistance to docility, productivity, and efficiency that are the hallmarks of a new kind of neoliberal idealism found in neuroscience. "It is time to remember," writes Malabou, "that some explosions are not in fact terrorist—explosions of rage, for example. Perhaps we ought to relearn how to enrage ourselves, to explode against a certain culture of docility . . ." (2008, 79). On its broadest level, a new politics of brain science emancipates the brain's explosive powers, and in this freedom to disobey, discovers the subject of a new "biological alter-globalism" (2008, 80).

This subject is not one that abides by the predicable model of continual self-improvement, efficiency, and self-management. Rather it is the subject as accident, or accidental subject, who progresses by fits and starts, who is characterized by gaps and traumas, who lacks a continuous narrative that organizes into a coherent 'life.' Malabou warns, "We must all of us recognize that we might, one day, become someone else, an absolute other, someone who will never be reconciled with themselves again . . ." (2012, 2). Born of and in an accident, something different, something new might appear that does not fit within the order of things and that suddenly disobeys all expectations. Such 'radical metamorphosis' emphasizes the explosive nature of plasticity in its destructive but also creative capacities to fabricate "a new person, a novel form of life, without anything in common with a preceding form" (2012, 18). Such changes are events that break with the teleological unfolding of capacities, talents, goals, or purposes. These strange changes Malabou finds in the works of Kafka and in the aftermath of traumatic brain injuries or in the sudden event of old age. All are accidental events that mutate the subject, sometimes beyond recognition.

One interesting example of the creatively destructive potential of the explosive plasticity of the brain can be found in Jason Padgett's autobiographical memoir *Struck by Genius: How a Brain Injury Made Me a Mathematical Marvel* (Padgett and Seaberg 2014). After a traumatic mugging, Padgett suddenly acquired acute mathematical synesthesia that allowed him to understand advanced physics and to draw complex mathematical shapes. Neither of these strange abilities could have been predicted in any way from Padgett's mathematically impoverished past. They were accidents that caused a kind of creative destruction and reconstruction of Padgett's brain, unleashing totally new insights, interests, and pleasures that sent him off on a radically novel voyage to understand himself and the implications of his intuitive sensitivity toward mathematical beauty. In this way, Padgett was forced to recognize himself *as a stranger*, as subject to that which was other, violent, disruptive, disorienting, surprising but also full of new possibilities. Openness to the strangeness of the accidental self thus came as a gift without explanation.

Here we move beyond any notion of the self-actualizing, self-regulating, self-managing entrepreneur or neoliberal subject of neuroscience who sculpts his or her brain in order to maximize productive outputs and performance quotas. The management of the brain's plastic flexibility gives way to an ethic and politics of encountering our internal otherness through accidental events. Malabou thus maintains an open promise that something new can emerge from within the plasticity of a brain that has been shackled to neoliberal ideology by the very science that is supposed to speak on its behalf.

LEARNING AS NEURO-IDEOLOGY

In this section, I want to begin by drawing a correlation between the rise of learning discourses and practices and the turn toward neuroscience in educational research. This correlation is important for demonstrating how neuroscience offers a neuro-ideology for justifying learning on 'objective grounds' and how learning offers a location or practice base for socializing this ideology as 'good common sense.'

As Maarten Simons and Jan Masschelein (2008) argue, "The word 'learning' has come to be indispensable for speaking about ourselves, others, and society" (391). Learning is essential not only for thinking about what happens in schools but in society and the economy writ large. Since we live in a knowledge economy and many of us are employed as knowledge workers, learning is a central concern, hence the need for employees to think of themselves as 'flexible' 'lifelong learners.' Drawing on Foucault's theory of governmentality, Simons and Masschelein emphasize the role learning plays in guaranteeing self-governance and, simultaneously, the ability of the self to be governed. Learning is precisely the mechanism by which neoliberalism can combine individual freedom and the welfare/health of the population overall. As a lifelong learner, one must regulate one's self according to social norms of efficiency, productivity, and optimization. Indeed, in policy statements concerning lifelong learning, Simons and Masschelein highlight the ease with which we come to describe learners as "managers" (2008, 400) of their learning. Like a manager, the lifelong learner is encouraged to come up with his/her own strategies for success, keep tabs on progress, and evaluate results for future improvements. Mechanisms of self-quantification are essential in this process so that the self can be translated into measurable 'data' for future learning.

Because learning is something one does on behalf of one's personal happiness and as an expression of one's freedom to self-actualize one's unique potentials, it is the optimal mechanism of neoliberalism, which economizes all aspects of life. As Foucault (2008) argues, the withdrawal of the state is a kind of governmentality wherein economic and social problems become individual problems of the care-of-the-self who must *learn* in order to be economically viable. In this sense, freedom to be self-determining becomes an economic resource. The lifelong learner is the entrepreneurial self, and the entrepreneurial self is the lifelong learner. Simons and Masschelein summarize as follows: "For the entrepreneurial self, this decision to learn is similar to an act of investment—to be precise, an investment in human capital that is expected to offer an income or return" (2008, 411). Without such investment into learning, the self is fundamentally put at risk of being abandoned by the neoliberal market which has *forced it to be free* in the first place (Simons 2006).

As Ernst Thoutenhoofd and Anne Pirrie (2013) argue, the narrow construction of self-regulated, lifelong learning that over-emphasizes personal autonomy and the personal fulfillment of economic goals is partly the outcome of the institutionalized dominance of cognitive psychology in educational research. I would like to push this argument further and suggest that neuroscience is now edging in on cognitive psychology's imperialist tendencies. Indeed, learning theories have increasingly come to neuroscience to solve certain educational problems. This is due in part to the fact that neuroscience promises that which educational philosophy or sociology could never dream of: giving a biological explanation of what learning *actually* is. John Clark (2005) summarizes this perspective as follows: "If we are ever to get to the bottom of explaining what learning is, it will be by rigorous and systematic empirical studies of brains . . ." (668). Learning thus becomes the science of brain-based learning. Expanding upon Malabou's thesis, I argue that if neurobiology is the central terrain of struggle to define the new materialism of plasticity, and if learning it the primary social mechanism in the popularization of neuroscience, then learning itself becomes an essential location for philosophical intervention.

Learning from the standpoint of neuroscience can be summarized in terms of neural plasticity or the "ability of neurons to change their structure and relationships to one another in an experience-dependent manner according to environmental demands" (Cozolino and Sprokay 2006, 12). Through "proper social relationships" neural plasticity can be stimulated, leading to increased learning outcomes. The definition of education becomes nothing more than "increased cognitive processing efficiency" (Collins 2007, 305) by the brain. All other definitions of education are merely second-order descriptions that should be eliminated in order to emphasize the structures and functions of the brain that are essential for 'learning' to occur.

The expert learner is one who has optimal neural efficiency. One of the major dimensions of this efficiency is long-term memory retention that enables the brain to connect past, present, and future so as to be maximally adaptable. Neuroscience has shed new light on the biological processes of memory, leading to a series of learning strategies, including ongoing repetition accompanied with emphasis. Repetition ensures neural networks are consistently activated, and emphasis ensures that the learner will be able to build on existing neural networks and modify them as new information becomes available. Plasticity here is seen as the continuous opening and closing down of synaptic connections as we fluctuate between remembering what has happened and experiencing new stimulation. Network integration can also be facilitated through narrative construction and reconfiguration that build a coherent story to guide future behaviors (Cozolino and Sprokay 2006).

Stress and learning is an important topic in this literature. Too little arousal means that students will be unmotivated to learn, but too much arousal can be equally damaging. Thus what is called for is a moderate trigger capable of stimulating neural plasticity without producing negative side effects (Cowan and Kandel 2001). Usha Goswami argues that to avoid stress, "the biological necessity for learning" should be "incremental questions," troubling the notion that education should cause major "conceptual change" (2009, p. 33). Decreasing stress enables learners to repair semantic and narrative aspects of the learning process that might diverge in moments of tension. Stated differently, brain-based learning advocates that optimal learning takes place when environments and activities are challenging without being threatening. Incremental questions function to improve neural coherence and cohesion across neural networks (the sensory, somatic, motor, affective, and cognitive processes in various locations throughout the brain). When integrated into rich environments of learning, such questioning can produce the optimal conditions for learning, which can be summarized as: relaxed alertness, orchestrated immersion, and active processing of experience for consolidating learning through neural pathways (Cain et al. 2005). On this view, brain plasticity balances the flexibility offered by learning with neural integration and coherence in order to achieve overall self-efficacy and self-motivation.

Increased efficiency is also emphasized in brain-based learning through "synaptic pruning" (Clark 2005, 682) whereby weaker neural contacts are eliminated and unused synaptic connections are closed off. Here the functionality of connections ensures their survival. Plasticity is therefore an expression of the survival of the fittest neurons. Because this process is potentially infinite (Diamond, in D'Arcangelo 1998, 21), neuroscientists advocate lifelong learning as a mechanism for preventing neural impoverishment, something which occurs when synapses go unutilized.

At this point, I would like to avoid typical conversations in the brain-based learning literature. These include questions concerning the exact relationship between causal claims made by science and normative claims made by educators, concerning how to translate between scientific discourse and learning discourse, concerning the role of education in defining the scope of future neurological research, and concerning categorical mistakes when talking about mental learning using neurscientific lingo. Instead, I want to return to my opening question but with an educational and neuroscientific twist: what is the spontaneous philosophy of those working in the field of brain-based learning? Here we can draw a line in the sand in relation to the question of brain plasticity. As outlined earlier, there are several definitions of plasticity offered. Each of these definitions is somewhat different, but what they all share in common is an emphasis on flexibility, adaptability, efficiency, productive capacity, brain health, and so forth. The symmetry between the neurological and the social creates a mutually supportive ideology for ongoing research and ongoing learning without ever recognizing how this circuit is a reflection of broader social, economic, and political influences found in neoliberalism.

The critique here is that current synergy between learning discourses and practices and neuroscience is symptomatic of neoliberal constructions of self-other relations that privilege lifelong learning in the name of optimizing efficiency, flexibility, adaptability, and so forth. (I am not concerned with the nature of this synergy so much as it exists in multiple, contested forms). The question of plasticity is therefore neither merely bio-mechanical nor political-ideological. It is rather *bio-political* through and through. The concept of plasticity found in my brief literature review is a location of struggle not only in terms of scientific definitions or in terms of learning processes but in terms of political and economic frameworks that make the very question of brain-based learning intelligible at this point in history.

For Malabou what is excluded here is another dimension of plasticity, the explosive/destructive possibilities of the brain. It is important to note the emphasis on decreasing stress levels, limiting big conceptual transformations for incremental questions, the focus on integration, coherence, and cohesion. All such concepts limit the plastic to the flexible, to the obedient, and to the docile, attempting to minimize the radical possibilities for brains to undergo surprising if not traumatic transformations that produce new selves. To allow for the existence of trauma in the classroom is not to advocate for teachers to induce such states, but rather to recognize that education (not merely learning) does, at times, involve accidents that produce their own kind of brain trauma. Here I am not suggesting that all traumas are productive (for instance, the trauma of child abuse or the trauma of poverty certainly should be alleviated), but rather that there are aspects of education that are traumatic. Advocates of brain-based learning pedagogy would see such trauma as something to be avoided, mitigated, or narrativized so as to reestablish the coherence of the neural network. They would avoid an important if not essential part of educational experience: the radical estrangement of one's self from one's self (the transformation of the self into a stranger, an unrecognizable other who is given over to the power of the accident). What Malabou reminds us is that such trauma is not merely destructive (as brain-based learning would suggest) but also radically creative in its own way, opening up a space where a new notion of subjectivity can emerge, new pleasures, new perceptual possibilities, and new forms of self. The newness of this destructive capacity to give form cannot necessarily be reincorporated into existing neural networks and is fundamentally disruptive of the coherency and orderliness proposed by brain-based learning. Further, the resulting neural configuration need not be composed of the fittest and most active neural synapses. Survival of trauma might be highly contingent, breaking free from the neo-Darwinism espoused by brain-based learning researchers and theorists. Indeed, terminology such as 'weak' or 'strong' do not work within an ontology of the accident where the rule is not evolutionary growth, advancement, and progressive mastery so much as disruptive, chance transformations. These institute abrupt breaks and starts with their own unprecedented origin points that could not be predicted by even the most sophisticated of instruments.

Allowing for the plasticity of plasticity into education means recognizing the fragility and precariousness of educational life. Whereas brain-based learning attempts to minimize the *indeterminacy* of life by playing up the form of 'strong' neural structures, Malabou's insistence on the accidental nature of ruptures indicates that the impossible does happen despite our safeguards, despite our planning, and despite our pedagogical intent. But again, this indeterminacy holds open a promise: that learning can be more than learning, that creation beyond creative intentionality can occur, and that the horizon of an alternative notion of the self can burst into the present without warning.

To undermine the spontaneous philosophy of brain-based learning is therefore to emphasize a split between the plastic and the plastique, the maintenance and restoration of flexibility (learning), and the potential for disobedience and creation (educational explosions). For Malabou, this means that we once again allow for creation in the classroom beyond what is prescribed. To move beyond mere flexibility is therefore to recapture the "genius" (Malabou 2008, 12) of plasticity. Here we can return once again to the example of Padgett who was "struck by genius" after a brain injury. The phrase "struck by genius" is important in this context because genius is not something *we can intentionally train*. Rather, genius comes from without, comes from an accidental meeting with that which is traumatic. Genius is therefore beyond mere management of the entrepreneurial self who selects experiences in order to maximize self-realization. Genius is located on the horizon of the dangerousness of plasticity as an explosive possibility found within our brains. To be genius is to be knocked on the head by the unanticipated, thrown off track, made strange—made other.

EDUCATION AS ACCIDENT: BEYOND NEURO-IDEOLOGY

Malabou argues that we must allow for creative destruction (genius) to occur in order to unleash the freedom of the brain and thus to overcome the neoliberal spontaneous philosophy of neuroscience. While she is speaking directly to philosophers, I would like to end by asking what the implications are if we assume she could be addressing educators. What would this mean? If we accept the explosive potentials of the brain, then we have to reformulate Malabou's question as follows: what should we do with our brains in education?

Under the sign of learning backed by neuroscientific data, it would seem that we should use or brains in the most effective, efficient, and stress-free way possible in order to become master learners. Currently, education as learning concerns the quantification of ever-increasing returns on an initial investment. Continual growth, performance, and excellent are sought, and neuroscience is the final salvation for understanding the causal networks in our brains responsible for desirable outputs. The teleological narrative structure of this salvation story should make us inherently suspicious of its ideological roots in religious idealism, now masquerading as a materialist science of neurons.

Yet the explosive nature of the plastic poses particular problems for educators. What is education if not a process of incremental growth that is cumulative, continual, and flexible? Indeed, to challenge such notions is not merely to critique current brain-based learning. It also cuts to the quick of several tried and true foundations of educational philosophy as such. John Dewey, for instance, is the quintessential educational philosopher of plasticity. As one of the primary conditions of growth, Dewey highlights the plasticity of the young. Dewey (1944) describes plasticity as the "power to modify actions on the basis of the results of prior experiences" (44), where growth is the "cumulative movement of action toward a later result" (41). For such cumulative movement to occur, there must be continuity between experiences. Indeed, one of the obstacles to what Dewey (1997) refers to as the "experiential continuum" (33) is discontinuity of experiences. He writes, "Each experience may be lively, vivid, and 'interesting,' and yet their disconnectedness may artificially generate dispersive, disintegrated, centrifugal habits. The consequence of formation of such habits is inability to control future experiences" (1997, 26), and in this sense, prevent further educational growth. If education is the "reconstruction and reorganization of experience which adds to the meaning of experience" (Dewey 1944, 76), then one must avoid ruptures, gaps, or breaks, for these would undermine the organic unfolding of experiences through time. The threat of the accident is precisely that meaning could not be reconstructed, that there would be a loss of this underlying organicism resulting in mis-educative experiences, ones that do not build toward the realization of one's aims.

In short, two alternatives must be avoided. First, Dewey (1944) refers to "fixity of habits" (48) as mis-educative in that they come to control us rather than us controlling them. Here we can think of the unthinking conformity to addictive behaviors. Second, Dewey warns against centrifugal experiences that lack continuous, cumulative effects. Not only do these two conditions prevent education from happening, but they transgress on the very order of nature itself. In *Art as Experience* (2005), Dewey states, "Nature and life manifest not flux but continuity, and continuity involves forces and structures that endure through change" (337). What is at stake in this claim is the naturalization and universalization of plasticity as flexibility.

Although progressives would find in Dewey an alternative to contemporary trends that link education to scientific positivism, what I want to highlight here is the underlying *continuity* between Dewey's influential treatment of human plasticity and the plasticity of brain-based learning today. Indeed, one could make the argument that neurological plasticity is the missing hinge that enables us to connect the observation of childhood plasticity and Dewey's broader claims that nature as such is plastic by design. This would also explain why critics of neuroscientific educational researchers find the pedagogical advice given to teachers nothing more than 'commonsense' progressive platitudes all trumped up with fancy neuroscience language. If this is the case, then offering critiques of plasticity as the spontaneous ideology of brain-based learning is not enough, for it leaves intact the underlying philosophy of education, which makes brain-based research *intelligible as educationally relevant.*

The new materialist critique of plasticity is therefore risky, and its gesture must dig deep in order to uncover the abiding repulsion to the ontology of the accident that forms the central taboo in modern philosophy of education. What would it mean to argue that the discontinuity introduced by the accident could produce educational results that do not conform to Dewey's model of growth through the experiential continuum? What kind of education is this that opens up to the space and time of rupture and explosion rather than flexibility and continuous modification?

If education is accidental, or composed of accidents, or allows for accidents as formative experiences, then what does this mean for educators who must now deal with the potential trauma, who must confront students whom they may *no longer recognize*? The educational accident places us on the far edge of what can even be recognized as educational. What should we do with our brains in education? This is no simple question, and indeed is perhaps more complicated than Malabou's original formulation. It seems that what is needed is not only an ontology of the accident (which Malabou offers with great richness and detail) but also an ethic of the accident that both remains sensitive to the fragility of childhood while also open to the freedom of neurological explosions. Without this sensitivity, then education becomes nothing more than preparation for socialization into a neoliberal world of entrepreneurial selves. Such a fate loses what is most important in education: the experience, even if traumatic, of genius.

156 Tyson E. Lewis

REFERENCES

Althusser, Louis. 1990. *Philosophy and the Spontaneous Philosophy of the Scientists and Other Essays*. London: Verso.

Cain, Renate N., Geoffrey Gaine, Carol McClintic, and Karl J. Klimek. 2005. *12 Brain/Mind Learning Principles in Action: The Field Book for Making Connections, Teaching, and the Human Brain*. Thousand Oaks, CA: Corwin Press.

Collins, John W. 2007. "The Neuroscience of Learning." *Journal of Neuroscience Nursing* 39 (5): 305–310.

Cowan, W. Maxwell and Eric R. Kandel. 2001. "A Brief History of Synapses and Synaptic Transmission." In *Synapses*, edited by W.M. Cowan, T.C. Sudhof, and C.F. Stevens, 1–88. Baltimore: John Hopkins Press.

Cozolino, Louis and Susan Sprokay. 2006. "Neuroscience and Adult Learning." *New Directions for Adult and Continuing Education* 110: 11–19.

Clark, John. 2005. "Explaining Learning: From Analysis to Paralysis to Hippocampus." *Educational Philosophy and Theory* 37 (5): 667–687.

D'Arcangelo, Marcia. 1998. "The Brains Behind the Brains." *Educational Leadership* 56 (3): 20–25.

Dewey, John. 2005. *Art as Experience*. New York: Perigee Books.

Dewey, John. 1997. *Experience and Education*. New York: Simon & Schuster.

Dewey, John. 1944. *Democracy and Education*. New York: Simon & Schuster.

Foucault, Michael. 2008. *The Birth of Biopolitics: Lectures at the Collège de France 1978–1979*. New York: Palgrave Macmillan.

Goswami, Usha. 2009. "Principles of Learning, Implications for Teaching: A Cognitive Neuroscience Perspective." In *New Philosophies of Learning*, edited by Ruth Cigman and Andrew Davis, 26–43. Chichester, UK: Wiley-Blackwell.

Hardt, Michael and Antonio Negri. 2004. *Multitude: War and Democracy in the Age of Empire*. London: Penguin Books.

Malabou, Catharine. 2012. *Ontology of the Accident: An Essay on Destructive Plasticity*. Malden: Polity Press.

Malabou, Catharine. 2010. *Plasticity at the Dusk of Writing; Dialectic, Destruction, Deconstruction*. New York: Columbia University Press.

Malabou, Catharine. 2008. *What Should We Do with Our Brains?* New York: Fordham University Press.

Padgett, Jason and Maureen Ann Seaberg. 2014. *Struck by Genius: How a Brain Injury Made Me a Mathematical Marvel*. New York: Houghton Mifflin Harcourt.

Simons, Maarten. 2006. "Learning as Investment: Notes on Governmentality and Biopolitics." *Educational Philosophy and Theory* 38 (4): 523–540.

Simons, Maarten and Jan Masschelein. 2008. "The Governmentalization of Learning and the Assemblage of a Learning Apparatus." *Educational Theory* 58 (4): 391–415.

Thoutenhoofd, Ernst D. and Anne Pirrie. 2013. "From Self-regulation to Learning to Learn: Observations on the Construction of Self and Learning." *British Educational Research Journal* 41 (1): 72–84.

10 Beyond a Representational Model of Mind in Educational Neuroscience

Bodily Subjectivity and Dynamic Cognition

Clarence W. Joldersma

Educational neuroscience is often heralded as putting education on a scientific footing through evidence-based practices (Blakemore and Frith 2005; Carew and Magsamen 2010; Petitto and Dunbar 2009; Posner 2010). This chapter is not an attempt to adjudicate these empirical claims. Rather, it gives a critique of and develops an alternative to the philosophical model of mind that frames much of such educational neuroscience, namely, a representational theory of mind correlated with a computational understanding of the brain. The chapter first problematizes representationalism and its computational cognate, arguing that educational neuroscience must move beyond the representationalist model. It then offers educational neuroscience another model of mind, one based in recent interpretations of Merleau-Ponty's idea of bodily subjectivity. This model is better for evaluating the possible contributions neuroscience might make to educational practice.

REPRESENTATIONALISM IN EDUCATIONAL NEUROSCIENCE

A central assumption in much neuroscience is the localization hypothesis, namely, the idea that particular mental activities are correlated with localizable areas of the brain. In the words of Posner and his associates, "the human brain localizes mental operations of the kind posited by cognitive theories" (Posner et al. 1988, 1627). Research correlating brain operations and cognitive processes often centers on various cognitive tasks identified by educational and cognitive theorists, trying to pinpoint their performances in localized brain areas. Built into the experimental design of such research is the correlative assumption that "the [cognitive] task can be decomposed into specific processes that can be independently manipulated" (Poldrack 2010, 147). Educational neuroscientist Stanislas Dehaene's research, for example, is guided by the localization hypothesis when he uses neuroimaging to look for local brain activity during simple cognitive tasks in arithmetic, such as subtraction or naming numerical digits (Dehaene 2008, 234). The localization hypothesis is operationalized by decomposing a subject's cognition and learning into its simplest elements and then looking for localized neural activity of these basic components. This typically involves an experimental setting of controlled manipulation of certain details of mental functions—reading, arithmetic, physical tasks, hearing, attention—and identifying localized effects in the brain using neuroimaging techniques. Other times a local area of the brain is stimulated and correlated with a subsequently occurring mental state or activity (Poldrack 2011). In general, the localization hypothesis undergirds much of the research and evidence of educational neuroscience.

The localization hypothesis dovetails well a philosophical theory of mind called computationalism (Horst 2011; Miłkowski 2013). A computation model takes cognitive processes to be like the operations of a computer (Fodor 1983; Jackendoff 1990; Joldersma 1994). In this approach, the mind is modeled as a computational machine that contains a set of rules for manipulating mental symbols. This approach shows up in educational theorizing. Cognitive scientist John Bruer describes minds as devices that "process symbols, use a small set of basic operations to manipulate them, and store them in memory" (Bruer 1993, 21). The mind for Bruer is a computing device. For example, in arithmetic, mental symbols are numerals such as 2 and 5 and computational rules include operations such as 'plus' and 'minus.' More generally, Bruer states, "There are two kinds of symbols: those that stand for input or data (what the computation is about) and those that stand for operations on the data" (Bruer 1993, 22). Bruer is saying that basic research supporting applied educational science should involve identifying computable symbols, both those that stand for mental content (input) and those that stand for mental operations. The goal is to discover how the mind constructs production-system programs that guide human action. The assumption is that educational research should focus its efforts toward discovering mental structures and their computational processes. Central to such research is the view that there is a science of mind, one whose central task is discovering and identifying mental symbols and their processing. Educational cognitive science often embraces a computational understanding of mind.

Key to the computationalist model is the doctrine of neural correlates, namely, that there is a one-to-one correspondence between mental states and brain states. Bruer articulates this assumption clearly, stating "Cognitive neuroscientists [should] look for neural correlates of cognitive processes" (Bruer 2008, 54). Recent neuroscience dovetails well with this assumption, for much of its research involves looking for the localized relations between cognitive tasks and neural activity. Neuroimaging methods such as fMRIs are central in such studies, showing where such simple elements of cognition occur in the brain: "Functional magnetic resonance imaging (fMRI) technology goes hand in hand with orthodox computational models" (Gallagher et al. 2013, 421). Imaging technologies are designed to detect functional segregation of brain areas, often through developing composite pictures of local areas of blood-oxygen depletion or some other proxy that occurs during simple cognitive tasks. This often is guided by a computational understanding of the brain and mind. Dehaene's work exemplifies this assumption. His studies look for correlations between localized neural activity and specific cognitive processes. For example, he finds evidence that "the left and right intraparietal sulci and the left and right precentral sulchi" areas of the brain are dedicated to a cognitively simple "number sense" (Dehaene 2008, 234). In another example, he reports that neuroimaging studies have identified a local brain area dedicated to the visual aspect of reading. Imaging studies indicate, he observes, "Whenever a good reader is presented with a written word, activation can be observed in an area of the left ventral visual region, located in the occipito-temporal sulcus" (Dehaene 2008, 238). Specific cognitive tasks are interpreted as having neural correlates in localized brain areas.

These localization studies not only give evidence for the assumption of neural correlates but suggest that particular mental activity depend foundationally on particular neural activity. Chris Frith states this doctrine in its classical clarity: "I firmly believe that there cannot be changes in my mind (mental activity) without there also being changes in brain activity" (Frith 2009, 23). Similarly, Thomas Metzinger articulates the idea of neural correlates when he states that a "set of neurofunctional properties in your brain [is] sufficient to bring about a conscious experience" (Metzinger 2009, 11). Frith and Metzinger are saying that differences occurring in the mind are not merely correlated to, but are caused by, particular brain activity. The search for neural correlates of cognition and consciousness is central in much neuroscience research (Raichle 1998; Rees et al. 2002; Tononi and Koch 2008). The goal is to uncover the causal mechanisms at the neuronal level of particular mental (cognitive) processes.

This idea in neuroscience echoes the classic supervenience thesis in philosophy of mind. Jaegwon Kim describes supervenience as the belief that there is a one-to-one correspondence between a mental state and a brain state, where any differences that exist between mental states correlate to corresponding differences between brain states (Kim 1984). Minds as symbol-manipulating devices require a one-to-one correspondence between the mental states and the brain states on which they supervene. Stronger than mere correlation, supervenience is the doctrine that changes in the brain will cause changes in the mind's contents.

Computational approaches typically assume a representationalist model of mind. The internal symbols are typically understood as mental representations. Representations are things that carry information about the world, and we know the world indirectly, through them. In Metzinger's words, "we know the world only by using representations . . ." (Metzinger 2009, 9). Although ultimately caused by a chain of events in the external physical world, their content arises independent of that context, as properties of the representation itself. A mental representation is a state of mind such as a particular belief, desire, hope, fear, or perception (Fodor 1981). These mental representations "function both as immediate objects of propositional attitudes and as domains of mental processes" (Fodor 1987, 18). The idea is that these internal states represent the world in some way—their contents are *about* something in the world external to the mind. In turn, the particular content of a mental representation is what distinguishes one from another, where two beliefs are different mental representations if they have different content. On this theory, mental states involve causal sequences of particular physical tokens. Particular neurological activity are physical tokens that make relevant information of the world available to the person by giving rise to mental representations whose contents are phenomenal (experienced) states.

The supervenience hypothesis is most plausible when mental content is construed in representational terms. In turn, the representationalist approach rides on the assumption that the phenomenon of mental content is to be explained with neural activity. That gives the mental content the right 'shape' for finding one-to-one correspondences between localized neural activity and the content of mental representations. The supervenience claim is that there is no difference in mental representation without a difference at the (localized) neuronal level. But there is but a short distance to saying that, already at the neuronal level, there are representations and that these already have mental content—(proto)mental properties, such as (proto)red and (proto)rectangular.

Representationalism shows up in recent educational neuroscience. One definition of that research is precisely the study of mental representations (Szűcs and Goswami 2007). This echoes cognitive science's earlier understanding. For example, Bruer states, "Cognitive scientists call these symbol structures *mental representations*. The idea of representation is fundamental to cognitive science" (Bruer 1993, 22–23; emphasis in original). Educational neuroscience's explanations of cognitive skills, on this reading, often appeal to states that carry information about the external world. For example, Dehaene's studies of numbers and reading exemplify representationalism. He states that humans take in information from the external world and convert this "into an internal approximate quantity code" and manipulate it by calculating processes that are "implemented at the neural level" (Dehaene 2008, 236). These internal codes and implemented internal rules for calculation are internal mental representations. Szűcs and Goswami describe these internal representations as "the activity of neural networks of the brain which code information in the form of electrical activity" (Szűcs and Goswami 2007, 114, 115). Many researchers in educational neuroscience assume the mind/brain to be a computational device that calculates over mental representations. Educational neuroscience centrally uses a representational theory of mind.

According to Bruer, a central feature of the representational model is interiority. He states, "Representations are the symbolic links between the external environment and our internal, mental world" (Bruer 1993, 23).

Representations are mental objects in an interior space that stand for (represent) something in the external world. The interiority position associated with representationalism has been with philosophy for a while. Descartes theorized that the mental was marked by interiority, that it was internal mental states that are known directly, and that consciousness was aimed at those states. Similarly, Locke argued that the mind is a presence room in which simple and complex ideas are found and experienced, where consciousness is a kind of perception of the ideas entering one's mind, including the power to know them as one's own thoughts (Aquila 1988, 544; Joldersma 1994). Recent philosophical positions in neuroscience echo this central feature of representationalism. Frith claims, "we do not have direct access to the physical world. It may feel as if we have direct access, but this is an illusion created by our brain" (Frith 2009, 40). Rather, there is a chain of causal events that intervene, and he concludes that the brain creates interior mental life. For example, if a person experiences the color 'red' and the shape 'rectangle' and construes these as properties of a red door, energy waves in the light portion of the spectrum bounce from the physical structure in the external world onto the sensory receptors of the eye, which causes neurons to activate, sending signals into particular groups of neurons in the brain. The activation of those neurons "somehow creates the experience of color and shape in my mind" (Frith 2009, 23). What we have direct access to, on Frith's account, is an internal representation of the external structure, constituted as the interior experience of a particular color and shape of a door. Similarly, Metzinger argues that conscious experience is exclusively internal. By this he means that "phenomenal content is determined locally, not by the environment at all but by the internal properties of the brain only" (Metzinger 2009, 10). The issue of consciousness is not about direct connection with the external world but about the way that interior mental life is structured—a purely internal affair.

BEYOND REPRESENTATIONALISM

There are both conceptual and methodological reasons for being skeptical of the representational model of mind in educational neuroscience. Methodologically, for neuroimages to correlate cleanly with mental representations, the images must unequivocally depict a clear and simple brain process distinct from other brain processes. Only then would we begin to have clear evidence that a localized brain activity is dedicated to a simple content that has a mental correlate. Neuroimages such as fMRIs are alluring in their clarity, and many are tempted to treat them as giving direct access to clear and distinct brain processes, and thus to what Metzinger calls intrinsic "neurofunctional properties." But neuroscience works with limited tools, both theoretically and technically (Gallagher et al. 2013, 421). Neuroimaging in particular is an incomplete tool, only able to give rise to complex composite images that are fundamentally ambiguous with respect to what causes their details. Depending partly on what technique is used, and depending partly on the limited nature of those techniques, a neuroimage's details might be caused by the generation of new neurons, growth and change in existing neurons, generation of new synapses, increases in white matter cells, or changes in the capillaries bringing blood to the region (Zatorre et al. 2012). Furthermore, many images are composites: for example, fMRI images are not single snapshots but composite pictures of many human subjects, typically of increases in blood flow in relatively large regions of the brain. These images therefore are methodologically limited, not able to give the requisite clarity and distinctness required to localize simple cognitive tasks in brain areas. Further, there is good evidence to suggest that particular regions of the brain are not modular, namely, dedicated solely to a single task. In his localization studies of simple arithmetic tasks, Dehaene states that it is wrong to hold that a single brain area acts as a number module: "There are no modules in the cortex" (Dehaene 2010, 186). In a localized brain region captured by imaging techniques as the hot spot for (say) 'number' in the cognitive task of number estimation, the neurons involved are about 15% of the total in that area. The other neurons in the same area are thought to be involved in a disparate set of activities, including touch, motion, location, and object size. Together, these objections raise important methodological questions about the scientific project of localization required to confidently draw conclusions about neural correlations between brain and mind, between local neural processes and particular mental representations.

But there are equally serious *conceptual* issues with the representationalist assumptions in educational neuroscience. The localization hypothesis coupled with the supervenience thesis is meant to give plausibility to the idea that particular content of a mental representation can be correlated with particular local neural activity (Poldrack 2011). But the claim about the mapping of localized brain activity onto specific mental representations is that this is not merely a formal *correlation*. Rather, as Alva Noë and Evan Thompson have argued recently, the neural correlation doctrine is something stronger, namely, a "matching-content doctrine" (Noë and Thompson 2004, 3). The claim is that intrinsic content properties of particular brain states have matching-content properties in mental states. This is the idea that for every conscious state (e.g., a simple cognitive task), there is "a minimal neural substrate that is nomically (as a matter of natural law) for its occurrence" (Noë and Thompson 2004, 4). They are pointing out that the correlation is construed as a causal structure—for every simple cognitive state there is a clear and distinct neural state that is necessary and sufficient for causing the content of the cognitive state. This is the defining feature of the neural correlation thesis; namely, *contents* of cognitive states are caused by neural substrates. This is also the central claim of traditional supervenience doctrine: no difference in mental content without a difference in the underlying brain-state content. The contents at each level match because of an upward causation.

The representationalist matching-content doctrine is meant as a context-free model of cognitive content. Mental content in this account is construed as non-relational, intrinsic properties of neural activity, such as a neural firing pattern of a local brain area. When the neural substrate is activated, the conscious state is thought to occur necessarily, because the neural substrate causes its occurrence and individuates its mental content. According to Noë and Thompson, the context-free character of content requires the strong assumption of a "one-one mapping (under some description) from features of conscious experience onto features of the minimal neural substrate" (Noë and Thompson 2004, 5). The matching occurs between the *content* of the neural activity and that of the content of the conscious state to which it gives rise. This is a narrow understanding of content, namely, that it is context-free: it is the pattern of *this* particular neural substrate that gives rise to *that* particular conscious content. The construal that mental content is context-free fits well with an internalist view of mind. Internalism interprets mental states as independent of what is happening in the outside world or even in other parts of the body. In traditional philosophy of mind, 'internal' is meant to exclude the relational properties of the mind or the brain—the individuation of content at the cognitive level and the neurological level are non-relational (Fodor 1987, 30–31). Recent neuroscience echoes this. The internalist assumption of representationalism frames the idea that neural substrates systematically match the content of cognitive states.

To get beyond representationalism, we need a different conception of mind and content. But for that we also need a different understanding of the brain. Tim Van Gelder was one of the first to challenge computationalism with his conception of brain as a dynamic, complex system (Van Gelder 1995, 1998), and recent scholarship in neurodynamics has continued this approach (Beer 2008; Engel 2011; Juarrero 2000; Schöner 2008; Tsuda 2001). On this construal, the brain is a dynamic system whose features include massive networking, parallel and distributed processing (exhibiting nonlinearity), and immense feedback loops (creating recurrent networks). Macro-scale patterns emerge out of micro-scale activity, a kind of emergent self-organization that in turn constrains and shapes the micro-activities that constitute them. When the brain is construed as a dynamic system, the particular elements of the brain are constrained and co-opted by higher-order, more global dynamic patterns of brain activity. The idea of emergent self-organization undermines the one-to-one correspondence of local brain activity and particular mental content.

But to view the brain as a dynamic system still means it could be interpreted in isolation. Many theorists go further in their reinterpretation of the brain by explicitly connecting it more intrinsically to the body and the world within which it is embedded. In turn, this requires a different conception of the body. For that I turn to recent interpretations of Merleau-Ponty's idea of bodily subjectivity. His ideas anticipate the current explorations of what is more recently called sensorimotor, embodied, and enacted approaches to perception and cognition (Gallagher 2010). Evan Thompson argues that a key to Merleau-Ponty's conception is that bodiliness describes a relation to the world, doing so in pre-objective terms. He states, "Merleau-Ponty maintains that the relation between self and world is not primarily that of subject to object, but rather what he calls, following Heidegger, being-in-the-world" (Thompson 2005, 409). Merleau-Ponty's claim is that the primal relation between self and world is first of all a practical relation. Thompson parses what this means:

> To belong to the world in this way means that our primary way of relating to things is neither purely sensory and reflexive, nor cognitive or intellectual, but rather bodily and skillful. Merleau-Ponty calls this kind of bodily intentionality "motor intentionality."
>
> (1962, p. 110, 137) (Thompson 2005, 410)

Motor intentionality is a skillful way of coping with the world; this is what the phrase being-in-the-world is meant to indicate. Some use the term 'embodied' for this, but this can be misconstrued as meaning that there is something non-bodily encased in the body. Merleau-Ponty's view is more radical, something Thompson indicates by using the word 'bodily' instead. Merleau-Ponty writes, "I am in it [my body], or rather I am it" (Merleau-Ponty 1962, 150). The term 'bodily' is short-form for the phrase, 'I am my body' which means *being* a bodily subject. The idea of bodily subjectivity precludes interpreting the body first of all as the object that the natural sciences describe. Experiencing one's own body as an object is to experience an object over against one's self as a conscious subject—the traditional subject-object relation. However, "most of the time one's body is not present as an intentional object, but is experienced non-intentionally and pre-reflectively. This kind of experience is consciousness of the body-as-subject" (Thompson 2005, 412). The body is neither a perceived object nor a felt means. Instead, the body, in its bodiliness, is constitutive of the person's subjectivity. Merleau-Ponty's notion of bodily subjectivity signals the unity of subjective experiences of the bodily self in the world. Thompson says, "for a bodily subject, it is not possible to specify what the subject is in abstraction from the world, nor is it possible to specify what the world is in abstraction from the subject" (Thompson 2010, 247). This means that one's subjectivity cannot be understood apart from bodily being-in-the-world.

The brain still has a vital role to play in this model but is interpreted differently. Rather than a physical mechanism to encode and manipulate representations (which at times rise to conscious states), the brain is viewed as part of the whole organism embedded and active in the world. In the words of Gallagher and his associates, "On this view, rather than representing or computing information, the brain is better conceived as participating in the action" (Gallagher et al. 2013, 421). They are saying that understanding the brain requires understanding it first of all as part of an active living body in the world. The brain functions in the manner that it does precisely because it is embedded in a bodily subject immersed in the world. Living creatures such as humans have limbs that grasp, eyes that focus in structured ways, and upright postures that help cope with specific environments in particular ways. The bodily subject as a whole interacts with its surrounding world. Therefore the secret to the human brain is its role in bodiliness. Rather than construing the brain as the organ for thinking as traditionally understood, namely, generating and manipulating mental representations understandable in isolation, the brain is foremost a participant in bodily action, playing central roles in the way a creature as a bodily whole interacts with its environment. Although the brain remains central, it is in the context of bodiliness; namely, the way the organism as a bodily subject responds to its dynamic surroundings.

Earlier I described the brain as a dynamic system to suggest an alternative to the computational model. But even this might fall short. When the brain is construed as a participant in bodily subjectivity, it cannot be adequately understood as an isolated dynamic system. Rather, we need to model the nervous system in its role of the bodily subject's being-in-the-world. The brain as a dynamic system is better described as embedded in the organism-environment coupling, which is itself a dynamic system. This coupling can be construed as a system in which the brain is embedded because its functioning is constrained by the organism-environment dynamics. Dobromir Dotov argues that it is helpful to construe the brain as "a (very large) set of latent open loops," which are shaped by bodily behavior. The bodily subject's interactions with the world constrain which dynamic brain loops might close and which might activate: "In given circumstances one of the loops will be closed, and thus selected out of the larger set, by a given configuration of the body and environment" (Dotov 2014, 6). The brain's functioning can fruitfully be construed as closing "the circuit of a given dynamic field spanning a configuration of brain, agent, and environment" (6), where the selection of the loop is offloaded to the larger dynamic system constituted by the bodily subject's coupling with its environment. At the same time, "the brain has to be sensitive simultaneously to multiple threats and opportunities in the environment and switch among them" (Dotov 2014, 6). To avoid unwanted, threatening environmental dynamics, the brain as a dynamic system needs to be able to switch to other dynamic organizational possibilities.

This accords well with Evan Thompson's account. The explanatory unit is the dynamic relation between bodily subject and its environment, including other bodily subjects. He states that the brain's basic logic of operation is to "couple movement and a stream of sensory activity in a continuous circular fashion" (Thompson 2010, 242). This puts the nervous system in context of body and world. The brain's function is intrinsically connected to a continuous circularity of motor movement and sensory activity as the bodily subject makes its way about in the world. The role of the nervous system is not to generate and manipulate physical symbols (mental representations), but to integrate the organism in a particular way, "holding it together as a mobile unity, as an autonomous sensorimotor agent" (Thompson 2010, 242). The brain and nervous system keeps these two sides in constant connection. How the bodily subject moves depends on what it senses, and what it senses depends on how and where it moves. In Merleau-Ponty's words, "every habit is both motor and perceptual" (Merleau-Ponty 1962, 152). This means that understanding the brain's functioning in the bodily subject involves appreciating its role in the mobile and sensing bodily subject, and that implies being embedded in the world. Thompson argues that "neural states are described not at the level of intrinsic neurophysiological properties or as mere neural correlates of mental states, but rather in terms of how they participate in dynamic sensorimotor patterns involving the whole organism" (Thompson 2010, 256–257). Neural activities in the brain need to be characterized in terms of how they take part in the skillful activity of the whole person actively embedded in the world. Brain states are best portrayed as participating in the larger nexus of sensory, motor, and cognitive activity. This situates descriptions of the brain in its role in bodily-being-in-the-world, including social interaction.

Thompson argues that this leads to a different understanding of mind. What we might call mind emerges in the reciprocal interactions among motor, sensory, and cognitive activity in the engagement with the surrounding world. The mind does not supervene on the brain, but rather the "mind is embodied in our entire organism and the world. Our mental lives involve three permanent and intertwined modes of bodily activity—self-regulation, sensorimotor coupling, and intersubjective interaction" (Thompson 2010, 241). By self-regulation he means the activities of maintaining and renewing (biotic) life, including the felt negative valences such as being hungry, sleepy, or afraid and positive valences such as such as being satiated, alert, or adventurous. These are consciously experienced mental states but intrinsically connected to continued maintenance of our bodiliness. By sensorimotor he means the way the person is coupled with the world through both action and perception, which are both always already emotionally charged. And by intersubjective interaction he means the dynamic interconnections between the experienced self and others cognitively and emotionally. All of these, together, constitute the mind or, more accurately, mental life. According to Thompson, "each individual human mind emerges from these extended modes of activity . . ." (Thompson 2010, 241). Mental life is always already bodily embedded in the world. The bodily character of mind, including its embeddedness in the world, means that isolating the mind—as something caused by the brain and as a set of experienced mental representations—is off the mark.

In this model, cognition is also understood differently. Scott Marratto argues that for Merleau-Ponty, "cognitive life is rooted in bodily movement and, in particular, in what is called 'coping' behavior" (Marratto 2013, 11). Cognition in his view is rooted in motility and perception, becoming "a living process." This means at least that for it to be cognition, it is an emergent dynamic that can't be decomposed into components, each of which would be parts of cognition and could add up to the whole. Merleau-Ponty's approach to cognition says Marratto, involves the idea that cognitive "behavior only becomes intelligible when we understand it as the enactment of a nexus of *meanings* linking an organism to its 'environment'. . ." (Marratto 2013, 17). Cognition is centrally something we *do*. It is a "skilful probing" in which "the world makes itself available to our reach" (Noë 2006, 216). Cognition more generally is subtended by and extensions of the same neural dynamic systems that support the sensorimotor skills of the bodily subject in its coming to grips with the world.

This clears the way for a different understanding of mental content. For Merleau-Ponty, content is relational: "the *behavior* of organisms in fact determines the *value* or *significance* of stimuli" (Marratto 2013, 17). Mental content on this reading is construed in terms of the experienced significance of incoming sensory information as the bodily subject deals with the dynamic, complex patterns that constitute its environment. Content arises in the relation of actively being situated in the world as "a kind of responsive activity on the part of the organism" (Marratto 2013, 17). We do not have to deny the obvious point that mental content depends on brain processes in some manner. But it does challenge the idea that a particular neural state has content matching the specific content of a conscious state, a context-free understanding of content. Marratto suggests that for Merleau-Ponty, mental content is intrinsically relational. Rather than construing mental content as a property of an internal state in isolation, it is construed as a function of a relation to something external to the bodily subject.

In the relational approach, we can understand content "in nonrepresentational, integrative, and dynamical terms" (Gallagher et al. 2013, 421). There are three aspects to this. First, the representational model is not helpful in understanding content. A representational model seems to push us toward a localization approach, searching for correlates of simple cognitive content in local brain areas. Second, content emerges in the dynamism of the organism-environment coupling, incorporating a multitude of more local sub-functions into an integrative whole as the bodily subject undertakes a task. And third, the emergent content is not static but is something essentially dynamic as the bodily subject makes its way about in the world.

Noë and Thompson suggest three more features of the mental content. Mental content has an inescapable coherence, is inherently experiential, and always actively attending to something; in their words, content is "structurally coherent, intrinsically experiential, and active and attentional" (Noë and Thompson 2004, 14). Each of these adds something to the idea of dynamic content. First, the *structural coherence* of content involves skillful mastery of sensorimotor relations. This relies on Merleau-Ponty's depiction of the structure of perceptual experience. For example, Merleau-Ponty argues that the structure of perceptual experience of (say) a butterfly relies on a figure-ground structure—no presence of a butterfly in one's experience without the background against which it is featured. Moreover, Noë and Thompson argue, "Figure-ground structure seems to be a global, non-atomistic property of visual experience" (Noë and Thompson 2004, 14). Although they acknowledge neuroscience has also been working on figure-ground analysis, they argue that this has not established the doctrine of content matching. The structural coherence of the content of experience is fundamentally different from that of its neural substrate. This is because the brain participates in something larger, a dynamic system, something with the familiar body parts of humans, for example—feet, hands, face, mouth, ears, eyes, and so forth. It is the whole person, as an active agent in its world, that responds, not the brain that happens to be housed in and nourished by a body. The secret to the brain is the body in the world. The secret to the structural coherence of perceptual content is the whole-being response to the circumstances within which the agent finds itself.

Second, our mental content is framed by a first-person dimension, making it *intrinsically experiential*. Noë and Thompson, drawing on the phenomenological tradition, suggest that part of, and central to, an experienced content is that it is always perspectival, from a first-person point of view. Dan Zahavi reminds us that, "Subjectivity is essentially oriented and open toward that which it is not, and it is exactly in this openness that it reveals itself to itself" (Zahavi 2005, 308). Mental content is a function of our bodily subjectivity. The butterfly one sees always stands "in a certain egocentric spatial relation to you, and as standing out against a background relative to you" (Noë and Thompson 2004, 16). With everything we know about neural substrates, there is little evidence that it experiences anything, let alone from a (certain) point of view (e.g., from its own egocentric space). That is, the content of neural substrates, if that concept is meaningful, is fundamentally different in kind. There is no correlative agreement between the contents of the two levels (neural and conscious), even if we might attribute content to the neural level.

Third, Noë and Thompson have a similar argument for the *active and attentional* features of conscious experience. By this they mean a number of things. When part of a perceptual object is occluded (hidden behind another object, say), a person doesn't experience only a part-object. Rather, we experience the whole object, centrally because we implicitly feel we could move around the occlusion to bring to view the hidden aspect of the object under attention. This means, they suggest, that the content of perceptual experience is "not so much a visual one as an attentional one" (Noë and Thompson 2004, 16). The object is foregrounded because of our attention to it, rather than because visually it is (say) in front of the background. Perhaps the 'content' of the neural substrate is determined by the causal mechanism. But the activity of attention rather than the passivity of light-wave reception is crucial in determining the content of a person's experience. They conclude that "the content of experience itself—the content of one's temporally extended, active, and attentional encounter with the environment—cannot be represented by neural representational systems as these are standardly conceived . . ." (Noë and Thompson 2004, 17). It is difficult to think what attentional content might look like at the neuronal level.

Something fundamentally relational and dynamic has been uncovered in this analysis of mental content. Noë and Thompson point out that, "perceptual content depends on the skilful activity of the whole animal or person, making use of its capacities for eye, head, and whole body movements, and for directed attention . . ." (Noë and Thompson 2004, 17). Mental content is not merely something inside the mind, as envisioned by theorists such as Frith, Metzinger, and Bruer. The content of experience is not an *internal* mental representation but a way of being-in-the-world as a bodily subject. Dan Zahavi states, "Rather than saying that we experience *representations*, it would be better to say that our experiences are *presentational*, and that they *present* the world as having certain features" (Zahavi 2005, 308; emphasis in original). Mental content is presentational, presenting the world as having certain features for a bodily subject already immersed in and dealing with the world. Even the more abstract content has this character, including mental rotation of objects and numerical magnitude (Badets and Pesenti 2010, 46; Engel 2011, 228).

We can describe the fundamental dynamic relationality of mental content in what J. J. Gibson calls affordances offered by the world. The door handle offers itself as graspable, the key-board as typable, and the chair as sitable. Affordances can roughly be thought of as the handiness of useful things (Heidegger 1996, 69; see also Gallagher 2008). Affordances are not objects with explicit characteristics, but relationalities associated with the bodily presence of someone situated in the world. The relational approach to understanding mental content is fundamentally different from the idea of an internal, context-free content that correlates with the content of a neural substrate. The relational approach obviates the need for the matching-content doctrine, which correlates representational content of conscious experience with representational content of neural substrates. This is in part because affordances connect closely to the sensorimotor dynamism of the bodily subject. Thompson states that everyday things in our lives "have motor senses or meanings . . . which elicit appropriate actions" (Thompson 2010, 247). The things in the world are first of all meanings to which the bodily subject can bring appropriate actions. The mug has the meaning of graspability for the hand that might enclose on it, and the sidewalk affords the possibility of walking. These are not meanings in themselves, objectively, but "by virtue of the orientation they have to our moving and perceiving bodies" (Thompson 2010, 248). For the bodily subject to make its way about in the world, its mental content is a unity of the meanings afforded by the things in the world and the bodily ability to interact with those meanings skillfully. Hubert Dreyfus suggests that the world's situations *solicit* the bodily subject to engage in skillful action (Dreyfus 2002, 367). Solicitations can be described, to use Susanna Siegel's term, as *experienced mandates*, experiences of the surrounding world that invite a person to act in a particular way. She says, "From your point of view, the environment pulls actions out of you directly, like a force moving a situation, with your actions in it, from one moment to the next" (Siegel 2014). Although ultimately Siegel retains representations in her model, her idea of experienced mandates actually alleviates the need for classic representationalism. Affordances are not objects to be perceived, spectator-like, via the senses, and *then* acted upon by an organized and deliberate set of motor actions. Rather, the affordances are experienced in the action itself, in the feeling of being moved by the environment to act in that way. It is in the invitation to act in particular ways, ways that the environment affords. There is a continual feeling of answerability that motivates the experience as mandated. This is not (propositional) content of an internal symbol occurring in the mind's presence room that then (subsequently) calls up another representation—a motor schema—to initiate action. Thompson states, "What it is to experience the world perceptually is to exercise one's bodily mastery or know-how of certain patterns of sensorimotor dependence between one's sensing and moving body and the environment" (Thompson 2005, 415). The bodily subject's interactions have a response character, a response to the feeling of answerability. This tightens further the sensory and motor connections of the bodily-being-in-the-world.

RETHINKING MENTAL CONTENT IN
EDUCATIONAL NEUROSCIENCE

Bodily subjectivity gives educational neuroscience a different framing model. Researching the brain and nervous system can rightly remain a central task in this alternative model. But the research will shift toward the brain's role in participating in the way the bodily subject interacts with the physical and social environment. Educational neuroscience might research how the learning brain is part of the bodily subject's learning activities, including the hands that reach and grasp, the eyes that focus, the upright postures freeing hands and locating eyes, and so forth (Gallagher et al. 2013). This shifts educational neuroscience research away from looking for neural correlates by suggesting it needs to think of the brain nonrepresentationally as an integrative and dynamic system. Or more to the point, the unit of explanation for educational neuroscience is not the brain in isolation. Rather, it is the dynamic relation between bodily subject (the learner) and its environment, including other bodily subjects, such as teachers. Research might include how the brain has its "own structural features that enable specific perception-action loops involving social and physical environments, which in turn effect statistical regularities that shape the structure of the nervous system" (Gallagher et al. 2013, 412–422). The brain as embedded, as a dynamic system, requires educational neuroscience to investigate the larger dynamic coupling between learner and teacher, between learners, and between learners and their environments. Further, if centrally the brain's role is anticipatory (Gallagher and Bower 2014), educational neuroscience would do well to investigate how neural processing participates in the dynamics of bodily subject's anticipatory aspects of processes such as perception and action. It could investigate how learning might involve "a kind of dynamic adjustment process in which the brain, as part of and along with the larger organism, settles into the right kind of attunement with the environment" (Gallagher and Bower 2014, 241). In this, educational neuroscience would expand the explanatory unit beyond the brain in isolation to the dynamic coupling between bodily subjects and their physical and social environments. If learning occurs in the interactive experiences of the bodily subject and the world, then educational neuroscience would do well to investigate the role the brain plays in that relationality. If full bodily subjectivity participates in the anticipatory processes of learning, educational neuroscience might show the centrality of the brain's anticipatory dynamics in virtue of its being part of that larger system.

Some educational neuroscience is heading in this direction. Stephen Campbell has taken this approach in his work on mathematics education. He states, "Embodied cognition provides mathematics educational neuroscience with a common perspective from which the lived subjective experience of mind is postulated to be manifest in objectively observable aspects of embodied actions and behaviour" (Campbell 2010, 318). He is capitalizing on the idea that there is a coupling between the learner as a bodily subject and the experienced world. Campbell's research is premised on the idea that learning isn't something that occurs in an interior presence room, but shows itself in the embodied actions of the bodily subject embedded in the world. Keith Sawyer and James Greeno also take this approach, arguing that "solutions of problems involving mathematical reasoning were better understood as emerging from interactions between people and resources in the setting than as products of mental operations with and on symbolic representations" (Sawyer and Greeno 2009, 348). For these educational neuroscientists and others, learning emerges in the dynamic system constituted by the coupling of bodily subject and world (Horn and Wilburn 2005, 752). On this construal, the study of learning involves what Sawyer and Greeno call situativity rather than a focus on the isolated changes within the mind's mental structures. In their research on mathematics learning, they find that "it is meaningless to assess whether someone has learned a particular topic of mathematics without taking into account the kind of activity system in which the person's knowledge is to be evaluated" (Sawyer and Greeno 2009, 349). Thus a paper-and-pencil test would not be a good 'activity system' to judge if a learner can use mathematics in an 'activity system' such as buying groceries. The use of the former to evaluate the latter is based on the idea that mathematical learning is located inside the head, as properties of mental representations. The situative approach is an alternative to the mental-representation model of learning. This also implies that educational neuroscience research cannot remain isolated in the laboratory with a focus on individual learners in fMRI machines (for example). If learning is an emergent phenomenon that arises in situations, that is, as a form of self-organization of a dynamic system constituted in the coupling of bodily subject and world, then educational neuroscience needs a more embedded approach.

In this paper, I have argued that educational neuroscience needs to get beyond a representational model of mind. In its stead I have offered a different construal of mind, one that brings together brain, body, and world. I have suggested that rather than mental representation and computation, we move to a dynamic systems understanding of the brain. In turn, I have suggested that the brain is best understood in the context of bodily subjectivity, embedded in a world. This is fundamentally a relational, dynamic construal of mental life, cognition, and learning.

REFERENCES

Aquila, Richard E. 1988. "The Cartesian and a Certain 'Poetic' Notion of Consciousness." *Journal of the History of Ideas* 49 (4): 543–562. doi:10.2307/2709673.

Badets, Arnaud, and Mauro Pesenti. 2010. "Creating Number Semantics Through Finger Movement Perception." *Cognition* 115 (1): 46–53. doi:10.1016/j.cognition.2009.11.007.

Beer, Randall D. 2008. "Dynamical Systems and Embedded Cognition." In *The Cambridge Handbook of Artificial Intelligence.*, edited by K. Frankish and Ramsey, 128–150. Cambridge University Press.

Blakemore, Sarah-Jayne, and Uta Frith. 2005. *The Learning Brain: Lessons for Education.* Vol. VI. Malden: Blackwell Publishing.

Bruer, John T. 1993. *Schools for Thought: A Science of Learning in the Classroom.* Cambridge, MA: MIT Press.

Bruer, John T. 2008. "Building Bridges in Neuroeducation." In *The Educated Brain: Essays in Neuroeducation*, edited by Antonio M. Battro, Kurt W. Fischer, and Pierre Le´na, 43–58. Cambridge, UK: Cambridge University Press. Retrieved from http://site.ebrary.com/id/10221463

Campbell, Stephen R. 2010. "Embodied Minds and Dancing Brains: New Opportunities for Research in Mathematics Education." In *Theories of Mathematics Education*, edited by Bharath Sriraman and Lyn English, 309–331. Advances in Mathematics Education. Springer Berlin Heidelberg. Retrieved from http://link.springer.com/chapter/10.1007/978-3-642-00742-2_31

Carew, Thomas J., and Susan H. Magsamen. 2010. "Neuroscience and Education: An Ideal Partnership for Producing Evidence-Based Solutions to Guide 21st Century Learning." *Neuron* 67 (5): 685–688.

Dehaene, Stanislas. 2008. "Cerebral Constraints in Reading and Arithmetic: Education as a 'Neuronal Recycling' Process." In *The Educated Brain: Essays in Neuroeducation*, edited by Antonio M. Battro, Kurt W. Fischer, and Pierre Le´na, 232–247. Cambridge, UK: Cambridge University Press.

Dehaene, Stanislas. 2010. "The Calculating Brain." In *Mind, Brain, and Education: Neuroscience Implications for the Classroom*, edited by David A. Sousa, 179–198. Bloomington, IN: Solution Tree Press.

Dotov, Dobromir G. 2014. "Putting Reins on the Brain. How the Body and Environment Use It." *Frontiers in Human Neuroscience* 8 (October): 1–12. doi:10.3389/fnhum.2014.00795.

Dreyfus, Hubert L. 2002. "Intelligence Without Representation—Merleau-Ponty's Critique of Mental Representation the Relevance of Phenomenology to Scientific Explanation." *Phenomenology and the Cognitive Sciences* 1 (4): 367–383. doi:10.1023/A:1021351606209.

Engel, Andreas K. 2011. "Directive Minds: How Dynamics Shapes Cognition." In *Enaction: Toward a New Paradigm for Cognitive Science*, edited by John Robert Stewart, Olivier Gapenne, and Ezequiel A. Di Paolo, 219–244. Cambridge, MA: MIT Press.

Fodor, Jerry A. 1981. *Representations: Philosophical Essays on the Foundations of Cognitive Science*. Cambridge, MA: MIT Press.

Fodor, Jerry A. 1983. *Modularity of Mind: An Essay on Faculty Psychology*. Cambridge, MA: MIT Press.

Fodor, Jerry A. 1987. *Psychosemantics: The Problem of Meaning in the Philosophy of Mind*. Cambridge, MA: MIT Press.

Frith, Chris. 2009. *Making Up the Mind: How the Brain Creates Our Mental World*. Hoboken, NJ: John Wiley & Sons.

Gallagher, Shaun. 2008. "Philosophical Antecedents of Situated Cognition." In *Cambridge Handbook of Situated Cognition*, edited by P. Robbins and M. Aydede, 35–52. Cambridge, UK: Cambridge University Press.

Gallagher, Shaun. 2010. "Merleau-Ponty's Phenomenology of Perception." *Topoi* 29 (2): 183–185. doi:10.1007/s11245-010-9079-y.

Gallagher, Shaun, and Matthew Bower. 2014. "Making Enactivism Even More Embodied." *Avant*, 5 (2): 232–247.

Gallagher, Shaun, Daniel D. Hutto, Jan Slaby, and Jonathan Cole. 2013. "The Brain as Part of An Enactive System." *Behavioral and Brain Sciences* 36 (04): 421–422. doi:10.1017/S0140525X12002105.

Heidegger, Martin. 1996. *Being and Time*, translated by Joan Stambaugh. Albany, NY: SUNY Press.

Horn, Jim, and Denise Wilburn. 2005. "The Embodiment of Learning." *Educational Philosophy and Theory* 37 (5): 745–760. doi:10.1111/j.1469-5812.2005.00154.x.

Horst, Steven. 2011. *Symbols, Computation, and Intentionality: A Critique of the Computational Theory of Mind*. Berkeley, CA: University of California Press.

Jackendoff, Ray S. 1990. *Consciousness and the Computational Mind*. Cambridge, MA: MIT Press.

Joldersma, Clarence W. 1994. *The Mind of Science: A Critique of Computationalism's Scientific Approach to Mind*. PhD dissertation. University of Toronto.

Juarrero, Alicia. 2000. "Dynamics in Action: Intentional Behavior as a Complex System." *Emergence* 2 (2): 24–57.

Kim, Jaegwon. 1984. "Concepts of Supervenience." *Philosophy and Phenomenological Research* 45 (2): 153–176. doi:10.2307/2107423.

Marratto, Scott L. 2013. *The Intercorporeal Self: Merleau-Ponty on Subjectivity*. Albany: State University of New York Press.

Merleau-Ponty, Maurice. 1962. *Phenomenology of Perception*. London: Routledge & Paul.

Metzinger, Thomas. 2009. *The Ego Tunnel: The Science of the Mind and the Myth of the Self*. New York: Basic Books.

Miłkowski, Marcin. 2013. *Explaining the Computational Mind*. Cambridge, MA: MIT Press.

Noë, Alva. 2006. *Action in Perception.* Cambridge, MA: MIT Press.

Noë, Alva, and Evan Thompson. 2004. "Are There Neural Correlates of Consciousness?" *Journal of Consciousness Studies* 11 (1): 3–28.

Petitto, Laura-Ann, and Kevin Niall Dunbar. 2009. "Educational Neuroscience: New Discoveries from Bilingual Brains, Scientific Brains, and the Educated Mind." *Mind, Brain and Education : The Official Journal of the International Mind, Brain, and Education Society* 3 (4): 185–197. doi:10.1111/j.1751–228X.2009.01069.x.

Poldrack, Russell A. 2010. "Subtraction and Beyond: The Logic of Experimental Designs for Neuroimaging." In *Foundational Issues in Human Brain Mapping*, edited by Stephen Jose Hanson and Martin Bunzl, 147–160. Cambridge, MA: MIT Press.

Poldrack, Russell A. 2011. "Inferring Mental States from Neuroimaging Data: From Reverse Inference to Large-Scale Decoding." *Neuron* 72 (5): 692–697. doi:10.1016/j.neuron.2011.11.001.

Posner, Michael I. 2010. "Neuroimaging Tools and the Evolution of Educational Neuroscience." In *Mind, Brain, and Education: Neuroscience Implications for the Classroom*, edited by David A. Sousa, 26–43. Bloomington, IN: Solution Tree Press.

Posner, Michael I., S.E. Petersen, P.T. Fox, and M.E. Raichle. 1988. "Localization of Cognitive Operations in the Human Brain." *Science* 240 (4859): 1627–1631. doi:10.1126/science.3289116.

Raichle, M.E. 1998. "The Neural Correlates of Consciousness: An Analysis of Cognitive Skill Learning." *Philosophical Transactions of the Royal Society of London. Series B: Biological Sciences* 353 (1377): 1889–1901. doi:10.1098/rstb.1998.0341.

Rees, Geraint, Gabriel Kreiman, and Christof Koch. 2002. "Neural Correlates of Consciousness in Humans." *Nature Reviews Neuroscience* 3 (4): 261–270. doi:10.1038/nrn783.

Sawyer, Keith R., and James G. Greeno. 2009. "Situativity and Learning." In *The Cambridge Handbook of Situated Cognition*, edited by Philip Robbins and Murat Aydede, 347–367. Cambridge and New York: Cambridge University Press.

Schöner, G. 2008. "Dynamical Systems Approaches to Cognition." In *Cambridge Handbook of Computational Cognitive*. Cambridge, UK: Cambridge University Press. Retrieved from http://fog.its.uiowa.edu/~icdls/dft-school/documents/DFT_Publications/cambridge_chapter_schoner.pdf

Siegel, Susanna. 2014. "Affordances and the Contents of Perception." In *Does Perception Have Content?*, edited by Berit Brogaard, 51–75. Oxford: Oxford University Press.

Szűcs, Dénes, and Usha Goswami. 2007. "Educational Neuroscience: Defining a New Discipline for the Study of Mental Representations." *Mind, Brain, and Education* 1 (3): 114–127. doi:10.1111/j.1751-228X.2007.00012.x.

Thompson, Evan. 2005. "Sensorimotor Subjectivity and the Enactive Approach to Experience." *Phenomenology and the Cognitive Sciences* 4 (4): 407–427.

Thompson, Evan. 2010. *Mind in Life: Biology, Phenomenology, and the Sciences of Mind.* Cambridge, MA: Belknap Press of Harvard University Press.

Tononi, G., and C. Koch. 2008. "The Neural Correlates of Consciousness: An Update." *Annals of the New York Academy of Sciences* 1124 (1): 239–261. doi:10.1196/annals.1440.004.

Tsuda, Ichiro. 2001. "Toward an Interpretation of Dynamic Neural Activity in Terms of Chaotic Dynamical Systems." *Behavioral and Brain Sciences* 24 (5): 793–809.

Van Gelder, Tim. 1995. "What Might Cognition Be, If Not Computation?" *The Journal of Philosophy* 92 (7): 345–381. doi:10.2307/2941061.

Van Gelder, Tim. 1998. "The Dynamical Hypothesis in Cognitive Science." *Behavioral and Brain Sciences* 21 (05): 615–628.

Zahavi, Dan. 2005. "Intentionality and Experience." *Synthesis Philosophica* 20 (40): 299–318.

Zatorre, Robert J., R. Douglas Fields, and Heidi Johansen-Berg. 2012. "Plasticity in Gray and White: Neuroimaging Changes in Brain Structure during Learning." *Nature Neuroscience* 15 (4): 528–536. doi:10.1038/nn.3045.

11 Enactive Hermeneutics and Natural Pedagogy[1]

Shaun Gallagher

Neural hermeneutics is a concept developed by the neuropsychologist Chris Frith (Frith and Wentzer 2013).[2] Frith works out this concept in terms of predictive coding models of brain function and a simulationist approach to social cognition. In this paper, I'll summarize the idea of neural hermeneutics and offer a critique from the phenomenologically informed perspective of embodied cognition. An alternative, 'enactive hermeneutics,' is proposed with a focus on social interaction, including the concept of natural pedagogy developed by Csibra and Gergely (2009). Enactive hermeneutics, I'll argue, productively allows for a more adequate understanding of the relations among embodied cognition, neuroscience, and education.

NEURAL HERMENEUTICS

Hermeneutics, the theory and practice of interpretation, has a long history that can be traced back to ancient Greece. In the development of hermeneutics, there is constant reference to education in the broad sense. In his dialogue *Ion*, Plato explores the role that the rapsode plays in interpreting the poets and the gods. Rapsodes, like Ion, in their performances, interpret the poets and allow the audience to gain understanding and insight. The insight that we get from Plato is that in this performance the rapsode is not fully in control. Prefiguring more recent understandings of such processes, expressed by philosophers like Heidegger (2008) and Gadamer (2004), the interpreter (and this means the educator too [see Gallagher 1992]) is caught up in a process that is much more complex and extensive than she can be aware of, and it ultimately expresses itself, for better or for worse, through her interpretation. The complexity and extensiveness at stake here is usually conceived in terms of the larger forces of culture and history, or sometimes in very specific structures of intersubjective engagement. More recently neuroscience has added a twist to this complexity that concerns forces inside the interpreter—the actual brains behind the interpretation.

In some cases, the concept of interpretational control is cast in terms of the truth or falsity of the interpretation. On some conservative conceptions, the correctness of the interpretation of a text, for example, is measured by whether it reflects the author's intention or the original audience's under-standing (e.g., Betti 1990; Hirsch 1967; Schleiermacher 1998). One gains control over this process by doing one's historical research and by brack-eting any biases that come from one's own interests, culture, or historical period. This view depends on a conception of truth as correctness, or *ade-quatio*, where the interpretation has to match the objective state of affairs. This concept of truth is challenged by Heidegger, who focuses on the more ancient concept of *aletheia*, or truth as a type of uncovering, where the ques-tion is about what the interpretation reveals rather than what it gets correct. Gadamer extends this idea by showing that it is impossible to control for all biases, that some biases are productive, and that what we call truth is really a product of a dialogue between interpreter and interpreted rather than something to be found objectively in the text.

Frith, in his outline of neural hermeneutics, acknowledges the difficulty in trying to take up the conservative view of hermeneutics where the major task is defined as "how to develop criteria for deciding when an interpretation is correct" (Frith and Wentzer 2013). He rightly considers this as problem-atic, and he understands the problem to apply, not just to the interpretation of texts, whose authors may be dead or otherwise unavailable, but also to intersubjective, face-to-face communication. Even if we are conversing with a living author, as Gadamer points out, the author has no privilege or con-trol in regard to his own text, since a text always goes beyond its author. Frith indicates that perhaps this goes even deeper, since it's not just a ques-tion of whether I or the author can understand a text but also whether I can understand the person with whom I am conversing.

> Even if I am talking with you face-to-face, I cannot access your mind to check whether my interpretation of what you have just said corresponds to what you intended me to understand. I can create a coherent story, but I can never get independent evidence about the correctness of my interpretations.
>
> (Frith and Wentzer 2013, 657)

There is, of course, a practical understanding that seems to be sufficient in cases of everyday communication, and we can judge whether we understand one another over the course of time if we find some consistency between ongoing understanding and behavior. This, however, does not put interpre-tational control in the interpreter's hands, since it still depends on processes that get worked out in time and the other's behavior, and it is still open to uncertainty, further revision, and even more interpretation. Nonetheless, as Frith notes, "in spite of this apparently insurmountable difficulty," we seem to manage to understand each other. Frith wants to know how this works.

Specifically, Frith, as a good neuroscientist, is interested in identifying the brain mechanisms that allow us to understand one another. On the nitty-gritty neurophysiological level, Frith is a champion of the predictive coding approach to understanding brain function; and in terms of social cognition, he favors theory of mind (ToM) approaches. In regard to this question, he focuses on how simulation and alignment support our understanding of others (Frith 2007).

Predictive coding is a more general theory of how the brain functions. For example, when we open our eyes and look at an apple, the brain generates a myriad of sensory signals. These signals require interpretation at a very basic neural level, since any particular visual sensory signal (i.e., any particular activation of neurons in the visual cortex) is ambiguous with respect to what the object of perception might be—an apple, a tomato, a baseball, etc. To resolve this ambiguity, on the basis of prior experiences or beliefs, our brain predicts the most likely cause of the sensory signal and then collects more evidence (more sensory signals) sometimes by taking action. The latter strategy is simply to move around and gather more sensory data that will confirm the original prediction or send prediction errors back to the brain, which then revises its prediction. In a dynamic process measured in terms of milliseconds, the brain comes to settle on the best interpretation by minimizing prediction errors (minimizing ambiguity). It perceives an apple. This applies not only to apples and other objects but also to other people and other minds.

> In principle the same mechanism can be applied when trying to understand the mental world of others. The major difference is that, unlike with [apples], the process goes in both directions: while I am trying to understand you, you are trying to understand me.
> (Frith and Wentzer 2013, 658; also see Friston and Frith (2014) for more detail about the predictive coding approach to social cognition)

Social cognition involves processes of perception and of folk-psychological inference. The brain starts with sensory evidence, perhaps in the form of observed behavior or spoken words; it then attempts to infer through a series of hierarchical interpretations the thought or belief or desire that causes the behavior. Importantly, moving away from more static ToM approaches that frame this process in terms of one person observing the behavior of the other, Frith acknowledges that this is a two-way, dyadic process.

> Here the sensory evidence might be the words I hear from which I infer the idea you are trying to convey. I can test my inference, not only by predicting what else you are likely to say, but also by saying something myself and predicting how you will respond. Meanwhile you will be applying the same strategy to what I say. When our prediction errors become sufficiently low, then we have probably understood one another.
> (Frith and Wentzer 2013, 658)

For Frith, however, the process is somewhat indirect. Since I don't have any direct access to your mind, the prediction errors that we are minimizing pertain to the difference between "my idea and my representation of your idea" (658). To be more precise, it's the difference between my original prediction of what you mean and subsequent interpretations based on more informed predictions.

Frith suggests that this formulation captures the sense of the hermeneutic circle, which he understands in the traditional terms of parts and whole. The whole can only be understood in terms of the parts, and the parts can only be understood in terms of the whole. "In the same way, in the predictive coding loop, the inferred cause (the idea, *the whole*) predicts the evidence, while, at the same time, the evidence (the words, *the parts*) modifies the inferred cause" (Frith and Wentzer 2013, 658).

Predictive coding is an explanation of the mechanism, but it doesn't explain the starting point. With respect to what others might be thinking, where do we get the first prediction? One possibility is that the first inference is made on the basis of a prior knowledge of folk psychology. Carruthers (1996) would call this a tacit theoretical inference that the brain makes; it gets tested out in the ongoing encounter and revised until we reach understanding. This would be a version of what is called "theory-theory" (TT). A different possibility, indicated by Frith, corresponds to simulation theory (ST). On this approach, I would predict your mental states on the basis of what my own mental states would be if I were in your situation or engaged in the kind of behavior that you are engaged in.

On some interpretations of ST, one can see close connections between traditional hermeneutics and contemporary neuroscience (see e.g., Stueber 2006). Simulation is often understood as a form of empathy, and versions of it can be found in the hermeneutical tradition in philosophers like Dilthey (see, e.g., Chenari 2009). ST is also associated with the mirror neuron system, which is activated both in cases when I am engaged in intentional action and when I see you engaged in intentional action (Rizzolatti et al. 2001). When I am observing your action, my motor system simulates it by activating the same neurons that activate when I do the same action (as well as mechanisms that inhibit me from doing the action in this case). Indeed, the same mirror system allows me to predict your next action or where your actions are headed, since it also codes for the goals of actions.

One objection to ST is that it presumes that the other person is similar to the perceiver. I've referred to this as the diversity problem (Gallagher 2012a), and it's been a classic objection to these kinds of theories. Both Max Scheler (1954) and Gilbert Ryle (1949) raised this objection against a forerunner to ST. Ryle, for example, argued that the logic of simulation isn't correct, because the idea of imputing to a variety of others what is true of my simulated action ignores the diversity of their actions. "[T]he observed appearances and actions of people differ very markedly, so the imputation to them of inner processes closely matching [one's own or] one another would be actually contrary to the evidence" (1949, 54).

For Frith, however, this problem can be mitigated through *alignment*, which is again tied to the mirror system. Alignment signifies the automatic tendency to imitate each other. We find this phenomenon in dyadic conversation, for example, where we mimic the gestures, facial expressions, emotions, intonations, and even the vocabulary of others. Even if we are somewhat different from each other, alignment "makes us more similar to the person we are interacting with and thereby makes motor and mental simulation more efficient" (Frith and Wentzer 2013, 658).

The notion of alignment is important because it points to processes that go beyond the brain processes of interaction that depend on the other person and perhaps on the particularities of the situation. It signals a 'collaboration' between partners who are engaged in discourse or action. I note that this is an optimistic hermeneutics, akin to the romantic hermeneutics of Schleiermacher, whom Frith cites in this connection. From Schleiermacher we can obtain a "better understanding of the text even than the original author" (Frith and Wentzer 2013, 659). Frith and Wentzer extend the argument:

> By the same argument a listener can have a better understanding of the speaker, than the speaker herself. This is because the listener will not only understand the message that the speaker intends to convey, but can also take account of signs, such as body language, indicating aspects of the message that the speaker was unaware of. This better understanding will be fed back to the speaker in the course of the conversation. Thus, through interactions with others we can achieve a better understanding of ourselves.
>
> (2013, 659)

Obviously there are cases in which we fail to understand others, where we fail to pick up on their bodily cues; and there are cases in which we oppose the other, fail to attain anything like alignment, and yet still understand each other. Just such cases motivate the thought, explicated by Gadamer in contrast to Schleiermacher, that we have a *different* understanding, not necessarily a better one: "We understand differently if we understand at all" (2004, 264). This means that we should still worry about the diversity problem.

ENACTIVE HERMENEUTICS

Accordingly there are still worries that alignment, especially in the theoretical context of simulation, does not go very far in solving the diversity problem. In this regard, one can cite empirical studies that show the import of cultural differences and that we do not empathize with members of an outgroup. We know, for example, that perceptual processes at the subpersonal level are already shaped, via mechanisms of plasticity, by environmental (including social and cultural) factors and prior experience. Indeed, this is consistent with the predictive coding approach that Frith himself takes. For example, there is a well-known difference between the way Westerners and Asians perceive and attend to visual objects and contexts (Goh and Park 2009). Not only are brain processes different relative to the use of different cultural tools and practices, also there are cultural variations in brain mechanisms specifically underlying person perception and emotion regulation (Kitayama and Park 2010). For example, relative to European Americans, Asians show different neural processing in response to images of faces that represent a social-evaluative threat (Park and Kitayama 2012). Social and cultural factors, then, have a physical effect on brain processes that shape basic perceptual experience and emotional responses. Such processes may interfere or prevent alignment, or make any alignment that appears a mere surface phenomenon.

Consider also a study by Xu et al. (2009) that dramatically demonstrates the neural effects of implicit racial bias. Specifically it shows that empathic neural responses to another person's pain are modulated by racial in-group/out-group relationships. Brain imaging from fMRIs shows decreased activation in the anterior cingulate cortex (ACC), an area thought to correlate with empathic response, when Caucasians viewed Chinese subjects undergoing painful stimulations (needle penetration) to the face, compared with ACC activation when they viewed the same stimulations applied to racial in-group members. Likewise when Chinese subjects view Caucasians in the same situation. Apparently we are simply less responsive to out-group members, and our brains display significantly less empathic-related activity when observing out-group members (Molnar-Szakacs et al. 2007). In-group members fail to understand out-group member actions, and this is particularly prominent for those out-groups who are disliked and dehumanized (Gutsell and Inzlicht 2010; see Gallagher and Varga 2014).

If such social and cultural factors interfere with alignment and undermine simulation, they are in fact real limitations to our understanding. Notwithstanding the limitations on alignment, however, I suggest that this notion, rather than simulation, points in the right direction, because it starts to consider more enactive, embodied aspects of our intersubjective interactions and to go beyond narrow considerations that concern brain function. Generally speaking, the alternative to TT or ST approaches is an approach that emphasizes embodied interaction and takes the unit of explanation to be brain-body-environment (where environment means both physical and social environment). Interaction theory (IT) argues that the mechanisms of social cognition are not entirely in the brain or inside the head. In this respect, TT and ST place the emphasis on finding such mechanisms within the individual, in either a ToM network that includes the temporo-parietal junction, medial parietal cortex, and medial prefrontal cortex (e.g., Saxe and Kanwisher 2003; Saxe et al. 2009) and correlates with the generation of theoretical inferences about the mental states of others, or the mirror system in premotor and parietal cortexes (Iacoboni et al. 2005) that constitutes internal simulations. The debate between TT and ST, indeed, can be framed as a debate about neural hermeneutics. In contrast, IT proposes that social cognition is more about what I'll call 'enactive hermeneutics.'

The enactivist model understands the brain as an integrated part of a larger dynamical system that includes body and (both physical and social) environment.[3] The explanatory unit of perception (or cognition, action, etc.) is not just the brain, or even two (or more) brains in the case of social cognition, but dynamic relations between organism and environment or between two or more embodied subjects. The processes of social interaction, accordingly, are not reducible to the neuronal processes or mechanisms found inside the individual's head; they include physical engagements with others in socially defined environments; they are characterized by embodied interactions and affective processes where distinct forms of sensory-motor couplings are generated by the perception and response to facial expression, posture, movement, gestures, etc., in rich pragmatic and social contexts.

The enactive approach doesn't rule out the importance of brain processes.[4] Mirror neurons, for example, may indeed play an important part in social cognition, not by simulating actions of others, representing a small version of them inside one's head, but by being part of larger sensory-motor processes that respond to different interaction affordances (e.g., Caggiano et al. 2009; Gallagher 2007). The emphasis falls on these larger attunement processes that allow an agent to perceive the other as someone to respond to or with whom one can interact. For the enactivists, 'attunement' is more appropriate than 'alignment,' since attunement may include negative and not just positive aspects. Sometimes understanding another, and in some cases mutual understanding, is accomplished in the social interaction itself where shared meaning (or some decision or even some misunderstanding) is instituted in a way that could not be instituted by brain processes alone inside the single individual (De Jaegher et al. 2010). Di Paolo and De Jaegher (2012) call this 'participatory sense making.' It involves a dynamic interactive process that goes beyond the individual participants in the same way that the meaning of a text goes beyond the author.

This is not the place to provide a full account of interaction theory or the scientific evidence it's based on (see Gallagher 2001, 2008, 2012b; Ratcliffe 2007; Reddy 2008). Rather, I want to focus on the notion that social cognition involves a dynamic interactive process of participatory sense making that goes beyond the individuals involved, since this takes us back to the issue of control (or lack of it). Here I'll provide one example and then go on to discuss the concept of natural pedagogy.

The example concerns the perception of emotion or, more precisely, what happens when we are engaged with others who are expressing a certain emotion. One can think of emotions as complex patterns that are constituted not just by internal phenomenal feelings but also by bodily and facial expressions, behaviors, action expressions, and so forth. On this view, emotion perception may be considered a form of pattern recognition (Izard 1972; Izard et al. 2000; Newen et al. 2015). That is, features of the emotion itself are perceptible, features such as facial expressions, movements, action-tendencies, vocal intonation, and the specifics of the intentional object and the situation. What we perceive when we perceive an emotion is a gestalt, an integrated set of perceptible phenomena that constitute, at least in part, the emotion.

Of course the neural underpinnings of emotion perception will be quite complex. It's important to know that, for example, the perception of another's face activates not just the face recognition area and ventral visual pathway, which corresponds to object recognition, but also the dorsal visual pathway that informs our motor system and facilitates motor control and action (Debruille et al. 2012). Consistent with the enactive view, this suggests that we perceive action affordances in the face of the other. We don't simply perceive a snapshot of a face in an instant, we *respond* in a temporal continuity to others' emotions as well as to their actions. Accordingly, an agent's perception of another's face presents not just objective patterns that one might recognize (identify) as emotions. Rather, it involves complex interactive behavioral and response patterns arising out of an active engagement with the other's face—not a simple recognition of objective facial features, but an interactive perception that involves the experience of significance or valence.

The idea that emotion is a pattern of aspects motivates the idea that the perception of emotion is a kind of pattern recognition, as indicated earlier. In some sense this is true, but it is not the whole story. To perceive an emotion, as a bodily expression, is not simply to recognize an object or a pattern, as if the task was to simply identify the emotion. This is often the way that emotion perception experiments are set up. A subject is presented with a picture of a face or a body and asked to identify the emotion. In contexts of real interaction with others, however, it is not a task of emotion identification but concerns how one responds to emotion. To perceive an emotion is to experience significance (De Gelder 2013). It is to become attuned to a valence that manifests itself as affectively relevant and has an effect on the perceiver, indeed, on the perceiver's whole body (Huis in 't Veld et al. 2014).

The idea that perception is merely the identification or recognition of an object or a pattern of features remains an overly cognitive and incomplete explanation. Moreover, this is as far as a predictive coding account goes—it explains a process of prediction and elimination of prediction errors that seemingly finishes when the brain has inferred, whether by theoretical inference (TT) or by simulation (ST), the correct mental state in the other's mind. In this respect, it seems to be a cold, calculating process in search of a correct answer. Simulation is often characterized as having one's system (or mental) state match the system (mental) state of the other, either automatically or through a multi-step process, but only for purposes of identifying the other person's mental state. That's the importance in ST of inhibitory mechanisms or of sequestering or quarantining the simulated states, which are regarded as pretend or vicarious states (e.g., Goldman 2006). Even empathy is considered to be a vicarious state rather than a real emotional feeling for the other that may have affective consequences for the empathizer (e.g., de Vignemont and Jacob 2012).

In contrast, an enactive hermeneutics would suggest that at some level, the experience of the gaze of another person directed at you *affects* you (in the strong sense of 'affect') (see e.g., Sartre 1956; Stawarska 2009). Likewise, your perception of the other's emotion *affects* you, even if this affect is not consciously recognized. Even when presented with masked, subliminal images of angry or happy faces or bodies, one's autonomic and peripheral systems register the emotion and respond (Tamietto 2013), and this response is part of what the perception is.[5] The perception of emotion is often an affective perception.[6]

This is part of how interaction works to establish not only understanding but real, existential engagement that takes the process beyond the control of the individuals toward a participatory sense making. This is not just confined to the case of emotion; it also applies to intentions, actions, and joint actions, including instances of communication, working together, and learning together.

NATURAL PEDAGOGY

The enactive processes of embodied interaction are important for learning in educational contexts. Fitting closely with the IT approach to social cognition, the concept of natural pedagogy (Csibra and Gergely 2009) provides an account of how we gain generalizable, conceptual knowledge. Some philosophers argue that children need language to gain access to the realm of concepts (e.g., Brandom 1994; Davidson 1975; Dummett 1993). For example, Davidson argues that attaining a concept of belief (or any concept) is not possible without being capable of speech or the interpretation of speech (1975, 170; see Davidson 2003; Margolis 2011). We might think that Gadamer also would consider language essential for conceptual understanding. Piaget, in contrast, argues that concepts may be acquired prior to language ability (Piaget and Inhelder 1969), and a number of philosophers agree, appealing to an internal system of mental representations (Bermudez 2003; and for different reasons, Fodor 1975; Pinker 1994). On the enactive view, however, neither language nor mental representation initiates or is required for conceptual abilities (i.e., abilities to acquire and use concepts), even if at some point language and external representations may facilitate concept acquisition and use. Rather, what initiates and facilitates conceptual abilities is something very specific in intersubjective interaction (Gallagher 2005).

Csibra and Gergely's (2009) notion of *natural pedagogy* addresses this question and suggests that it is not a spoken word, or language, *per se* (or language alone) that allows for the development of conceptual ability. Csibra and Gergely (2009, 148) define learning as a conceptual accomplishment that involves "acquiring new information" and being able to use it later when necessary. It requires generalizing information to new situations—learning not just individual facts that apply only to the one immediate situation in which they are learned but also learning to apply concepts to different objects, locations, or contexts. How is it possible to do this when in the learning process we are actually located in only one particular situation at a time—how do we know that the information we gain about X in this situation applies to X in other situations (the *problem of induction*) if it is not through language *per se*? A more standard explanation in terms of language is that children learn by associating the word they hear with the object referenced. They hear a word like 'apple' a number of times, always in association with the particular kind of fruit. After a number of instances, they learn to associate the word with the thing. Some kind of statistical learning mechanism in their brain establishes the association (firing together—wiring together); in predictive coding terms, it becomes a prior. Indeed, predictive coding has been used to explain associative learning, and associative learning plays an important role in facilitating prediction by providing the priors that ground it (Schultz and Dickinson 2000). On this view, repetitive passive observations are sufficient. Infants, however, tend to learn faster than can be accounted for in this way. Indeed, in some cases, they can learn generalizable knowledge from a single instance. How is that possible?

Csibra and Gergely (2009) argue, in this respect, for the importance of ostensive communication. Specifically, certain interactive aspects of communicative practices lead to conceptual learning. Infants, prior to speech, are not passive assimilators; they are more proactively receptive to communications because they are sensitive to ostensive signals that indicate they are being addressed. In contexts of ostensive communicative interaction, infants develop referential expectations and are biased to interpret such communications as conveying information that is generalizable.

Here are some examples. If by ostensive demonstration where I get the infant's attention by meeting his or her gaze, for example, and by addressing the demonstration explicitly to him or her, I show the infant two airplanes and say that 'airplanes fly'; the infant learns not just that these two airplanes fly, he or she learns generic knowledge about airplanes. The information "is generalizable to other members of the category and to variable contexts" (Csibra and Gergely 2009, 148). The communication of knowledge in this way, however, is not limited to linguistic communication.

> If I show you by manual demonstration how to open a milk carton, what you will learn is how to open that kind of container (i.e. you acquire kind-generalizable knowledge from a single manifestation). In such cases, the observer does not need to rely on statistical procedures to

extract the relevant information to be generalized because this is selectively manifested to her by the communicative demonstration.

(148)

What's important is that the communication is interactive, in the sense that it is ostensively directed at the learner, or that the learner is being actively guided. Such a pattern of learning is fundamentally different from situations in which the learner is passively observing or overhearing something. On a passive osmosis method like that, even over the course of several repetitions, the child does not necessarily generalize what it sees or hears.

Ostensive communication means

(1) there is some indication or sign that the communication or demonstration is meant to be communicative (and not just an accidental happening), and
(2) there is some sign that specifies the addressee so that the infant knows she is being addressed.

Csibra and Gergely show that the clearest ostensive cues involve direct gaze toward the addressee and mutual eye contact. Infants have an innate tendency to look to the eyes and to join in mutual gaze. In addition, auditory cues (e.g., motherese intonation) can capture the infant's attention: "young infants tend to follow gaze shifts only when these are preceded by an ostensive signal such as eye contact or infant-directed greeting" (2009, 151). Since the attention of the infant must be directed to an object, clearly situations of joint attention seem a natural place for this to occur. Besides pointing or manipulation/demonstration, one can use eye direction (infants expect to find a referent when they follow gaze).

Based on experimental studies, Csibra and Gergely show that infants in such circumstances "expect to learn something generalizable rather than just become informed about particular episodic facts that obtain only in the 'here-and-now'" (2009, 151). For example, when an agent looks at a particular object and expresses a certain emotion on his face (joy, disgust, fear, etc.), fourteen-month-olds interpret this "as conveying valence information about the referent [rather] than [simply] expressing the subjective attitude state of the communicator towards the object" (151). Eighteen-month-olds apply this to other people. That is, they generalize to the idea that other people will also like or dislike or fear the object, respectively (Gergely et al. 2007). But this happens only when this is communicated to them in an ostensive manner (Egyed et al. 2007).

Csibra and Gergely (2009) also cite evidence of another difference between osmosis (passive learning) and ostensive (interactive) situations. In the latter situation, but not the former one, the nine-month-old focuses and learns about the permanent features of an object (e.g., its visible features), which can be referenced and re-identified later in different situations. For example, she ignores information about the current location of a moveable object, which is irrelevant for future re-identification or for the identification of other members of its kind. In the non-communicative or osmosis situation, in contrast, the infant is more likely to detect changes in an object's location than its permanent appearance features (Yoon et al. 2008).

Csibra and Gergely thus conclude from this that infants

> display interpretive biases that suggest that they expect to learn generic and shared knowledge from such communicative acts. For example, infants expect that ostensive signals will be followed by referential signals, pay preferential attention to generalizable kind-relevant features of objects that are referentially identified by demonstrative communicative acts addressed to them . . . and assume that communicated valence information about objects (i.e. whether they are evaluated positively or negatively) is shared by others.
>
> (Csibra and Gergely 2011, 151)

IMPLICATIONS FOR EDUCATION

In the case of natural pedagogy, something transpires that goes beyond what predictive coding predicts, and beyond any simulative matching, and beyond embodied alignment in the here and now. Neural hermeneutics does not adequately explain the kind of phenomena involved in emotion perception, in shared intention formation, or in natural pedagogy, all of which are characterized by significant aspects of embodied interaction. In such cases, face-to-face interaction becomes constitutive of a dialogical, dynamic understanding that is not just epistemic (involving truth understood as correctness). Of course the issue of correct interpretation, and certainly normative aspects, may be involved, since there is always a chance of misunderstanding. A child may mistakenly generalize something that should not be generalized. In generalizing what one learns, however, just as in emotional engagement with another, or in forming shared intentions to jointly act in a certain way, something, which remains significant to the process and which may be *the* significant thing, extends beyond the control that either or both of the agents may have.

In the natural pedagogical setting, the child picks up on the significance of the other's intent (even if that intent is ambiguous and may be so even to the other person). To the extent that the kind of joint attention involved in natural pedagogy is a 'basic' joint action (Fiebich and Gallagher 2013), the two agents are engaged in an interaction from which meaning, which transcends the immediacy of the present situation, emerges. This is the notion of participatory sense making. One can point to the relevant phenomenon in natural pedagogy, the ostensive address that makes it a specific type of interaction rather than a passive observation. Although it is not clear why this leads precisely to generalized knowledge,[7] it is clear that this kind of interaction (or participatory sense making) is what leads the child to generalize what she learns. It is the interaction (or a derivative type of observation[8]) that constitutes the social cognition, and to the extent that the meaning that emerges from the interaction transcends either of the participants, one should not take this meaning to be something under the control of either one.

In a very real way, this sense-making process is the setting up of the priors that inform the predictive dynamics of brain function. These are, to borrow a phrase from Jesse Prinz (2004, 55), "set up to be set off." There is, in this regard, a hermeneutical circle that involves the brain-body-environment and not just the working of the brain. In response to the other's ostensive address, the child's cognitive system (an integrated brain-body system) attunes itself to the object's salience or value in the very perception of it, not just in a process of epistemic identification but in a way that includes bodily affective, peripheral, and autonomic changes (as explained by Barrett and Bars 2009, see endnote 2). This is a response that is set off based on prior experience—prior interactions with this particular person, prior manipulation of like objects, and so forth—as well as interests and expectations that have been shaped in that prior experience. One can easily think of such encounters initiating transformative processes of assimilation or accommodation to form new associations and priors that set up the system, shaping new predictions that drive ongoing experience, again involving not just the brain but a whole body adjustment, which is a complex one in the case of intersubjective interaction. This hermeneutical circle, I contend, is more enactive than simply neuronal. At least in regard to such processes, what it describes is educational experience.

NOTES

1. The author acknowledges support received from the Marie-Curie Initial Training Network, "TESIS: Toward an Embodied Science of InterSubjectivity" (FP7-PEOPLE-2010-ITN, 264828), European Commission Research, and the Humboldt Foundation's Anneliese Maier Research Award.
2. The phrase 'neural hermeneutics,' as far as I know, was originally used by Francisco Varela and appeared in print in May 2003, in Varela and Depraz (2003), and almost simultaneously as the title of Frith's keynote lecture to the Annual Meeting of the Organization of Human Brain Mapping in June of that year (Frith 2003).
3. For an explication of neural hermeneutics that is closer to this enactivist perspective, see Thompson et al. (2005); Varela (2006); and Varela and Depraz (2003, 213). For more on hermeneutics and cognitive science, see Gallagher (2004).
4. Indeed, enactive concepts of interaction and attunement may be expressed in predictive coding terms that emphasize two 'directions of fit.' The first involves updating predictions or adjusting priors on the basis of ongoing perceptual experience—the world to brain direction. The second is the idea of active inference, where we act on the world to directly shape or resample it in such a way as to test our prior expectations. This can be thought of as a kind of dynamic

hypothesis testing (as in PC) or as a dynamic adjustment process (as in enactivist models). See Gallagher and Allen (under review) for more detail.

5. Barrett and Bar (2009) offer a way to think of this in terms of an embodied predictive coding model that is closer to the enactive one. Their *affective prediction hypothesis* "implies that responses signaling an object's salience, relevance or value do not occur as a separate step after the object is identified. Instead, affective responses support vision from the very moment that visual stimulation begins" (1325). That is, along with the perception of the environment, we undergo certain bodily affective changes that accompany this integrated processing. As we engage with others, our bodies are already configured into overall peripheral and autonomic patterns based on prior associations. What predictive coding models call 'priors,' which include affect, are not just in the brain but involve a whole-body adjustment. (Also see Gallagher and Allen, under review; Seth 2013; and Seth et al. 2012).

6. This does not rule out the idea that one might have an affective response to some object (as, e.g., in the aesthetic experience one might have in looking at a beautiful stand of trees or in looking at the aftermath of clear-cutting a forest), but the affective perception of another person's emotion is defined by a particular set of social affordances that trees don't offer.

7. One explanation may be evolutionary. Csibra and Gergely (2011) call it 'natural' pedagogy and argue that it is an evolutionary adaptation. Csibra and Gergely (2009) suggest that the tendency to generalize ostensively demonstrated information is simply an innate mechanism.

8. The experiments cited to support the requirement of ostensive communication in natural pedagogy were conduced with infants ten to eighteen months old. In older children, however, it's not clear that ostensive communication is a necessary requirement in cases where children take some practice as normative; less ostensive, more implicit cues that suggest the practice is familiar, i.e., that indicate that it is a well-known practice, also allow for the child at three years of age to grasp the agent's intention as generalizing for that practice (Schmidt et al. 2011). In these experiments, the children simply observed the action of an agent in playing a game without interacting with the agent, although they were allowed to play with the pieces after the observation and prior to the demonstration that they understood the practice in normative terms, i.e., as involving specific rules. On the enactive interpretation, observation is a form of enactive perception, already informed by interaction, so what the child sees and understands, even in the observational mode, are social affordances—possible actions that the child can take in regard to the other person or *with* the other person in regard to the world. On this view, one should distinguish between passive observation and active observation where action-orientation and interaction are still the basic factors. In predictive coding terms, the notion of 'active inference' comes close to this idea.

REFERENCES

Barrett, L.F., and M. Bar. 2009. "See It with Feeling: Affective Predictions During Object Perception." *Philosophical Transactions of the Royal Society B: Biological Sciences* 364 (1521): 1325–1334.

Bermudez, J. 2003. *Thinking Without Words*. Oxford: Oxford University Press.

Betti, E. 1990. "Hermeneutics as the General Methodology of the *Geisteswissenschaften*." In *The Hermeneutic Tradition: From Ast to Ricoeur*, edited by G. Ormiston and A. Schrift, 159–197. Albany, NY: SUNY Press.

Brandom, R. 1994. *Making It Explicit: Reasoning, Representing, and Discursive Commitment.* Cambridge, MA: Harvard University Press.

Caggiano, V., L. Fogassi, G. Rizzolatti, P. Thier, and A. Casile. 2009. "Mirror Neurons Differentially Encode the Peripersonal and Extrapersonal Space of Monkeys." *Science* 324 (5925): 403–406.

Carruthers, P. 1996. "Simulation and Self-Knowledge: A Defence of Theory-Theory." In *Theories of Theories of Mind,* edited by P. Carruthers and P.K. Smith, 22–38. Cambridge, UK: Cambridge University Press.

Chenari, M. 2009. "Hermeneutics and Theory of Mind." *Phenomenology and the Cognitive Sciences* 8 (1): 17–31.

Csibra, G., and G. Gergely. 2009. "Natural pedagogy." *Trends in Cognitive Sciences* 13: 148–153.

Csibra, G., and G. Gergely. 2011. "Natural Pedagogy as Evolutionary Adaptation." *Philosophical Transactions of the Royal Society B: Biological Sciences* 366 (1567): 1149–1157.

Davidson, D. 1975. "Thought and Talk." In *Inquiries Into Truth and Interpretation,* edited by D. Davidson, 155–170. Oxford: Oxford University Press.

Davidson, D. (2003). "Responses to Barry Stroud, John McDowell, and Tyler Burge." *Philosophy and Phenomenological Research* 67 (3): 691–699.

Debruille, J.B., M.B. Brodeur, and C. Franco Porras. (2012). "N300 and Social Affordances: A Study with a Real Person and a Dummy as Stimuli." *PLoS ONE* 7 (10): 1–9.

De Gelder, B. 2013. [nt]. Conference Presentation. *The Scope and Limits of Direct Perception.* Copenhagen. December 13, 2013.

De Jaegher, H., and E. Di Paolo. 2007. "Participatory Sense-Making." *Phenomenology and the Cognitive Sciences* 6 (4): 485–507.

De Jaegher, H., E. Di Paolo, and S. Gallagher. 2010. "Does Social Interaction Constitute Social Cognition?" *Trends in Cognitive Sciences* 14 (10): 441–447.

de Vignemont, F., and P. Jacob. 2012. "What Is It like to Feel Another's Pain?" *Philosophy of Science* 79 (2): 295–316.

Dummett, M. 1993. *Seas of Language.* Oxford: Oxford University Press.

Egyed, K. I. Kiraly, K. Kreko, and G. Gergely. 2007. "Understanding Object-Referential Attitude Expressions in 18-Month-Olds: The Interpretation Switching Function of Ostensive-communicative Cues." Poster presented at the Biennial Meeting of the SRCD, Boston, August 2007.

Fiebich, A., and S. Gallagher. 2013. "Joint Attention in Joint Action." *Philosophical Psychology* 26 (4): 571–587.

Fodor, J. 1975. *The Language of Thought.* Cambridge, MA: Harvard University Press.

Friston, K., and C. Frith. 2014. "A Duet for One." *Consciousness and Cognition.* doi:10.1016/j.concog.2014.12.003.

Frith, C. 2003. "Neural Hermeneutics: How Brains Interpret Minds." Keynote Lecture at the 9th Annual Meeting of the Organization of Human Brain Mapping, New York.

Frith, C. 2007. *Making Up the Mind: How the Brain Creates Our Mental World.* Oxford: Blackwell.

Frith, C.D., and T.S. Wentzer. 2013." Neural hermeneutics." In *Encyclopedia of Philosophy and the Social Sciences,* edited by B. Kaldis, 657–659. Thousand Oaks: Sage Publications, Inc. doi: http://dx.doi.org/10.4135/9781452276052.

Gadamer, H.-G. 2004. *Truth and Method* (2nd rev. edition), translated by J. Weinsheimer and D.G. Marshall. New York: Crossroad.

Gallagher, S. 1992. *Hermeneutics and Education.* Albany, NY: State University of New York Press.

Gallagher, S. 2001. "The Practice of Mind: Theory, Simulation, or Primary Interaction?" *Journal of Consciousness Studies* 8 (5–7): 83–107.

Gallagher, S. 2004. "Hermeneutics and the Cognitive Sciences." *Journal of Consciousness Studies* 11 (10–11): 162–174.

Gallagher, S. 2005: *How the Body Shapes the Mind.* Oxford: Oxford University Press.

Gallagher, S. 2007. "Simulation Trouble." *Social Neuroscience* 2 (3–4): 353–365.

Gallagher, S. 2008. "Inference or Interaction: Social Cognition without Precursors." *Philosophical Explorations* 11 (3): 163–173.

Gallagher, S. 2012a. "Empathy, Simulation and Narrative." *Science in Context* 25 (3): 301–327.

Gallagher, S. 2012b. "In Defense of Phenomenological Approaches to Social Cognition: Interacting with the Critics." *Review of Philosophy and Psychology* 3 (2): 187–212.

Gallagher, S. and M. Allen. in press. "The Future of the Social Brain." *Synthese.*

Gallagher, S., and S. Varga. 2014. "Social Constraints on the Direct Perception of Emotions and Intentions." *Topoi* 33 (1): 185–199.

Gergely, G., K. Egyed, and I. Király. 2007. "On Pedagogy." *Developmental Science* 10: 139–146.

Goh, J.O., and D.C. Park. 2009. "Culture Sculpts the Perceptual Brain." *Progress in Brain Research* 178: 95–111.

Goldman, A.I. 2006: *Simulating Minds: The Philosophy, Psychology, and Neuroscience of Mindreading.* New York: Oxford University Press.

Gutsell, J.N. and M. Inzlicht. 2010. "Empathy Constrained: Prejudice Predicts Reduced Mental Simulation of Actions During Observation of Outgroups." *Journal or Experimental Social Psychology* 46: 841–845.

Heidegger, M. 2008. "On the Origin of the Work of Art." In *Basic Writings*, edited by D.F. Krell, 143–212. New York: Harper Collins.

Hirsch, E.D. 1967. *Validity in Interpretation.* New Haven: Yale University Press.

Huis in 't Veld, E.M., G.J.M. Van Boxtel, and B. de Gelder. 2014. "The Body Action Coding System I: Muscle Activations During the Perception and Expression of Emotion." *Social Neuroscience* 9 (3): 249–264.

Iacoboni, M., I. Molnar-Szakacs, V. Gallese, G. Buccino, J.C. Mazziotta, and G. Rizzolatti. 2005. "Grasping the Intentions of Others with One's Own Mirror Neuron System." *PLoS Biology* 3 (3): e79.

Izard, C.E. 1972. *Patterns of Emotions: A New Analysis of Anxiety and Depression.* New York: Academic Press.

Izard, C.E., B.P. Ackerman, K.M. Schoff and S.E. Fine. 2000. "Self-Organization of Discrete Emotions, Emotion Patterns, and Emotion Cognition Relations." In *Emotion, Development, and Self-Organization*, edited by M.D. Lewis and I. Granic, 15–36. Cambridge, UK: Cambridge University Press.

Kitayama, S., and Park, J. 2010. "Cultural Neuroscience of the Self: Understanding the Social Grounding of the Brain." *Social Cognitive & Affective Neuroscience* 5 (2–3): 111–129.

Margolis, E., and Laurence, S. 2014. "Concepts." *The Stanford Encyclopedia of Philosophy*, edited by E.N. Zalta. Retrieved from http://plato.stanford.edu/archives/spr2014/entries/concepts

Molnar-Szakacs, I., A.D. Wu, F.J. Robles, and M. Iacoboni. 2007. "Do You See What I Mean? Corticospinal Excitability during Observation of Culture-Specific Gestures." *PLoS One* 2: e626.

Newen, A., A. Welpinghus, and G. Jukel. 2015. "Emotion Recognition as Pattern Recognition: The Relevance of Perception." *Mind and Language* 30 (2): 187–208. doi: 10.1111/mila.12077.

Park, J., and S. Kitayama. 2012. "Interdependent Selves Show Face-induced Facilitation of Error Processing: Cultural Neuroscience of Self-threat." *Social Cognitive & Affective Neuroscience* 9 (2): 201–208. doi: 10: 1093/scan/nss125

Piaget, J., and B. Inhelder. 1969. *The Psychology of the Child*. New York: Basic Books.

Pinker, S. 1994. *The Language Instinct: The New Science of Language and Mind*. London: Penguin.

Prinz, J., 2004. *Gut Reactions: A Perceptual Theory of Emotion*. New York: Oxford University Press.

Ratcliffe, M. 2007. *Rethinking Commonsense Psychology: A Critique of Folk Psychology, Theory of Mind and Simulation*. Basingstoke: Palgrave Macmillan.

Reddy, V. 2008. *How Infants Know Minds*. Cambridge, MA: Harvard University Press

Rizzolatti, G., L. Fogassi, and V. Gallese. 2001. "Neurophysiological Mechanisms Underlying the Understanding and Imitation of Action." *Nature Reviews Neuroscience* 2: 661–670.

Ryle, G. 1949. *The Concept of Mind*. New York: Barnes and Noble.

Sartre, J.P. 1956. *Being and Nothingness*, translated by H.E. Barnes. New York: Philosophical Library.

Saxe, R and Kanwisher, N. 2003. "People Thinking About Thinking People: The Role of the Temporo-Parietal Junction in 'Theory of Mind.'" *NeuroImage* 19 (4): 1835–1842.

Saxe, R.R., S. Whitfield-Gabrieli, J. Scholz, and K.A. Pelphrey. 2009. "Brain Regions for Perceiving and Reasoning About Other People in School-Aged Children." *Child Development* 80 (4): 1197–1209.

Seth, A.K. 2013. "Interoceptive Inference, Emotion, and the Embodied Self." *Trends in Cognitive Sciences* 17 (11): 565–573. doi:10.1016/j.tics.2013.09.007.

Seth, A.K., K. Suzuki, and H.D. Critchley. 2012. "An Interoceptive Predictive Coding Model of Conscious Presence." *Frontiers in Psychology* 2: 1–16. doi:10.3389/fpsyg.2011.00395.

Scheler, M. 1954. *The Nature of Sympathy*, translated by P. Heath. London: Routledge and Kegan Paul. Original: *Wesen und Formen der Sympathie*. Bonn: Verlag Friedrich Cohen, 1923.

Schleiermacher, F. (1998). *Hermeneutics and Criticism: And Other Writings*, edited by A. Bowie. Cambridge, UK: Cambridge University Press.

Schmidt, M.F., H. Rakoczy, and M. Tomasello. 2011. "Young Children Attribute Normativity to Novel Actions without Pedagogy or Normative Language." *Developmental Science* 14 (3): 530–539.

Schultz, W., and A. Dickinson. 2000. "Neuronal Coding of Prediction Errors." *Annual Review of Neuroscience* 23 (1): 473–500.

Stawarska, B. 2009. *Between You and I: Dialogical Phenomenology*. Athens, OH: Ohio University Press.

Stueber, K.R. 2006. *Rediscovering Empathy: Agency, Folk Psychology, and the Human Sciences*. Cambridge, MA: MIT Press.

Tamietto, M. 2013. "Attentional and Sensory Unawareness for Emotions: Neurofunctional and Neuroanatomical Systems." Conference Presentation. *The Scope and Limits of Direct Perception*. Copenhagen, December 13, 2013.

Thompson, E., A. Lutz, and D, Cosmelli. 2005. Neurophenomenology: "An Introduction for Neurophilosophers." In *Cognition and the Brain: The Philosophy and Neuroscience Movement*, edited by A. Brook and K. Akins, 40–97. Cambridge, UK: Cambridge University Press.

Varela, F. 2006. "Neural Synchrony and Cognitive Functions." In *Self-organization and Emergence in Life Sciences*, edited by B. Feltz, M. Crommelinck, and P. Goujon, 95–108. Dordrecht: Springer.

Varela, F., and Depraz, N. 2003. "Imagining: Embodiment, Phenomenology and Transformation." In *Buddhism and Science: Breaking New Ground*, edited by A. Wallace, 195–232. New York: Columbia University Press.

Xu Y., X. Zuo, X. Wang, and S. Han. 2009. "Do You Feel My Pain? Racial Group Membership Modulates Empathic Neural Responses." *Journal of Neuroscience* 29 (26): 8525–8529.

Yoon, J.M.D., M.H. Johnson, and G. Csibra. (2008) "Communication-Induced Memory Biases in Preverbal Infants." *Proceedings of the National Academy of Science USA* 105: 13690–13695.

12 Some Problems with the Neuroscience Research Program

Nicholas C. Burbules

Neural microcurrents carry within them the spark of every varying impulse and response, conscious and unconscious. The brain waves recorded on neatly squared paper in trembling peaks and troughs are the mirrors of the combined thought-pulses of billions of cells. Theoretically, analysis should reveal the thoughts and emotions of the subject, to the last and least. Differences should be detected that are due not only to gross physical defects, inherited or acquired, but also to shifting states of emotion, to advancing education and experience, even to something as subtle as a change in the subject's philosophy of life.

—Isaac Asimov, Second Foundation
(New York: Doubleday 1953), pp. 107–108.

Asimov's optimistic science fiction, more than sixty years ago, about the potential for science to detect through 'neural microcurrents' even the content of one's philosophy of life is a harbinger for much of what is being claimed for neuroscience today. The essays in this collection address a number of reasons to question such claims. I am clustering these criticisms under five headings: methodological, conceptual, theoretical, political, and educational. Many specific criticisms in these chapters cut across those five categories, but I hope they are useful in interrelating the main arguments these authors have put forth.

METHODOLOGICAL CRITICISMS

The chapters including this kind of criticism mainly address the role of fMRI (functional magnetic resonance imaging) brain scans as a tool for studying brain activity. But it is important to note that there are other tools as well: conventional magnetic resonance imaging (MRI), electroencephalograms (EEG), magnetoencephalography (MEG), positron-emission tomography (PET), and others. As Derek Sankey and Minkang Kim point out in their chapter, different techniques (for example, EEG and fMRI) may yield different results. Clarence Joldersma explains:

[F]or neuroimages to correlate cleanly with mental representations, the images must unequivocally depict a clear and simple brain process, distinct from other brain processes . . . . Neuroimaging is a limited tool, only able to give rise to complex composite images that are fundamentally ambiguous with respect to what causes their details. Depending partly on what technique is used, and depending partly on the limited nature of those techniques, a neuroimage's details might be caused by the generation of new neurons, growth and change in existing neurons, generation of new synapses, increases in white matter cells, or changes in the capillaries bringing blood to the region.

But there is a deeper issue, which is that the misleading verisimilitude of a visual image may give the impression that one is seeing "what is really going on" in the brain. As Paul Smeyers summarizes:

The studies are correlational . . . . Far too often readers assume that fMRI techniques enable researchers to capture "visual proof" of brain activity without taking into account the complexities of acquiring the data and processing the images. To ease the task of interpreting and reporting results, neuroimaging studies often highlight responses in specific brain regions; however, these regions are rarely the only ones that produced activity. Moreover, every human brain is distinctive, so the fMRI studies look at areas of agreement across brains, which often vary greatly. In fact, laboratories often use their own techniques to test and analyze the messy and inconsistent data across participants and trials.

This analysis parallels work in the social studies of science that explain the social construction of scientific images and reveal the deeply conflicted ways in which even a group of experts, looking at "the same" scientific image, can offer very different interpretations about what it illustrates (see Latour and Woolgar 1979; Lynch and Woolgar 1990). Joldersma draws a similar conclusion:

Brain images are the result of a complex process, including scrupulous experimental design, decisions about what constitutes normal and abnormal, rigorous control over other aspects of the subject's actions during the experiment, artificial constructions required for measuring brain activity, equilibration of the raw data to match other brain measurements from other subjects, turning the numerical data into presentable brain images, and matching variations in quantities with a color scheme overlain onto a contour map of the brain area. Each of these steps requires assumptions, not only about anatomy and physiology but also about human nature . . . . To produce these seemingly simple pictures of localized brain activity requires complex, interdisciplinary data gathering and mathematical manipulation. The images are the result of a great deal of processing and synthesizing . . . . Brain images are under-determined by the data from which they arise.

For non-experts, the thick layer of assumptions and methodological choices hidden behind the apparent transparency of a visual image is, of course, especially seductive. Smeyers quotes Pasquinelli: "The ignorance of basic facts about the making-of of brain images can mislead the layperson into believing that an image of the brain is sufficient to prove the existence of a mental state—an attitude described as 'neurorealism.'"

Finally, as Bruce Maxwell and Eric Racine point out, a significant portion of basic research that supports inferences about human brain functioning is actually based on other animals:

A second issue concerns the applicability of neuroscience evidence to the ordinary life contexts. The biological research concerned with inves-tigating the influence of stress on specific neuro-endocrine pathways reviewed earlier is experimentally contrived and highly technical. A sig-nificant portion of it is also animal-based.

This will raise a number of questions later when I turn to some of the theo-retical assumptions behind brain research, notably the separation of brain function from the self-conscious thought processes of a *human* subject.

CONCEPTUAL CRITICISMS

Of a more purely philosophical nature are the criticisms that neuroscience is founded on conceptual confusions about making inferences concerning thoughts or the mind based on observations about activity in the brain. Philosophers call this a 'category error.'

Joldersma attributes this error to a series of assumptions inherent to the neuroscience research program. First, 'computationalism':

A computation model takes cognitive processes to be like the opera-tions of a computer. The mind is typically modeled as a computational machine that contains a set of rules for manipulating mental symbols. . . . Key to the computationalist model is the doctrine of neural correlates, namely, that there is a one-to-one correspondence between mental states and brain states. . . . Specific cognitive tasks are interpreted as having neural correlates in localized brain areas.

Joldersma quotes Frith and Metzinger, offering an even stronger thesis, which states, "differences occurring in the mind are not merely correlated to, but are caused by, particular brain activity."

Even if it were true that every mental state matched up with a distinct brain state ("I am thinking about a cat on a mat."), it would be a mistake to say that the brain state *caused* the mental state. It could, for example, be the opposite: that mental states, and changes in mental states, cause changes in brain states. But there are also reasons to doubt that every mental state matches up with a distinct brain state: would every time one thinks about a cat on a mat fire exactly the same neurons? Why would one expect that to be so?

Joldersma identifies a related problem, which he terms 'representationalism': "internal symbols are typically understood as mental representations. Representations are things that carry information about the world, and we know the world indirectly, through them." He goes on:

> But there are equally serious *conceptual* issues with the representationalist assumptions in educational neuroscience. The localization hypothesis coupled with the supervenience thesis is meant to give plausibility to the idea that particular content of a mental representation can be correlated with particular local neural activity . . . The claim is that intrinsic content properties of particular brain states have matching-content properties in mental states. . . . This is a narrow understanding of content, namely, that it is context-free: it is the pattern of this particular neural substrate that gives rise to that particular conscious content. The construal that mental content is context-free fits well with an internalist view of mind. Internalism interprets mental states as independent of what is happening in the outside world, or even in other parts of the body. . . . To get beyond representationalism, we need a different conception of mind and content. But for that we also need a different understanding of the brain . . . When the brain is construed as a dynamic system, the particular elements or parts of the brain are constrained and co-opted by higher-order, more global dynamic patterns of brain activity. The idea of emergent self-organization undermines the one-to-one correspondence of local brain activity and particular mental content.

Another conceptual issue is 'brainism,' a certain kind of mistaken synecdoche that confuses the part with the whole. Emma Williams and Paul Standish skeptically quote Blakemore and Young: "the brain knows things, reasons inductively, constructs hypotheses on the basis of arguments, and its constituent neurons are intelligent, can estimate probabilities and present arguments." Williams and Standish contrast this view with Hacker's response: "On the current neuroscientist's view, it's the brain that thinks and reasons and calculates and believes and fears and hopes. In fact, it's human beings who do all these things, not their brains." And Williams and Standish conclude that neuroscientists "have come to ascribe to constituent parts of human beings attributes that logically apply to the whole . . . *[B]rains don't think, human beings do.*" As we will see directly, this conceptual argument lays the foundation for a much wider theoretical critique.

Smeyers, drawing from Bakhurst, makes the philosophical move to put the thinking subject back in the center of the discussion:

> What goes missing in any third-person, physical description of the brain states is, Bakhurst argues, the subjective dimension: "all that is observable are the neural correlates of mental activity, not mental activity itself." To this he adds that from a personalist position, beginning from the premise that the human mind is a psychological unity, a person's mental states are not just a rag-bag collection of representations. "One way to put this argument about psychological unity is to say that brainism . . . struggles to make sense of the first-person perspective. A person does not typically stand to her own mental states as to objects of observation."

THEORETICAL CRITICISMS

The next set of concerns draw from these methodological and conceptual shortcomings to argue that the brain-centric model of thought cannot possibly offer a complete basis for understanding the mind because it does not include—cannot include—factors that are essential to mental life. In these chapters, there are four main lines of theoretical elaboration I want to summarize and show their relation to one another: the relation of brains to persons, the relation of thinking and acting, the fact of embodiment, and the relevance of context and culture.

Returning to the point that brains do not think—people do—the issue is not just terminological. Sankey and Kim argue that

> all living structures are complex, emergent, self-organizing, dissipative systems . . . Consciousness is an "emergent property"; our conscious deliberative minds "emerge from the immense complexity of human brains; that is what highly complex brains do." Calling consciousness an emergent property does not explain it, much less does it explain it away, but it does locate it at the appropriate level of organization and description.

Human brains are active, networked, adaptive systems, not just a collection of specialized regions that map onto specific cognitive functions. Human consciousness is self-aware, self-monitoring, and self-adjusting; while some aspects of mental activity have brain function correlates, the *processes* of thought cannot be identified with the *processes* of brain function. Deron Boyles calls this theoretical perspective neuropragmatism: "Where neuroscience attempts to identify clusters of neurons, neuropragmatists, following

Dewey, seek to understand the transactional continuity of the cluster of neurons in a brain in a nervous system in an organism in an environment—all of which change."

One reason why thought cannot be equated with brain function is that part of much thinking involves acting, and the kinds of experiences that arise from acting, as Joldersma points out, include "techniques such as fMRI require artificial stillness inside a machine, thereby narrowing the human experience to an artificially simple sliver." Especially in a context like learning, successful acquisition of a concept, a skill, a dispositional capacity involves things that we do and not only things happening in our brains. This is particularly true in learning that directly involves bodily movement and activity (dance or sports); but the same argument can be extended to areas that appear to be more purely cognitive, such as mathematics.

The fact is that human brains exist inside human bodies. Drawing from the ideas of Maurice Merleau-Ponty, Joldersma lays out the argument:

> The brain functions in the manner that it does precisely because it is embedded in a bodily subject. Living creatures such as humans have limbs that grasp, eyes that focus in structured ways, and upright postures that help cope with specific environments in particular ways. The bodily subject as a whole interacts with its surrounding world . . . . Mental life is always already bodily embedded in the world . . . This clears the way for a different understanding of mental content. For Merleau-Ponty, content is relational: "the behavior of organisms in fact determines the value or significance of stimuli." Mental content on this reading is construed in terms of the experienced significance of incoming sensory information as the bodily subject deals with the dynamic, complex patterns that constitute its environment. . . . Our mental content is framed by a first-person dimension, making it intrinsically experiential . . . . The content of experience is not an internal mental representation but a way of being in the world as a bodily subject.

Joldersma's argument recalls the famous thought-experiment about whether a brain, preserved in a vat and hooked up to a computer, could still be an experiencing, conscious human brain. We are embodied creatures, and our bodies exist in a world external to them, a world that is constantly changing and unpredictable. Our dynamic interactions with the world through perception, movement, and diverse human doings are shaped by our bodies, and the kinds of bodies we have; hence human thought and experience can never be conceived as purely a function of our brains. (This is one reason, for example, that virtual reality systems are exploring haptics as well as perceptual mechanisms; participants in virtual 3-D worlds experience a range of bodily sensations, not all of them pleasant, as they experience, move through, and act in these environments. I have seen people 'riding' a virtual roller coaster sway and lose their balance, even though they are standing motionless on a flat floor. Some even vomit. See Burbules 2005)

Drawing these arguments together, the subjectivity of thought, its relation to experiencing and doing, and the situation of experiencing and doing in a human body, all vastly complicate the notion of mental states as simple correlates of brain states. None of these conditions can be adequately represented themselves as brain states. But then the arguments in this book go one step further, because these aspects of bodily experiencing and doing are not merely individual but also social: they exist in a context of culture and convention. Shaun Gallagher writes that

> not only are brain processes different relative to the use of different cultural tools and practices, also there are cultural variations in brain mechanisms specifically underlying person perception and emotion regulation . . . Social and cultural factors, then, have a physical effect on brain processes that shape basic perceptual experience and emotional responses.

Williams and Standish address this point by talking about Ludwig Wittgenstein's famous account of what it means to follow a rule. Rejecting what Charles Taylor calls an 'intellectualist' account, Williams and Standish argue that

> the intellectualist account appears to lose sight of the part played by convention in the following of rules . . . Another way of putting this is to say that it is through what people do together that rules and possibilities of correctness come into view and come to be . . . [A]ctivities . . . require conventions, communities, and concerns to make them possible.

Hence it is not possible to model thought merely through the states that exist within a brain; thought is constantly relating to these social and cultural factors—factors that are essential to the *meaning* of ideas.

POLITICAL CRITICISMS

A very different kind of critical angle is to look at the effects and consequences of the emphasis on neuroscience explanations of mental activity on society. Several chapters focus on those concerns.

A number of chapters (Boyles, Joldersma, Williams and Standish) point out the expanding marketplace for ostensibly neuroscience-based products that trumpet their capability to build mental capacity. Products with names like Brain HQ, Brain Gym, Fit Brains, Lumosity, etc., suggest that the same ethos of self-improvement that drives consumers to the gym or to buy home exercise equipment can now drive investments in brain improvement as well. Boyles sees "a lucrative commercial industry resulting from such enthusiasm."

The common theme across several chapters is that the emphasis on neuroscience as a basis for educational reform represents the dominance of a 'neoliberal' way of thinking. Citing Victoria Pitts-Taylor, Joldersma says,

in popular usage, neural plasticity has been employed, on the authority and popularity of neuroscience, to frame humans as permanently open to enhancement and modification, ready to change as the economic circumstances warrant. . . . Neoliberalism replaces an ethic of state care with an emphasis on individual responsibility and market fundamentalism.

In fact, the issue of brain plasticity comes up in different chapters. It might appear that plasticity is a progressive notion, since it entails that the brain isn't functionally hard-wired but can develop new neural pathways over time; for example, some people who suffer damage to some regions of the brain that are normally allocated to certain functions can retain those functions when other parts of the brain adapt to take them over. Unfortunately, some authors note, this idea of plasticity can be accommodated to ideals of personal perfectionism (via the commercial brain exercise products described earlier) or neoliberal conceptions of the perpetually learning self—the self-managed factotum of the learning society.

For Joldersma, as just noted:

New techniques allow scientists to look at a wide variety of experiences in examining how the adult brain is structurally transformed by its environment . . . Moreover, plasticity research is also discovering how to deliberately enhance brain plasticity . . . [B]rain plasticity can easily become a competing discourse, framing problematic political and economic differences as natural and internal.

Tyson Lewis develops a parallel argument about the articulation of 'brain plasticity' and a neoliberal view of the self, drawing from the work of Catherine Malabou:

[P]lasticity has come to prominence. This fact is perhaps most prevalent in cerebral plasticity and the capacity of synapses to modify their structure. Instead of code, the brain presents itself through cerebral images that are best described in relation to political metaphors (populations or assemblages) rather than as forms of writing. This insight then led Malabou from a critique of metaphysics and deconstruction to a critique of neuroscience as the central sphere to struggle over the meaning of plasticity today . . . If the plastic notion of the brain has liberated us from certain false models, including the brain as central telephone exchange and as computer, it has also limited the freedom of the brain by constraining it to a flexible, de-centered, neural network metaphor that merely recapitulates the broader logic of neoliberalism. . . . If neuroscience has produced a certain possibility for reimagining free-dom, this freedom is equally constrained by the current of neoliberal ideology underpinning flexible plasticity. Where is there room in the brain for resistance . . . resistance to flexibility without reverting back to a rigid notion of the brain? Questions of the spontaneous philosophy of neuroscience thus spill over into political questions and vice versa.

EDUCATIONAL CRITICISMS

The most extensive range of criticisms in these chapters, drawing from all sorts of concerns already noted, are with the attempt to derive specific impli-cations from neuroscience for education. In fact, all the chapters touch on this issue in one way or another.

One line of criticism starts with the relation between much of the dis-course surrounding neuroscience and a broadly neoliberal vision of the human subject in society and extends that to the context of education itself. Joldersma summarizes, "In this educational discourse, important student skills include becoming competitive and autonomous, transforming the self into a responsible subject who fits well into the neoliberal workplace." Williams and Standish suggest that this distorts the meaning of the term 'learning' itself: "it can be said that such modes of talking succeed in perpet-uating the instrumental and functional conception of learning and thinking that has, in recent years, come to prominence."

Lewis extends this argument, drawing from the work of Maarten Simons and Jan Masschelein:

> I want to begin by drawing a correlation between the rise of learning discourses and practices and the turn toward neuroscience in educa-tional research. This correlation is important for demonstrating how neuroscience offers a neuro-ideology for justifying learning on "objec-tive grounds" and how learning offers a location or practice base for socializing this ideology as "good common sense." . . . Indeed, learning theories have increasingly come to neuroscience to solve certain educa-tional problems. This is due in part to the fact that neuroscience promises that which educational philosophy or sociology could never dream of: giving a biological explanation of what learning actually is. . . . Learning thus becomes the science of brain-based learning.

Some authors in this collection address the potential for neuroscience as a support for learning in certain areas: Sankey and Kim, for example, point out a reason to be concerned about 'neuromyths' that exaggerate the educa-tional potential of neuroscience, but they also conclude that

> neuroscience can both inform and misinform the educational task of cul-tivating moral values. Educators should view neuroscience with critical

eyes. We have cautioned against proliferating neuromyths in education and the use of neuroscience to support pet theories in ways that can appear highly contrived. We have also taken neuroscience to task for its adherence to hard determinism and ontological reductionism. However, we have turned to neuroscience in our quest for the neurobiological origins of moral values, and when exploring the nature of moral intuition.

Maxwell and Racine come down more on the skeptical side of this question. Citing the hypothesis that

> reasoning is overwhelmingly used to rationalize people's preconceived ideas about ethical issues and in the service of social ends (e.g., demonstrating to one's peers that one endorses some socially accepted point of view on an ethical issue), rather than to find the ethically 'right' answer to ethical problems," they argue that, "This kind of result not only suggests that explicit moral reasoning is not a single psychological process. It suggests that the parallel psychological processes that play a major role in shaping moral judgments are opaque to reasoners themselves. . . . As convincing as this position may seem on the face of it, there are two reasons why we should not endorse the behavioral ethics perspective on the importance of teaching about moral reasoning in ethics education. First, it misplaces the main educational interest of 'models of moral reasoning' in ethics education. Second, it underestimates 'not knowing the right thing to do' as a factor contributing to unethical behavior."

For Pradeep Dhillon, neuroscience has real potential for understanding aesthetics and the impact of the arts:

> This line of argument provides warrant for the recent turn to neuroscience in aesthetics. The work of neuroscientists such as Semir Zeki reminds us that certain lines and colors (and their spatial relations) are more salient than others in the construction and appreciation of artworks; the salience of a given feature depends upon how it correlates with neurophysiological processes within the visual cortex. . . . [T]hese and other developments in cognitive neuroscience and visual neuroprocessing go some way toward providing us with a clearer sense of the necessary epistemological dependencies that we seek. Just because we cannot yet point with precision to all the determinate relations between non-aesthetic and aesthetic properties does not mean that we must give up on the existence of such a relation and its consequences for aesthetic merit, even beauty. . . . In other words, neuroscience gives us some insight into the ways in which different kinds of non-aesthetic properties are related to aesthetic properties, and neuroscience also gives us ways in which these aesthetic properties of a work are themselves often appropriate to other aesthetic properties of a work (and are intended

to be). . . . Such a development—a new way of reading images through naturalized aesthetics—suggests that we are at an exciting moment of developing a more level approach to aesthetic and art education, one that reminds us of our shared humanity even as we continue to appreciate the particularities that make for specific cultural practices and traditions. In adapting this new way of reading images, we can use aesthetics to create possibilities for educating toward a greater awareness of previously disparate worlds.

In a third educational domain, child upbringing, Maxwell and Racine offer a mixed assessment:

> Responsive childcare, Leach concludes, favors the development of a nervous system that reacts appropriately to life's stresses and may protect children against the risk of neuropsychological conditions such as anxiety and depression later in life . . . The view that there is a single universally 'healthy' or 'normal' stress-response system for humans, however, is hard to square with another key concept in developmental neuroscience, i.e., 'brain plasticity.' The stress-response system, like other neurological systems, undergoes structural changes in response to its environment such that the 'adaptiveness' of a neurological system is a function of the environment in which that system operates . . . The rhetorical appeal of neuroscience justifications for educational interventions and family policy is not innocuous hype. [P]olicy or practice proposals, which are poorly grounded epistemologically, risk diverting resources away from more effective strategies for promoting child welfare and positive development . . . Neurorealism therefore describes a form of naïve realism propelled by public fascination for contemporary neuroscience. A general rhetorical appeal of neuroscience-based explanations has been observed both in studies of media coverage of neuroscience . . . and in research in social psychology on how non-experts evaluate the evidential strength of neuroscience explanations.

Here, then, is the core issue for critics: the misjudged appeal of neuroscience to offer a scientific, brain-based model of learning vastly oversimplifies the actual dynamics of learning, reinforcing other trends (testing, teacher-proof approaches to curriculum design, and some trends in educational technology) to regard teaching and learning in a scientifically instrumental fashion. The particular ways that neuroscience research gets interpreted at the level of policy, and implemented at the level of practice reinforces these trends and creates false expectations about the perfectibility of learning and the learner.

Pressing this point further, the reception of neuroscience also distorts and misunderstands the complex nature of *teaching*. Boyles decries what he calls *Mind-Brain Education*:

MBE advocates are already publishing research that trumpets what brain functions are most important for success in school, how to identify the parts of the brain "responsible" for those functions, and what models and strategies exist for "maximizing" brain control for increased success in learning.

Smeyers terms this approach *neuroeducation*:

> Close inspection of these claims for a direct connection between particular 'brain-based' tools and teaching approaches reveals very loose and often factually incorrect links . . . the direct application of neuroscience findings to the classroom has not been particularly fruitful . . . (Ansari, Coch, and De Smedt, in Patten and Campbell 2011, 41). Unless the neurological mechanism that lies behind (and which is made explicit) could be directly influenced, it is not clear what the educational implications are that surpass those already available on the basis of relevant research in for example educational psychology. That neuroscience offers a description (or even explanation) in terms of neurological concepts and theories does not in itself warrant an educational surplus value. This remains to be argued and established . . . Education is not about getting information into students' heads or of implanting skills in them (Bakhurst 2008, 428).

The famous Coleman Report of 1966 shook up the educational establishment by suggesting the school influences were relatively ineffective in counterbalancing the far more powerful influences of home life, social and economic status, and other environmental factors largely beyond the control of schools to alter (Coleman et al. 1966). This sobering conclusion that unequal educational outcomes are a complex social problem, and not just a matter of improving instruction, has been resisted by the educational profession ever since—the consequences of that conclusion are just too discouraging. The trends in neuroscience, one might say, are anti-Coleman: reducing educational problems to brain problems and suggesting that scientifically grounded instructional techniques can fix learning. There are two obvious problems with this agenda: one, already reviewed at length here, is that, as Joldersma argues, "the unit of explanation for educational neuroscience is not be the brain in isolation. Rather, it is the dynamic relation between bodily subject (the learner) and its environment." Gallagher puts it this way:

> Neural hermeneutics does not adequately explain the kind of phenomena involved in emotion perception, in shared intention formation, or in natural pedagogy, all of which are characterized by significant aspects of embodied interaction. In such cases, face-to-face interaction becomes constitutive of a dialogical, dynamic, understanding that is not just epistemic (involving truth understood as correctness).

Finally, as Smeyers summarizes, "education is a communicative endeavour, not an engineering problem" (Bakhurst 2008, 428).

This raises the second problem, which goes to the heart of the neuroscience research program: *teaching does not mean causing changes in brain activity*. It simply cannot be conceived that way. Nor can changes in brain activity be taken as a measure or indicator of successful teaching. Returning to the Wittgensteinian argument, understanding or learning are not matters of what happens inside someone's head, even though this is how we sometimes talk about them; they are matters of what people can *do*. Teaching is a practical, contextual, interpersonal activity composed entirely of doings and eliciting from learners certain doings in which and through which education happens (or doesn't happen). Admittedly, those doings are murky indicators, indirect, and subject to interpretation (and misinterpretation). But the aspiration to read through those doings to some foundational level of objective 'fact' about what is or isn't in the learner's head is a recurrent illusory hope; neuroscience is simply the latest and most extreme version of that hope.[1]

NOTE

1. This essay has benefited from other readings, outside of this volume, that have helped to inform my understanding of neuroscience: Bakhurst 2008; Davis 2004, 2013; Geake 2008; Howard-Jones 2008; Immordino-Yang 2011; Purdy and Morrison 2009; Schrag 2011, 2013; Smeyers forthcoming; Varma et al. 2008.

REFERENCES

Bakhurst, David. 2008. "Minds, Brains and Education." *Journal of Philosophy of Education* 42 (3–4): 415–432.
Burbules, Nicholas C. 2005. "Rethinking the Virtual." In *The International Handbook of Virtual Learning Environments*, edited by Joel Weiss, Jason Nolan, and Peter Trifonas, 3–24. Dordrecht: Kluwer Publishers.
Coleman, James S., Ernest Q. Campbell, Carol J. Hobson, James McPartland, Alexander M. Mood, Frederic D. Weinfeld, and Robert York. 1966. *Equality of Educational Opportunity*. Washington, DC: Office of Education, US Department of Health, Education, and Welfare, US Government Printing Office. OE-38001.
Davis, Andrew. 2004. "The Credentials of Brain-based Learning." *Journal of Philosophy of Education* 38 (1): 21–36.
Davis, Andrew. 2013. "Neuroscience and Education: At Best a Civil Partnership: A Response to Schrag." *Journal of Philosophy of Education* 47 (1): 31–36.
Geake, John. 2008. "Neuromythologies in Education." *Educational Research* 50 (2): 123–133.
Howard-Jones, Paul. 2008. "Philosophical Challenges for Researchers at the Interface Between Neuroscience and Education." *Journal of Philosophy of Education* 42 (3–4): 361–380.
Immordino-Yang, Mary Helen. 2011. "Implications of Affective and Social Neuroscience for Educational Theory." *Educational Philosophy and Theory* 43 (1): 98–103.

Latour, Bruno, and Steve Woolgar. 1979. *Laboratory Life: The Construction of Scientific Facts*. Princeton, NJ: Princeton University Press.

Lynch, Michael, and Steve Woolgar, eds. 1990. *Representation in Scientific Practice*. Cambridge, MA: MIT Press.

Purdy, Noel, and Hugh Morrison. 2009. "Cognitive Neuroscience and Education: Unravelling the Confusion." *Oxford Review of Education* 35 (1): 99–109.

Schrag, Francis. 2011. "Does Neuroscience Matter for Education?" *Educational Theory* 61 (2): 221–237.

Schrag, Francis. 2013. "Can This Marriage Be Saved? The Future of 'Neuro-Education.'" *Journal of Philosophy of Education* 47 (1): 20–30.

Smeyers, Paul. Forthcoming. "Neurophilia: Guiding Educational Research and the Educational Field?" In *Educational Research: Discourses of Change and Changes of Discourse*, edited by Paul Smeyers and Marc Depaepe. Dordrecht: Springer.

Varma, Sashank, Bruce D. McCandliss, and Daniel L. Schwartz. 2008. "Scientific and Pragmatic Challenges for Bridging Education and Neuroscience." *Educational Researcher* 37 (3): 140–152.

Contributors

Deron Boyles is Professor of Philosophy of Education in the Department of Policy Studies, Georgia State University (Atlanta, GA). His research interests include school commercialism, epistemology, critical pedagogy, and the philosophy of John Dewey. His books include *American Education and Corporations: The Free Market Goes to School* (Falmer 2000) and (co-authored) *The Politics of Inquiry: Education Research and the "Culture of Science"* (SUNY 2009). His edited volumes include *Schools or Markets?: Commercialism, Privatization, and School-Business Partnerships* (Lawrence Erlbaum 2005) and *The Corporate Assault on Youth: Commercialism, Exploitation, and the End of Innocence* (Peter Lang 2008). He recently published "Brain Matters: An Argument for Neuropragmatism and Schooling," *PES Yearbook 2013*.

Nicholas Burbules is Edward William and Jane Marr Gutgsell Endowed Professor in the Department of Education Policy, Organization, and Leadership in the College of Education and an affiliate of the Unit for Criticism and Interpretative Theory at the University of Illinois at Urbana/Champaign (Urbana, IL). He is also the Director of the Ubiquitous Learning Institute, served as Editor of *Educational Theory* for more than twenty years, and helped establish *Education Review*. Recent publications include (with W. Kohli) *Feminisms and Educational Research* (R&L Education 2013) and (with M. Peters and P. Smeyers) *Showing and Doing: Wittgenstein as a Pedagogical Philosopher* (Paradigm 2010).

Pradeep Dhillon is Associate Professor of Linguistics in the Department of Educational Policy, Organization, and Leadership, University of Illinois at Urbana-Champaign (Urbana, IL). She holds courtesy appointments in Linguistics, Comparative Literature, and the Unit for Criticism and Interpretive Theory. Her research straddles philosophy of language (both Analytic and Continental) and mind, aesthetics, and international education; and she has a strong interest in Kantian value theory as it relates to aesthetics, cognition, and human rights education. She is the Editor for *the Journal of Aesthetic Education* and has served as the Chair of

Education for the American Society for Aesthetics. She has presented papers on neuro-aesthetics at several international philosophy conferences and has organized a two-part interdisciplinary symposium titled "Art and the Brain" (2006–2007). She has published widely within her areas of research interest. Her publications include the co-edited volume (with P. Standish) *Lyotard: Just Education* (Routledge 2000, 2013), the edited volume *Somaesthetics and Education* (University of Illinois Press, September 2015), and *Kant: The Art of Judgment*, (Continuum Press, Philosophy, in preparation).

Shaun Gallagher is Lillian and Morrie Moss Professor of Excellence, Department of Philosophy, University of Memphis (Memphis, TN) and is also Professorial Fellow on the Faculty of Law, Humanities, and the Arts at the University of Wollongong (New South Wales, Australia). His research covers a number of fields, including phenomenology, philosophy of mind, cognitive science, and hermeneutics, especially the topics of embodied cognition and intersubjectivity. Recent publications include *Phenomenology* (Palgrave Macmillan 2012) and *The Phenomenological Mind* (Routledge 2012). He is co-editor-in-chief of *Phenomenology and the Cognitive Sciences.*

Clarence W. Joldersma is Professor of Education, Education Department, Calvin College (Grand Rapids, MI). He has a broad range of research interests, including Levinas and twentieth-century French phenomenology, philosophy of mind, philosophy of science, sustainability, and social justice. Recent publications include the book *A Levinasian Ethics for Education's Commonplaces: Between Calling and Inspiration* (Palgrave 2014) and the essays "Benjamin's Angel of History and the Work of Mourning in Ethical Remembrance," *Studies in Philosophy and Education* (2014) and "An ethical *Sinnegebung* Respectful of the Non-human: A Levinasian Environmental Ethic," *Symposium* (2013).

Minkang Kim is Senior Lecturer in the Faculty of Education and Social Work, University of Sydney (Australia). Her teaching and research focus is the application of dynamic systems theory (DST) to the study of human development and learning, with particular interest in the non-linearity of human development and how, in an increasingly global world, social, emotional, and moral development are occurring in intercultural contexts. Recent publications include "Cultivating Teachers' Morality: The Pedagogy of Emotional Rationality," *Australian Journal of Teacher Education* (2013), (with Derek Sankey) "Towards a Dynamic Systems Approach to Moral Development and Moral Education: A Response to the JME Special Issue," *Journal of Moral Education* (2009), and "A Dynamic Systems Approach to Moral and Spiritual Development," in the *Routledge International Handbook of Education, Religion and Values* (2013).

Tyson E. Lewis is Associate Professor of Art Education and Art History in the College of Visual Arts and Design at the University of North Texas (Denton, TX). His scholarship focuses on the intersections between a phenomenology of perception, biopolitics (as the politics of the body), and art education/aesthetic appreciation. He is author of three books, including *Education Out of Bounds: Reimagining Cultural Studies for a Posthuman Age* (Palgrave 2010), *The Aesthetics of Education: Curiosity, Theatre, and Politics in the Work of Paulo Freire and Jacques Ranciere* (Continuum 2012), and *On Study: Giorgio Agamben and Educational Potentiality* (Routledge 2013). He has also co-edited (with Megan Laverty) *Art's Teachings, Teaching's Art: Philosophical, Critical, and Educational Musings* (Springer 2015).

Bruce Maxwell is Associate Professor in the Department of Education at the University of Quebec (Trois-Rivières, Quebec), where he teaches professional ethics in education, approaches to ethics education, and the "ethics" segment of the course Teaching Ethics and Religious Cultures. His research focuses on professional ethics and professional ethics education, moral development and education, and ethical and policy issues in education. Recent books include *Professional Ethics Education: Studies in Compassionate Empathy* (Springer 2008) and he co-authored the *Issues in Canadian Education* (Oxford 2015). Recent articles, with Eric Racine, include "Does Research in Affective Neuroscience Justify Responsive Early Childcare?" *Neuroethics* (2012).

Eric Racine is Director of the Neuroethics Research Unit (Institut de recherches cliniques de Montréal—IRCM) and Associate IRCM Research Professor. He is Adjunct Professor in the Department of Neurology and Neurosurgery, McGill University (Montreal, Quebec), an Affiliate Member of the Biomedical Ethics Unit, McGill University, and an Assistant Research Professor in the Department of Medicine and Social and Preventive Medicine (Bioethics Programs, University of Montreal). His research is involves developing a pragmatic framework for bioethics based on empirical research and exploring its implications in concrete questions related to the ethical application of neuroscience in research, patient care, and public policy. He is associate editor of the journal *Neuroethics*. Recent publications, with Bruce Maxwell, includes "The Ethics of Neuroeducation: Research, Practice and Policy," *Neuroethics* (2012).

Derek Sankey is an Honorary Associate in the Faculty of Education and Social Work, University of Sydney (Australia). His research and teaching focus on the application of dynamic systems theory to the notion of the human self and its education. He has a long interest in the interface between the natural sciences and the humanities, which he approaches with a background in philosophy of science. Recent publications include "Education and the Philosophy of Mind and Brain," in *Philosophical Reflections for Educators* (Cengage Learning 2008), "Future Horizons: Moral Learning and the Socially Embedded Synaptic Self," *Journal of Moral Education* (2011), with Minkang Kim, "Towards a Dynamic Systems Approach to Moral Development and Moral Education: A Response to the JME Special Issue," *Journal of Moral Education* (2009), and "A Dynamic Systems Approach to Moral and Spiritual Development," in the *Routledge International Handbook of Education, Religion and Values* (2013).

Paul Smeyers is Research Professor for Philosophy of Education at Ghent University and Extraordinary Professor of Education and Society, Faculty of Psychology and Educational Sciences, KU Leuven (both in Belgium) and Honorary Extraordinary Professor at Stellenbosch University, South Africa. He is Associate Editor of *Educational Theory* and Chair of the Research Community in Philosophy and History of the Discipline of Education established by the Research Foundation Flanders, Belgium. Recent publications include the co-authored book (with Richard Smith) *Understanding Education and Educational Research* (Cambridge 2014), the co-edited volumes *Educational Research: The Attraction of Psychology* (Springer 2013), and *Evidence Based Educational Policy: What Evidence? What Basis? Whose Policy?* (Blackwell 2009).

Paul Standish is Professor and Head of the Centre for Philosophy of Education at UCL Institute of Education. His research spans a broad philosophical range, including questions in ethics and education, democracy and citizenship, new technology, and higher education. His work capitalizes on the productive tensions in the relation between Analytical and Continental philosophy. His most recent books include *Education and the Philosophy of the Kyoto School* (Springer 2012) and *Stanley Cavell and the Education of Grownups* (Fordham University Press 2012), both co-edited with Naoko Saito. He was Editor (2001–2011) and is now Associate Editor of the *Journal of Philosophy of Education*.

Emma Williams is Assistant Professor in the Centre for Education Studies, University of Warwick. She was previously Philosopher-in-Residence at Rugby School, where she taught philosophy across the curriculum and co-developed interdisciplinary courses for the new A Level Qualification: The Extended Project. She has a background in philosophy, particularly Post-Kantian European Philosophy, and the Philosophy of Education. Her work explores the themes of language, rationality, and subjectivity within the context of education. Her publications include *The Ways We Think* (Wiley-Blackwell 2016), "Out of the Ordinary: Incorporating Limits with Austin and Derrida," *Educational Philosophy and Theory* (2014), and "In Excess of Epistemology: Siegel, Taylor, Heidegger and the Conditions of Thought," *Journal of Philosophy of Education* (2015).

Index